STRIKE IT RICH IN PERSONAL SELLING

STRIKE IT RICH IN PERSONAL SELLING

TECHNIQUES FOR SUCCESS IN DIRECT SALES, MULTI-LEVEL AND NETWORK MARKETING

Gini Graham Scott, Ph.D.

AVON
PUBLISHERS OF BARD, CAMELOT, DISCUS AND FLARE BOOKS

STRIKE IT RICH IN PERSONAL SELLING is an original publication of Avon Books. This work has never before appeared in book form.

AVON BOOKS
A division of
The Hearst Corporation
1790 Broadway
New York, New York 10019

First Avon Printing, September 1985

AVON TRADEMARK REG. U. S. PAT. OFF. AND IN
OTHER COUNTRIES, MARCA REGISTRADA, HECHO EN
U.S.A.

Printed in the U.S.A.

OPB   10   9   8   7   6   5   4   3   2   1

Contents

v

Part V Building a Sales Organization

Part VI Organizing Special Events to Build Your Own Business or Help Your Sales Group

STRIKE IT RICH IN PERSONAL SELLING

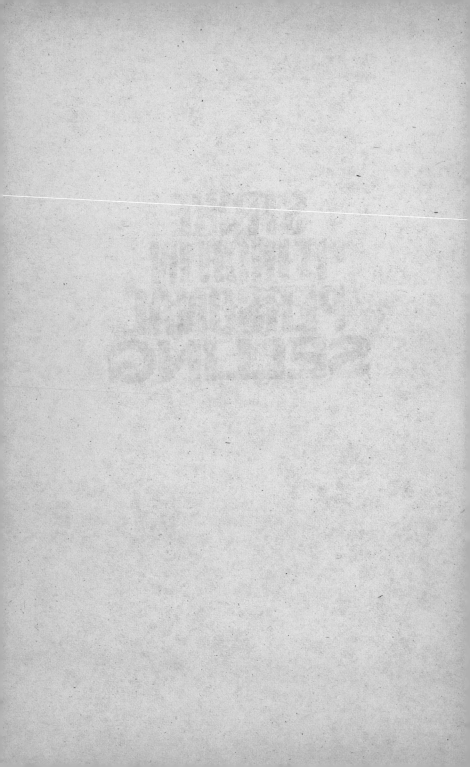

Part I

INTRODUCTION

Chapter 1

DIRECT SELLING AND MULTI-LEVEL MARKETING

In the last few years, there has been a tremendous growth in direct sales, party plan, and multi-level companies, spurred in part by recent developments in technology and the economy. The computer and communications revolution, the recession, and the decline of major industries have been particularly influential, and books such as *Megatrends* by John Naisbitt describe these changes at length.

These trends have led to a burst of entrepreneurship and the explosion of new start-up companies. At the same time, an alternative marketing system to distribute these new products and services has grown rapidly alongside the traditional retail-wholesale market. And this marketing system is direct sales.

The tradition of direct selling, of course, is very old. It goes back to preindustrial times, when a person with a product to sell simply contacted friends and neighbors or set up shop in a temporary market, a bazaar in a public square, or even by the side of the road. The itinerant salesman who went around from town to town in a small cart during the 1800s in America is part of this tradition.

3

Later, with the industrial revolution, direct-sales people not only sold their own products, but, increasingly, they represented larger companies and got a commission on sales. And then, in the 1940s, direct selling took a new twist with the emergence of the first of the multi-level marketing (MLM) companies—Nutrilite Systems and Stanley Home Products. The difference was that now, salespeople not only got a commission on the products they sold directly, but they also got a bonus or override for recruiting other people to sell the product. The commission structure went down more than one level—hence the term *multi-level*.

In the 1950s, Amway and Shaklee contributed a genius for marketing and organization-building to the MLM industry, and as a result each developed a massive sales network, to market household and health products respectively. Today, both companies have about one million distributors each, and together have about $2 billion in sales. The main strategy used by distributors for these companies includes home meetings, personal demonstrations, and larger business opportunity meetings and rallies. Although the distributors do sell a large number of products at retail, a major concern is recruiting prospects to become part of the sales network, too.

Using a slightly different approach that features party plan demonstrations by a network of well-trained consultants, Mary Kay launched what was to become a multimillion-dollar skin care and cosmetics empire in the 1950s. In this kind of sales program, the distributor works with a host or hostess to set up a sales demonstration and party. Although the distributor may hope to interest some customers in becoming distributors and putting on sales parties, too, the focus is initially on retail sales.

For a time there was some question about the legality of the MLM sales plans, and Amway ended up battling the U.S. government for about a decade. But in a 1979 decision, Amway's multi-level plan got a clean bill of health. Since then, the floodgates have opened, and thousands of new MLM companies have emerged, including some that have become well known, including Forever Living, Herbalife, and Neo-Life, with over fifty thousand distributors each.

Meanwhile, direct sales and party plan companies without multi-level programs have continued to grow, although the distinctions between what is multi-level or not have become fuzzy indeed, because in some of these "non-multi-level" companies, distributors do recruit other distributors.

Technically, any company where a distributor does this recruiting might be considered an MLM company—although many companies use other terms or deny the MLM connection because the term *multi-level* has recently gotten mixed up with pyramid schemes, chain letters, and assorted dubious recruiting schemes. For example, the Mary Kay company presents itself as a direct sales or party plan company and claims it is not an MLM company because its marketing plan only goes down two levels. And other firms with plans that pay commissions down several levels describe themselves as "network" or "personal" marketing companies to emphasize the personal interaction that occurs between the distributor, customers and other distributors in the network.

In fact, the marketing plans of all these companies vary extensively, whatever name they use. But what these companies do share in common is the freedom the distributor has to market the product or service according to his or her personal style. Whether the distributor is called a sales representative for a direct sales company, a sales associate for a party plan company, or a distributor for a multi-level company—and whatever the commission—the basic principle is the same. The individual has wide latitude in deciding the best way to sell a product or service, subject to company guidelines, and can use a great deal of creativity in using marketing and promotion techniques.

In fact, in MLM and party plan companies, the individual

is an independent contractor, essentially a small entrepreneur, who is creating his or her own business with the products of the company he or she represents. And whereas a sales representative for a direct sales company is typically limited to a specific territory, the party plan or MLM distributor can sell wherever he or she wants.

Sales reps and distributors also vary in the amount of time they commit to marketing a product or service. Some do it part-time; some full-time. Some represent one company; some more than one. Many operate out of their own homes; others set up small offices or distribution centers. Some emphasize sales through personal contact and variously employ one-on-one presentations, sales parties, or opportunity meetings. Others rely much more on mail order or telemarketing techniques. The techniques are almost as varied as the people who practice them.

And the names people are called vary widely, too, depending on the kind of company they represent and the role they play. For example, people may be called counselors, advisers, sales associates, sales representatives, distributors, or any number of other names. But for simplicity I use the terms *direct-sales person, sales associate*, or *distributor* interchangeably to refer to anyone involved in direct sales.

This book is designed to help all of these people—anyone in any form of direct sales—to market any product or service effectively, whether that person is a sales rep, independent distributor, or even an entrepreneur creating a direct sales network from scratch. Also, it is designed to help the person who wants only to sell direct to customers and the person who wants to build a sales team, too.

Part I sets the stage by describing the basic characteristics of direct sales programs, and it focuses particularly on multi-level (or personal or network) marketing because many people still aren't clear about what a multi-level company is and how it differs from other direct sales companies or from pyramid and chain letter schemes.

Part II begins with a discussion of the kind of attitude you need for success in marketing, because this is where success begins—your outlook and approach.

Part III deals with the topic of choosing a good product or service to market, how to select a good company and sales leader or sponsor to work with, and how to get properly prepared to go out and sell—whatever the product or company.

Part IV covers the technique for getting customers and distributors. Though some direct-sales people may be interested only in getting customers, I have covered these two topics together, since many distributors do both at the same time. If you're not interested in recruiting a sales team, just skip over these parts.

Then, in Part V, the techniques for creating and maintaining a successful sales organization—the next step after you have recruited a sales network—are discussed. Again, if you're not building a sales group, skip this part.

Part VI covers some special events that can be useful in making sales and building your organization.

Finally, Part VII deals with the basics of running a small business. It is oriented to the person who has never run a business before and may be starting the business out of his or her home.

At one time I considered having an extensive Resources and Directory section. But this industry is changing so rapidly that after six months, most of the listings I collected were out of date. Addresses and phone numbers changed, or organizations dropped out of existence entirely. So I have only listed a few major resources, which one can contact for more extensive and regularly updated information.

Chapter 2

TYPES OF DIRECT SALES PROGRAMS

There are four types of direct sales programs you can get involved in: a direct sales company that has a network of sales reps to show the product line, a party plan program with counselors and advisers, a multi-level, network or personal marketing company with independent distributors, or your own entrepreneurial venture.

This chapter will discuss each of these avenues of marketing briefly and distinguish them from other forms of marketing. Then, it will describe multi-level, network, or personal marketing at length, since this is the newest form of direct sales, the most complex, and the one which is subject to a great deal of controversy and confusion today.

DIRECT SALES AND OTHER FORMS OF MARKETING

The three major categories of marketing are retailing, mail order or direct mail, and direct sales.

Retailing: This is the most common form of marketing today. You go to a store and buy something at retail. In turn, the retailer gets his or her products from one of three sources: a wholesaler or distributor, a sales rep who takes orders from the manufacturer, or from the manufacturer himself.

Mail Order or Direct Mail: In mail order, you purchase something from an ad (usually in a magazine or newspaper, sometimes on TV) which directs you to mail in your payment. In direct mail, you receive a flyer or catalogue in the mail, and again you make your purchase by mail.

Direct Sales: In direct sales, a representative from the company contacts you personally. This person may be an outside employee for the company, a commissioned salesperson, or an independent entrepreneur distributing the products for one or more companies. He or she may call you on the phone, use a telemarketing system, go door to door, sell to you from a booth at a trade show or consumer fair, organize a sales party for you, or otherwise sell direct.

Types of Direct Sales Programs

Though four major types of direct sales programs exist, there often is much overlap in fitting particular programs into these categories. The best rule of thumb is to categorize the company by its primary focus.

Traditional Direct Sales Program: In this program, the direct-sales person works for the company as a sales representative, and is usually assigned a limited territory in which to sell the company's products. The individual is usually closely supervised by the company, and may even have specific hours to work in the field. He or she may sometimes be supplied leads by the company, too, and can variously call on individuals, organizations, stores, or companies. Normally the salesperson will be interested only in selling to customers and will not be involved in recruiting others to market the line. However, if the company is large enough, there will be a sales management structure, with sales managers assigned to oversee several salespeople in an area and perhaps some regional or national managers to oversee the local managers. All of these managers will get overrides on the salespeople they supervise, and possibly a salary.

Party Plan: In this situation, the salesperson is frequently called a counselor, consultant, adviser, or sales associate, and usually sells by putting on a sales party. He, or more usually she, can sell items such as dishes (Tupperware), cosmetics (Avon and Mary Kay), or more recently, sensual adult products. In some party plan programs, the sales associates are hired directly by the company; in others, the distributor can do some recruiting—usually from among the more interested customers who attend a party. Typically, the sales associate organizes a sales party by finding a willing host or hostess who invites some friends, neighbors, or business associates. Once the party is arranged, the sales associate does the presentation, sells products at the party, usually gives the host or hostess a commission, and later may follow up with customers to see if they need more products, might be interested in hosting their own party, or perhaps would like to represent the company.

Entrepreneurial Venture: This kind of program is basically one you create yourself. You buy some product wholesale from a manufacturer, or you work out arrangements to secure a service wholesale. Then you work it via direct sales yourself, however you want—to friends, to business associates, at flea markets, for conventions, and so on. You aren't quite a distributor for another company, since you are marketing these products under your own name, and you have no guidelines from the company to follow on how to market its goods. Essentially, you are free to do what you want.

Multi-Level Marketing (also called Network Marketing or Personal Marketing): This method may share elements with other types of marketing since the MLM category describes a company with a certain kind of marketing and compensation plan involving several levels of group organization and commission payment, but does not refer to the particular selling methods used (such as traditional direct sales, party plan, or mail order). Although most sales methods can be adapted to this plan, multi-level marketing until recently has been primarily a program involving direct personal sales. But now more and more MLM distributors are using direct mail and mail order. The key difference between MLM and other forms of sales is that the multi-level distributor is not only seeking to sell to customers retail but also is looking for distributors to sell the product or service to others. The multi-level distributor then trains these distributors to find and train others and not only gets a sales commission or profit on his or her own sales but gets a commission, bonus, or override when the distributors in his or her sales group make sales, too.

Another distinguishing characteristic of MLM is that the salesperson, usually called a distributor, sales associate, or consultant, is an independent contractor who may sell anywhere, although he or she is usually subject to company guidelines regarding advertising and the manner in which the product can be sold. (For example, even though the distributor can sell anywhere in the country, certain kinds of places—such as retail stores and trade shows—may be off limits.)

Recently, companies have coined all sorts of names to refer to multi-level programs, such as "network marketing" and "personal marketing." But there seems to be no real difference between the companies using these names. The main reason for using them seems to be the controversial image surrounding MLM. Many members of the general public still confuse MLM with pyramid schemes and chain letters, and many shady operators are still trying to legitimize illegal pyramids and letters by calling them MLM opportunities. So it's no wonder that many legitimate companies with multi-level marketing plans are calling their programs something else. But however these terms are used—multi-level, network marketing, personal sales, and so forth—they refer to the same basic thing—MLM.

THE BASICS OF
MULTI-LEVEL MARKETING

Multi-level programs have recently experienced rapid growth because MLM offers the possibility of high earnings—since it operates on the principle of multiplication of effort. You create an organization to market the product or service, and your earnings are based on what the members of your team earn as well as on your own efforts. And in turn, when you select a good program and promote it effectively, you can develop an extremely large sales organization, for you help your immediate team members develop their own teams, and their organizations become part of your group.

So you build your success on the success of others, and you play a crucial role in helping your distributors succeed by teaching them what to do. In short, a key principle of MLM is that you succeed by helping others succeed, too.

Another reason MLM has become popular is that you are not just selling a product to a customer and going on to make more sales. Instead, you are sharing the product and business opportunity with the distributors you sponsor and teaching them to do the same, so you create a warm, supportive organization to market the product.

You might think of MLM this way: it involves creating a

marketing network by sharing a product or service with a few people; then they share it with a few people; then they share and so on, until soon, there is an ever-growing network of people involved in distributing the product. And the larger your own network grows and the more product your network sells, the more you earn.

HOW MUCH YOU CAN EXPECT TO EARN IN MLM

Currently, some MLM superstars are making $50,000, $100,000, even $200,000 a month in big companies like Amway, Shaklee, and Herbalife, just as top performers attain big earnings in any industry. And some have become millionaires many times over, which shows what is possible.

But it is important to realize that making this kind of money takes perseverance, usually full-time effort for a year or more, plus a measure of luck. Also, these top earners represent only a tiny percentage of the millions of MLM distributors.

More generally, people in MLM pursue this as a sideline, spending a few hours a week in order to earn a few hundred dollars extra a month. According to many MLM experts, it takes about six months to a year for the average person to earn about $700 to $1,400 a month working about five to six hours a week. When one of the major industry publications, *Multi-Level Marketing News*, did a 1982 study of their readers, who are probably more active than the average multi-level distributor, they found the average respondent made about $11,000 a year marketing the products of about four different companies.

However, the specific earning picture varies greatly from program to program, since growth patterns differ widely. So you can get a better picture of what is typical if you ask what the average distributor earns when he or she starts in the program and what the active distributor earns on the average each year. Yet these averages are only guidelines, for, ultimately, how much you earn is up to you, since you are an independent contractor, your own boss. So you can work as much or as little as you want, and wherever you want since there are no territories. But if you want to do well, be prepared for hard work ... just as you have to work hard to be successful in almost anything.

Recently, all sorts of programs—usually called national sponsoring clubs or recruiting services—have sprouted offering to do all the work for you in return for a membership fee. But in reality, these programs are glorified pyramid schemes that don't usually work, because they soon run out of enough new persons to make the program pay off for any but the few on the top. And even if one does get a sales organization from this effort, frequently those who join buy very little or nothing at all and expect others to do the work—so the result usually is an extremely ineffective sales group. Therefore, be assured, MLM, like any form of direct sales, takes hard work.

HOW YOUR INCOME AND ORGANIZATION GROW IN MLM

In traditional direct sales programs, income is based on one's personal sales. You get a commission for whatever you sell. But in MLM, your income depends on several factors: the size of your group, how much product your group purchases and sells, and the size of your commission at each level in your organization. Although some MLM companies distinguish between different types of earnings—such as *commissions* for your direct sales and *bonuses* or *overrides* when people in your sales group sell something—to make the topic easier to talk about, I call them all commissions.

You have to work out the figures yourself for each program,

since every marketing plan differs in various respects: the number of levels, the commission rate at each level, the amount of product consumers and distributors are likely to buy, the minimum purchase requirement, if any, to get a commission, and so on.

But the basic principle of building an MLM organization and making it grow and pay off is the same. So let's look at what happens when you build an organization.

First, there's just *you* marketing the product. Initially, you may be buying at wholesale and selling some product at retail, which is one way to earn money as well as to introduce people to the product who might later become part of your sales team.

But a key principle in MLM is then to start building your organization by locating others to sell the product as soon as you can. Once you find these people, teach them not only to sell the product but to find others to be distributors, too. That's how you build an MLM sales team and get your team members to build their own teams, so your organization grows.

The MLM Principle of Multiplication

In typical MLM presentations, you'll hear about how your organization grows geometrically through the principle of multiplication. For example, suppose you know two persons, and they know two persons, and they know two, and so on. If this growth pattern continues, your team will look like this if it grows to four levels:

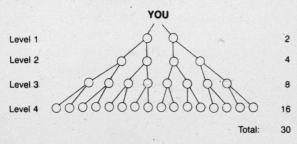

	YOU	
Level 1		2
Level 2		4
Level 3		8
Level 4		16
	Total:	30

You only knew two persons but you have gotten thirty into your organization.

Now suppose you and each of your team members recruited an average of three distributors each. Your growth pattern to the fourth level would look like this:

You
3
9
27
81
———
120

Now when you add one more person, the growth of your group will theoretically multiply like this:

You	You	You
4	5	6
16	25	36
64	125	216
256	625	1296
———	———	———
340	780	1554

Then, by adding in your average commission earnings for each person in your organization, you can see what you potentially might earn. For example, suppose you get an average monthly commission of $10 per person. Your total monthly commission based on the size of your organization might look something like this:

```
  120 persons  = $  1,200
  340 persons  = $  3,400
  780 persons  = $  7,800
1,554 persons  = $15,540
```

Then, if you are able to build an even larger organization, your income potential can increase that much more. Significantly, though—and this is one reason MLM has become so popular—you don't have to sign up the world to build a large group. In fact, you shouldn't. You should focus on working with a few individuals and training them to build a group, too. But they have to be the right people—those who will put the necessary effort into building an organization. You may have to sponsor a dozen, two dozen, three dozen persons to find them. But when you do, the key principle of MLM is to concentrate on helping those few select persons be successful.

In short, an MLM sales program works best when you *build deep, not wide*. If you build wide, you end up spending too much time recruiting new people yourself, and you won't have the time to help your direct recruits learn how to sponsor and teach others. *So the key is to work with a few people and teach them to do what you do.* Then, your organization grows. (If you are going to be explaining MLM to others, you can use Charts 1 and 2 to help you do this.)

Gini Graham Scott

WHAT AN MLM ORGANIZATION LOOKS LIKE IN PRACTICE

Now, no MLM organization will look perfectly like those on the organizational charts just described. These are really hypothetical examples of what your organization might look like if each person in your group recruited a certain average number of persons.

But in reality you'll have numerous persons in your organization who perform very differently. For example, you might have one hotshot who brings in ten recruits, another who brings in three, several who do nothing at all, and some who average about four to six each. And they, in turn, will have persons who perform differently. So your organization is likely to look something like this:

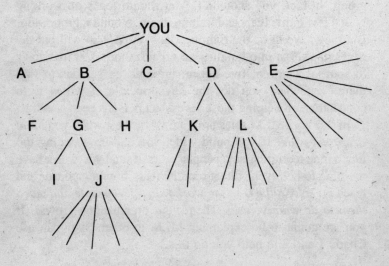

18

CHART 1: HOW YOU MULTIPLY YOUR EFFORTS IN MULTI-LEVEL

You and Your Recruits
Share the Program with
an Average of Two Persons

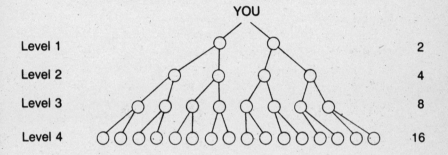

Level 1		2
Level 2		4
Level 3		8
Level 4		16

You and Your Recruits
Share the Program with
an Average of Three Persons

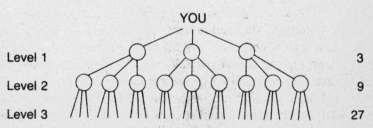

Level 1		3
Level 2		9
Level 3		27

CHART 2: BUILDING AN ORGANIZATION— WHAT HAPPENS IF YOU EACH BRING IN AN AVERAGE OF:

	2 Persons	3 Persons	4 Persons	5 Persons	6 Persons
	YOU	YOU	YOU	YOU	YOU
Level 1	2	3	4	5	6
Level 2	4	9	16	25	36
Level 3	8	27	64	125	216
Level 4	16	81	256	625	1296
Level 5	32	273	1024	3125	7776
Total:	62	393	1364	3905	9330

BUT IS MLM PYRAMID?

Inevitably, multi-level selling gets compared to the pyramid. Certainly, the diagrams presented earlier show a pyramid structure. But when people say MLM is a pyramid, they are referring to the illegal pyramid and chain letter schemes that have been repeatedly exposed for the scams they are.

It is important to recognize the crucial differences.

First, multi-level marketing is a *legitimate* way of moving merchandise. As long as a multi-level company adheres to key guidelines, to be discussed in detail in chapter 6, "Selecting a Good Product or Service," a multi-level program is perfectly legal. In fact, some of the biggest companies today are involved in multi-level—either by marketing products themselves with a multi-level sales plan or by supplying products to MLM companies. For example, some of the big corporate names include Beatrice Foods (supplies foods to an MLM company) and Kodak Films (some film products are distributed multi-level).

A key difference between an MLM program and an illegal pyramid is that multi-level marketing actually moves a valuable product or service, and all payouts are made for sales of that product or service, not on recruitment. By contrast, an illegal pyramid usually offers no product that has any value, and it operates on the principle of making payments for recruiting others. So, generally, only money moves through the network created by a pyramid, and no one gets any valuable product in return for the money that is paid.

Other major differences are that in MLM there are consumers who want to purchase a product or service, and consumers do not have to become distributors to make a purchase. Also, distributors do not have to buy the product to market it, although most do. By contrast, in the pyramid, everyone has to join the network to participate.

The differences are also obvious in the results of participation. In a legitimate MLM program, everyone benefits, because consumers get valuable products and services, while those selling them reap rewards for their marketing efforts— and these rewards can be great, indeed, because of the team-building multiplication effect. By contrast, a pyramid is a get-rich-quick scheme in which only a few people benefit, because they have been the first to get involved. They get the money which flows up the pyramid. But when the inevitable saturation occurs, the people on the bottom of the pyramid run out of new prospects and lose money.

In short, like other forms of direct sales, multi-level marketing provides the basis for building a long-term business which offers a valuable product and good service, while a pyramid scheme produces a few winners and a lot of losers who get hurt because nothing is purchased, only money is passed along. You can see these differences summarized in Chart 3.

CHART 3: THE DIFFERENCES BETWEEN MLM AND THE PYRAMID

Multi-Level Marketing	The Pyramid
A completely legal form of business.	An illegal rip-off scheme.
Based on the principle of sponsoring and teaching others, to help them succeed in an ongoing business.	Based on the principle of getting in first or very early, so one can sign up others and encourage them to do the same.
Involves moving valuable products or services from the producer to the consumer.	Involves moving money from someone on the bottom of the pyramid to someone on top. (Occasionally a product may be offered, but it is usually of little value; and the product is incidental to the emphasis on recruiting persons to sign up and give money to someone else.)
Consumers can purchase products and services without getting involved in the marketing program; conversely, those marketing the program do not have to purchase products to market them (though it helps).	Everyone has to join the pyramid to participate; and no valuable products are offered to the consumer. Some pyramid programs do have products, but they are not sold retail, just moved among recruits, and generally no one actually uses the products.

Multi-Level Marketing	The Pyramid
A recognized form of business as long as the company adheres to applicable state laws; in turn, multi-level distributors and companies gain assorted tax benefits from the government.	A get-rich scheme that is regarded as a fraud by the government; participants are thus subject to various fines and punishments.
Those who join the program later can make more than those who joined before them, based on their efforts, since there are always new consumers and potential distributors for the program.	Those who join the program later usually make much less and eventually lose money, because, after a while, the market becomes saturated or the scheme is exposed for what it is.

THE ADVANTAGES OF A DIRECT SALES OR MULTI-LEVEL BUSINESS

Direct sales and multi-level businesses are growing at a rate of about 30 percent annually, because these have a number of major advantages for the person who wants to start a business. Most of these advantages exist in any form of direct sales; some are true of MLM businesses in particular (summarized in Chart 4).

CHART 4: THE ADVANTAGES OF A DIRECT SALES OR MULTI-LEVEL BUSINESS

1. You can purchase the product at wholesale as a consumer.
2. You use and sell a better-quality product at a lower price, since the company can put more into the prod-

Gini Graham Scott

CHART 4: THE ADVANTAGES OF A DIRECT SALES OR MULTI-LEVEL BUSINESS (continued)

uct—because it puts less into marketing and promotion.

3. You have the freedom of being in business for yourself, of choosing your own hours and how much time you want to spend on your business.
4. Very little start-up capital is needed—usually less than $100.
5. Overhead is low, since you can run your business from your home.
6. You are not required to stock inventory, although it's good to have some on hand for samples.
7. There are no territorial restrictions—sell the product anywhere.
8. High earning potential exists, since you can expand your earnings as your organization grows.
9. You offer a personal service.
10. You can work with members of your family, since you work at home.
11. You can have fun, travel, meet new friends, and enjoy positive learning experiences.
    ...And you can probably think of other advantages.

1. *If you are already using the product as a consumer, you get extra savings as a distributor or sales rep,* because you can purchase the product at wholesale.

2. *You get to use and sell a better-quality product at a lower price.* Since the direct sales or MLM company has a team of independent business persons marketing and promoting the product, it doesn't have to do as much advertising and promoting itself. As a result, it can spend that money on the product itself or on the commissions it pays to those in the field.

3. *You are in business for yourself and have the freedom and tax advantages that go with this.* You can choose your own hours and decide how much time you want to devote to the business. Also, you can use the business as a tax shelter to reduce your taxes on your income. For example, if you are in a 25 percent tax bracket, you are spending about three months of the year working for the government just to pay taxes. But by having your own business, you can get back some or most of this, so you are spending these months working for yourself.

4. *You can go into a direct sales or MLM business for very little money—usually less than $100.* And in return, the income potential can be quite high if the business is successful. By contrast, in most businesses, the start-up costs are tremendous, while the risks are high. *Multi-Level Marketing News* magazine did a survey of typical costs to launch a small retail business and found the costs ranged from $7,000–$30,000 at the low end (to start a travel agency: $7,000–$24,000; a barbershop: $15,000–$25,000; a plant store: $11,000–$24,000) to $50,000 or $100,000 or even more for certain kinds of businesses. (For example, it's around $60,000–$100,000 to start a camera shop; $50,000–$60,000 for a hardware store; $50,000–$100,000 for a medium-sized restaurant.) Then, if you look at the failure rate, you'll see that 60–80 percent fail within five years, according to statistics from the Small Business Administration.

The franchise boom, which started in the late 1940s, occurred because franchising offered a way to reduce the failure rate, by providing franchise holders with a proven formula for success and training. And franchising has proved to be an extremely successful way to step into a growing business of your own. However, you still need high levels of capital. (For example, a McDonald franchise is over $100,000.) But in a good direct sales or MLM company, you get both the training and the opportunity to use the company name for a minimal investment.

5. *There is little overhead*, because you can run a direct sales or MLM business from your home.

6. *You are not required to stock any inventory, though you should have some inventory on hand, if only for samples*. In most sales businesses, you have to have an extensive inventory, and if something doesn't sell, you're stuck with it. But in most direct sales and MLM companies today, distributors can deal direct with the company. So you just need enough product to supply your retail customers and new distributors who need samples.

7. *You have no territorial restrictions in all MLM companies and in many direct sales companies*. With no restrictions, you can sell the product anywhere. In most sales positions and in a franchise, you are limited to a certain area.

8. *In MLM and network marketing companies, you can expand your earnings based on what others in your group do*. In traditional retail, direct sales, and franchise operations, you are limited to what you or your own store produces. But in MLM or network sales, your earning potential can expand exponentially, because you can build a large, growing organization that makes money for you.

9. *You offer personal service to customers, and today, that's a real plus*. In this age of discount house, department store, and catalogue showroom shopping, customers can easily feel like just a number; and typically, store clerks don't know

much about the product—just what it says on the box. But you can provide personal service. Moreover, yours is one of the few businesses today that can offer to bring the product to the customer.

10. *A direct sales business is ideal for a couple or a family* since it can be based in the home, and working together can bring everyone closer together, too.

11. *The business provides an opportunity for fun, travel, new friends, and positive learning experiences* . . . and you can probably think of other advantages.

So, with all these advantages, it's not surprising direct sales and MLM are among the fastest-growing forms of business today.

BUT IS DIRECT SALES SELLING?

Some people try to claim multi-level or network marketing isn't selling and describe it as "sharing," since an essential part of it is sharing, teaching, and sponsoring, and "selling" has acquired some negative connotations in our culture. People associate selling with fast-buck operators, with high-pressure salesmen, with sales hype that turns a product message into pure puffery, and with the act of convincing someone to buy something he or she does not need or want, or can't afford. But these are simply abuses, and selling is a perfectly respectable, honorable calling.

In fact, the most successful salespeople know that effective selling involves responding to real needs and real desires, and providing a valuable service by supplying a product or service that answers those needs and wants. Such salespeople are true professionals, and in general, successful salespeople can make more money in America than persons in any other profession—more than doctors, lawyers, professors, even Supreme Court judges.

So there is nothing wrong with being in sales, and there is no reason to make direct sales or MLM sound as if it isn't sales. Of course it is selling. An essential part of it is sharing, teaching, and sponsoring. But in the end, a product or service is sold, too.

Sometimes, direct sales or MLM people try to recruit others by claiming that they aren't involved in selling, because many persons feel they can't sell anything, regardless of their opinion of the selling profession. They believe it takes a special kind of person to sell something, and when they hear about any kind of marketing, they think, "Oh, no, I can't do that. I don't know how to sell." Or they think, "I don't feel right about selling something to my friends."

But these people are wrong on two counts:

1. All of us are salespeople to some degree. *We* are always selling ourselves, even if we do not think so. When we apply for a job, we have to sell ourselves to our prospective employer. When we hire people, we have to sell them on the advantages of working for us or our company. And even when we meet people, we are in effect *selling* them on the fact that we are a nice person to know. And they are *selling* us. Similarly, if we ask someone to do something for us, persuade someone to go with us somewhere, go out on a date, or ask someone to get married—all that is *selling* in some form. It may not involve directly moving a product or service, but we are *selling* someone on something—on us, on taking some action, on feeling a certain way.

2. When people think about selling, they are often thinking about the negative, high-pressure aspects of selling a product

STRIKE IT RICH IN PERSONAL SELLING

no one wants. But another way to think of selling is as a means of giving information and sharing an opportunity that will bring someone a valuable benefit. Also, there are quiet, gentle ways to do this, discussed in chapter 9, "Basic Sales Principles," so no one feels any pressure.

Thus, these forms of marketing definitely involve *selling*, but they involve *sharing, teaching*, and *sponsoring*, too. Selling is just the final step. After sharing the message, you persuade or sell people on the benefits of the program. Then, you sponsor and teach them how to share the message and sell others. And there's nothing wrong with doing this . . . we sell each other on ourselves all the time.

You may want to enphasize the sharing and teaching aspects of marketing to a person who initially resists the idea of selling when you present your program as a business opportunity. But, yes, direct sales and MLM are selling . . . and that's perfectly fine.

Part II

MAINTAINING
THE RIGHT ATTITUDE
FOR SUCCESS

Chapter 3

THINKING SUCCESS

In order to be successful in any kind of marketing or sales, you have to start with the right attitude. You have to think and feel success. And you have to direct your efforts to achieving your goals.

Hundreds of persons whose names are now known in every household—such as the Wright brothers, Thomas Edison, Dustin Hoffman, Burt Reynolds, and Barbra Streisand—met failure again and again when they were first starting out. But they persevered, and the rest, as the saying goes, is history.

There are some excellent success books, tapes, and training courses around. Become familiar with these, if you aren't already. Not only will these materials give you the basic principles in more depth than possible here, but steeping yourself in success principles and surrounding yourself with success-oriented people will help you stay on course.

Remember . . . you normally can't expect success to come to you overnight. You'll find that sometimes the going seems hard; sometimes people say no to your message. But if you have chosen a good product or service to market, have clear goals, maintain the right attitude, and keep working, you'll make it. You have to know that, believe it fully, and stay on course.

Not everyone is going to say yes to you; and you can't let that get you down. Rather, you have to regard getting a yes as a question of numbers. No matter how good your product, in most cases, about 50 to 75 percent of those you contact will be interested, and about a third of these will be interested in marketing the product, too. And perhaps 5 to 10 percent will become star performers. So you have to play the numbers game and realize that for every no you are closer to getting a yes.

You have to, as the song says, "accentuate the positive." No matter what anyone says, if you are sure of your product and your goals, if you maintain the right attitude, you can convey your enthusiasm and belief—and that's what you need to be successful in marketing anything.

THE BASIC PRINCIPLES OF SUCCESS

The basic principles of success were first outlined by Napoleon Hill in the 1920s, after he spent twenty years researching the reasons that extremely successful people become successful. In 1900 Andrew Carnegie hired him to put together a success course, and he spent the next twenty years interviewing achievers. He started his first success course in 1922, and then spent the rest of his life, about forty years, continuing to study success.

These principles provide a kind of road map to success, and to be successful in marketing, as in any other endeavor, you must follow the right road. This chapter describes the basic principles Napoleon Hill discovered. For further information, look at Napoleon Hill's books on success: *Think and Grow Rich*, *Success through a Positive Mental Attitude*, *The Master Key to Riches*, and *The Laws of Success*.

Napoleon Hill's Twelve Keys to Success

1. *Have a positive mental attitude*. Your thoughts play a crucial role in creating your reality. If you think positively, you tend to manifest positive situations and attract successful, positive people to you. By contrast, a negative attitude sows the seeds for negative experience.

2. *Have sound physical and mental health*. You have to be physically and mentally fit to put your best energies into achieving your goals.

3. *Go the extra mile*. Be willing to do that little bit extra. Be willing to try again. Even if you run into obstacles, stick with what you are doing until you achieve your goal. Most people tend to give up easily; but for real success, you need to persist, persist, persist!

4. *Have harmony in human relations*. You need to be understanding and to work comfortably with others to succeed—particularly if you are seeking to build a sales team to market your product.

5. *Be free of fear*. Many people are literally afraid of success and fear doing something different that will better their life. Or they are skeptical and claim something can't be done, because they are afraid of being wrong. But the person who is successful has overcome fears and is confident of attaining ultimate success.

6. *Have a hope of achievement*. You have to pick goals that are realistically possible, and you must realize that everyone has the ability to succeed. Further, you have to be committed to wanting to achieve.

7. *Have faith*. You must believe you can do it. More than that, you must open yourself to believing you have an inner power that will enable you to succeed. Then, by opening yourself in this way, you become open to the powers of the universe, which will give you the added strength you need.

8. *Be willing to share your blessings*. You must be willing to help others share your good fortune and succeed, too. In marketing and sales, as in other areas of life, you cannot do it alone; and so, to get others' support, you must help and support them, too.

9. *Choose a labor of love*. You must commit yourself to doing something you really want to do; otherwise you are sure to lose interest, enthusiasm, and the motivation to succeed. Likewise, regardless of what you are marketing, you must choose a product you really believe in and one you really want to promote.

10. *Have self-discipline*. You must be able to control your emotions and attitudes when you work with others and to stay in charge when you give a sales presentation. Also, you must have the self-control to stick to what you are doing and carefully schedule your activities according to your priorities.

11. *Have economic security or feel economically secure*. It's hard to think seriously about "making a million" or getting to the top if you aren't economically secure or don't feel that you are. It can take several months to start earning a substantial income in launching a business and building a sales network, so in the meantime, you should have a firm economic base through resources you can fall back on or by working on something else. Then, you can more comfortably and rationally begin building your business, and you won't convey the image

of someone who is desperately striving to make it. If you are economically secure, you can be relaxed about how you present your message, and you will be more convincing as a result.

12. *Have the capacity to understand people.* The key to success in any kind of sales is recognizing where the other person is coming from so you can respond to his or her needs and wants. To do this, you must be willing to listen and find out what the other person is about. Then, by being understanding, you can create a win-win situation, where you gain success by giving that person what he or she wants.

Other Important Success Principles

1. *Whenever you encounter some adversity, look for the seed of an equivalent benefit.* In other words, whatever happens, always view it from the positive side. Thus, consider any defeat, any obstacle, as a challenge or learning experience. Then, go on. No failure is really a failure unless you see it that way. Rather, it is another event that gives you a chance to grow and learn more.

For example, if a series of prospects say no, use this experience as an opportunity to assess what you are doing and improve upon it. Maybe your presentation could be better; maybe you need to listen more carefully to your prospect. Whatever the difficulty, learn from your defeats and change accordingly, to make your future experiences more successful.

2. *Concentrate on building up your weaker areas.* You've heard it said, "A chain is no stronger than its weakest link." When you build a business or sales team, that principle is likewise true. So from time to time, evaluate what you are doing and notice any gaps. Do you have problems with no-shows at your sales presentations? Is it difficult getting those

in your organization to follow through? What other problem areas are there? Examine the situation, determine where your biggest problems lie, and work on correcting those first.

3. *Be enthusiastic*. Selling is based on transferring your enthusiasm for a product or service to someone else. So even if you have had a bad day and don't *feel* enthusiastic, *act* enthusiastic, and you will become that way. Or if necessary, do something to build up your enthusiasm. How? Think of the things you like to do that make you feel good, and then do something like that. It also helps to write down a list of the things you like to do and pull it out when you feel down. Get yourself feeling enthusiastic and acting enthusiastic, and your enthusiasm will radiate outward and help you make your sale.

4. *Develop your imagination to turn your ideas into reality*. Your imagination is an incredible resource. By developing it, you can come up with all sorts of creative ideas to help you promote your product or service. Also, using your imagination, you can visualize what you want to happen, and by imagining this intensely, you can make what you visualize occur.

For example, if you want to be a successful person, visualize yourself in that role, then act the part. At first it may seem foreign to you, but as you continue to visualize and play the part, you'll become that person. You become what you think and imagine; you simply need to start rehearsing for that part.

5. *Focus your attention*. No one achieves success if they are scattered and fragmented or drift through life. You have to concentrate your efforts and attention on achieving a specific goal, and mobilize your powers to achieve that.

For instance, when you focus on a specific product, you are continually thinking about ways to promote it, and therefore take advantage of every opportunity to do so. Say you are promoting a health product. You might jump at a chance re-mark, such as "I'm tired," to explain how your product might help. Or if someone mentions organizing a party, you might think of a way to include your product and offer: "Let's give out some samples as party favors." By contrast, when your attention isn't focused, you miss opportunities like these. You are thinking about too many things, and so it becomes difficult to generate creative, productive ideas.

6. *Develop accurate thinking and acquire all the facts you need.* You have complete control over what you think and therefore have the power to gain any knowledge you need. And indeed you should acquire it, because knowledge is power.

In marketing, having the facts is particularly important, because your credibility and ability to sell a product depend on this. You have to know what you are talking about, and when you do, others know it. You will be confident and speak knowledgeably and convincingly. Conversely, when you don't have this knowledge it will become painfully apparent, and you will surely fail.

Additionally, when you have the facts, you can make a good, reasoned decision, such as whether to promote a particular program, and you needn't let your emotions sway you into making a bad judgment. Of course, in the long run, go with your intuition or sixth sense; but first have accurate knowledge. Then, you can safely let your intuition run free. So look to experts, consultants, books, whatever you need—and before you jump into action, get the facts!

7. *Budget your time.* Time is money. You only have so many hours in the day. So allot your time carefully when you plan how to achieve success by setting priorities and distrib-uting your time accordingly. Then, if you encounter competing pressures that take your time away from what you want to do, learn to say a clear, firm no.

Besides listing priorities, it also helps to set up general guidelines for what you need to do and when. For example, in your datebook, sketch out what you plan to do in the morning, afternoon, and evening, and realistically set aside enough time to accomplish each task. As you need to, be flexible and change your time budget, but use your budget as a guide.

We are taught to budget our money and not spend more than our limit. So if time is money, why not budget time! Successful people do.

8. *Take personal initiative*. Don't just wait for things to happen; make them happen! It is sometimes said that there are three kinds of people: "Those that make it happen, those that wait for things to happen, and those who don't know what's happening." Well, the only ones who are successful are those who act.

So avoid putting off decisions and procrastinating. Usually, people who do this are afraid to act. They are afraid of being wrong. But the secret of success is not to worry about making mistakes. Sure, you'll make them. But that's how you learn— by seeing any obstacles or defeats as steps on the path to success.

So act! Act! Act! All leaders have this quality. They take initiative and act. The people who hang back end up as followers. But following never brought anyone big success. The people who succeed big, *act*!

9. *Develop a pleasing personality*. Since success depends on working in harmony with others and in understanding them, it helps to have a pleasing personality so people will like to be around you. And as every salesperson knows, when you are selling, you are not just selling a product; you are also selling yourself.

Thus, you want a positive, outgoing, attractive personality

40

that makes others want to be with you and work with you, and convinces them you are a success.

Try listing the qualities you think of when you characterize an attractive, successful person—such as cooperative, understanding, helpful, enthusiastic, friendly, warm, interesting, and so on. Then, note if you need to work on further developing any of these qualities. If so, think of things you can do to develop these traits and do them. For example, to be more outgoing, participate in activities that bring you into groups of people, such as throwing parties or giving speeches. Even if you feel uncomfortable at first, do it, because after a while, you'll develop a new way of being with others, and this personality trait will become a natural part of you.

10. *Surround yourself with positive, supportive people.* Your own attitude is conditioned by those in your environment, and even if you try to be positive, negative critical people will inevitably pull you down. So when you encounter such people, and you will, simply be polite and let them go. Then, concentrate on being around positive people.

In fact, draw on these persons for help and ideas. According to Napoleon Hill, one tool for success is creating a "mastermind alliance" made up of people who support your idea, have the abilities needed to help carry it out, and want to assist you in seeing it realized. Such a group can be used to brainstorm new ideas, create action plans, and implement them. Indeed, any sales team you join or create is much like this—positive, supportive people working with you to achieve personal goals.

Every outstanding success has been based on cooperative effort, and marketing is no different. You need to work with other positive people to achieve your success.

11. *Develop the habits of success.* We develop habits, because it's easier to run our life that way. Then, we don't have

to think about what we are doing each time we do something; we just do it unconsciously and it gets done.

It's the same with achieving success. We get used to doing things a certain way and may not realize that some of these activities interfere with our achieving success. It's as if our thoughts flow through our brain like a river, coursing through the same path again and again, unless we do something to change the channel.

So it's important to assess our present habits and see if we have any bad habits detracting from our success so we can change. For example, we may want to get rid of the habits of being lazy, irritable, dishonest, or just drifting through life. To do so, we must begin consciously thinking and acting in the desired way; then, gradually, as we build up new habits, they will become automatic, and we will change. The key is repeating the new pattern frequently and with intensity, for this shows we really want to change and believe we can. Since we become what we think and believe, the change we desire will eventually occur.

CHART 5: MAJOR SUCCESS PRINCIPLES

The Twelve Basics (According to Napoleon Hill)

1. A positive mental attitude
2. Sound physical and mental health
3. Going the extra mile
4. Harmony in human relations
5. Freedom from fear
6. Hope of achievement
7. Faith
8. Sharing your blessings
9. A labor of love
10. Self-discipline
11. Economic security
12. The ability to understand others

Other Important Success Principles

1. Look for benefits in your defeats
2. Work on building your weakest areas
3. Be enthusiastic
4. Develop your imagination
5. Focus your attention
6. Develop accurate thinking and get the facts
7. Budget your time
8. Take personal initiative
9. Develop a pleasing personality
10. Surround yourself with positive, supportive people
11. Develop the habits of success

Chapter 4

STAYING ON THE PATH TO SUCCESS

THE IMPORTANCE OF PERSISTENCE

To be successful, you must persist. The going may not always be easy, but you need to reaffirm your goals continually, repeat personal affirmations, accept the obstacles that come as challenges and learning experiences, and move on.

Now and then you may read of instant success. But mostly, you must be prepared for some solid hard work to achieve your ends.

And don't let the skeptics discourage you. In the beginning, some of the worst skeptics may be friends and relatives, who are used to seeing you as a certain kind of person. So they may not be ready, able, or willing to see you in the new role you want for yourself. Or they may not be interested in changing their own way of life, and may feel your relationship with them threatened if you change. Thus, they may try to deflect you from the path, saying things such as, "Oh, don't work so hard," or "Don't be silly. No one makes that kind of money."

So if you talk to people about what you are doing and they respond this way, don't let their comments discourage you or turn you from your goals. Simply acknowledge their comments and don't argue. They may come around eventually when you are successful, and you can always contact them again. Or they may never be ready. Just treat their comments as a duck does water, and let any negatives roll off your back. You know what you want—just focus on that.

ASSOCIATE WITH
SUCCESS-ORIENTED PEOPLE

It's crucial to associate with people who believe as you do. In *The Joy of Reaching the Top*, Dr. Dan Ford describes how persons tend continually to fall or rise to their own level wherever they may be. He met three men in Chicago who were going to move to Los Angeles. One was earning $100 a week as a dishwasher, another, about $200 a week as a factory worker, and a third, $1,000 a week as a salesman. When he saw them three months later in Los Angeles, they were doing and making about the same thing. The point is that people tend to get into ruts and stay comfortable doing what they have done before, because change is uncomfortable.

However, when you are headed for the top, you must be willing to change to get there, and that may mean having to leave some individuals behind. You can offer them the opportunity to join you; but if they don't want to change, that's their privilege. You can't make them change. And remaining close to these persons can hold you back, particularly if they are critical of what you want to do, because they can make you lose heart.

It's a well-known fact: just as like attracts like, people with similar attitudes, interests, and values tend to stick together. And the people you associate with influence you.

So to be successful, associate with successful people. Even if you are not quite where you want to be yet, join groups and participate in activities with those who are successful or want to be.

And don't let feelings of envy or jealousy get you down. Remember, most of these persons worked hard to get where they are and are working just as hard to stay there. So they deserve the rewards of their hard work. Moreover, soon you will be in this position if you follow their example. Thus, stick around these people and use them as models. Talk to them about how they made it. Learn from them. Observe how they dress. Notice how they talk. And be aware that most of them are upbeat, positive, active, go-for-it individuals. Also, ask for their suggestions on other people you can contact. Successful people can help you succeed if you let them.

Conversely, avoid being around negative persons as much as you can. You may not be able to do so entirely. There may be a crank at work who complains all the time. Your mother may call you frequently to tell you about the latest problems of the relatives. Your seatmate on a plane or a guest at a party may start pouring out his or her troubles to you.

But as much as possible, cut down on the negative contacts or turn them into positive ones. For example, when the complainer at work starts to complain, you can rightly say you have another important task to do. You can tell your mother you don't want to hear about all the problems—instead, you'd like to hear about the good things that happened to family members. Or tell your complaining seatmate politely that you'd like to relax. And if someone at a party revels in the negative, you can graciously move away.

In short, to stay upbeat and positive, stay around upbeat, positive persons, who leave you feeling motivated, self-confident, and good.

TECHNIQUES TO KEEP YOURSELF MOTIVATED

When you're working toward success, it's also important to keep yourself continually motivated. Some strategies you can use include the following:

Give Yourself Material Rewards. Set yourself a goal, and when you achieve it, give yourself a reward. Or if you feel down, reward yourself to experience a lift. Even something small can have a motivating effect. Symbolically, you're telling yourself "I'm worth it" or "I can do it."

Put Up Pictures or Photographs of Objects You Want. Make a want book or want list. Then, look at this book or list from time to time, and visualize yourself getting the desired objects and using them. These serve as reminders to keep on going to achieve your goal. Also, thinking about what you want frequently helps to plant the vision of having it firmly in your subconscious.

Compete with Yourself. Many successful people set their own personal goals and don't worry about what others are doing. The advantage of this approach is that you work on realizing your own potential and are not held back by a concern with what everyone else is doing. Remember, everyone has his or her own plan or purpose, and to be successful, you should focus on achieving your own goals.

Review the Success of Others. Read the biographies of successful men and women. Notice the obstacles they had to overcome and the techniques they used to attain success. You will be able to identify with the experiences of many of these people, and their efforts to gain their goal will inspire you to work toward your own. Also, their stories will give you models to emulate and ideas you can apply in your own efforts toward success.

Motivate Yourself by Motivating Others. People who teach or lead others know this principle works. They may not feel like teaching or leading that day, but they must do it. Then, as they perform in that role, the excitement and enthusiasm of others wears off on them, and soon they are feeling motivated again. So, find ways to motivate others to perform, and you'll find your efforts to do so are self-motivating, too.

Start Now! Don't wait. The sooner you act, the sooner you'll reach your success goals. And if you procrastinate, you may find one excuse after another never to begin: "I'm not ready," "I need more information," "I have to think about things for a while."

Sometimes, of course, it's necessary to weigh alternatives and make decisions. But often, these concerns become excuses that interfere with action, because you'll never be as ready as you would like to be or have as much information as you want. In addition, you can always weigh more alternatives.

However, you can learn more and improve your decision-making abilities as you act. So if you need to do so, take some time to make a reasoned decision about what to do. But then, *ACT! Go for it!* You may make some mistakes. But we learn through acting. *So make a decision and do it now!*

SUCCEEDING BY AFFIRMING YOUR SUCCESS

Another great motivator to keep you on the success path is affirming you have achieved what you want to achieve, as if it has already happened. Or affirm you have become the person you want to become.

Doing so accomplishes two things. First, you remind yourself of your goals and so remotivate yourself to achieve. Secondly, by seeing yourself as having already achieved these goals, you put that thought into your subconscious or you reinforce thoughts that are already there. Then, since your subconscious has tremendous powers to actualize what is deeply etched in thought, your thoughts will eventually be manifested in action, if you think them long and hard enough.

To illustrate: you probably have met some constant complainers. Everything bad seems to happen to them. They have accidents. They are frequently sick. They can't find a job. The weather is terrible. And on and on. Well, one reason they have all this bad luck is their attitude. They pay attention to the negative, and as a result tend to draw negative experiences into their life.

By contrast, you can draw success into your life by looking on the positive side and constantly reminding yourself that you already have the success you want. Then, in time, that success will manifest, because your thoughts have created the right setting for that reality to come into being.

Thus, whatever your success goals, concentrate on their coming to pass. Write them down and review them—at least twice a day—and when you do, say them over and over to yourself. Get relaxed, close your eyes, and actually see yourself as you want to be. Visualize having attained what you want. And most importantly, imagine that your success is happening *now*! You have achieved it and are experiencing and living it *now*!

Two ideal times to do this are in the morning when you wake up and at night before you go to bed. These are normally quiet times when you can be alone, and at these times, your subconscious is particularly receptive, for you can put aside the cares of the day and relax.

In fact, you can make this a very special time to further reinforce the reality you are creating with your mind. For example, you might have a special place or chair that you go to when you imagine your success. You might light a candle, turn on some soft music. Then, devote five to ten minutes to actively making affirmations and seeing your goal accomplished.

Also, you might try making affirmations with members of your sales team, since the group effort will provide further support for each of you, as well as bring you closer together to create a better-functioning team. One way to do this is to set aside a small part of a group meeting and then ask everyone to relax, close their eyes, and imagine having attained a personal goal.

Another way to use affirmations, if you are artistically inclined, is to draw some pictures of yourself achieving the goal you want . . . or to create a collage from magazine photos. Then, as you draw or look at these pictures later, the images will reinforce your conviction you are going to achieve your goal.

You can use the accompanying chart (Chart 6) to write out your affirmations. A few sample affirmations follow to get you started, but you should write down your own affirmations in your own words. Then, as you review and concentrate on them, say them to yourself, and as you achieve your goals, make a new affirmations list.

Some Examples of Affirmations:
I draw success, abundance, and good things to me.
I surround myself with wonderful, beautiful, successful people.
My life is filled with complete abundance. I have everything I want or need.
I am living the full life I want. I have a wonderful family,

CHART 6: MY AFFIRMATIONS FOR SUCCESS

(Spend at least 5 minutes twice a day on reviewing these affirmations and visualizing yourself experiencing them. Review them all, but select one or two to experience more intensely each session).

1.

2.

3.

4.

5.

6.

7.

8.

9.

10.

a beautiful home, the car I have always wanted, and I can travel whenever and wherever I want.

I have a winning, persuasive personality, and when I eagerly tell people about my business, they are eager to participate, too.

I am strong, powerful, and have absolute control over my life.

HOW TO RAISE YOUR SPIRITS WHEN YOU FEEL DOWN

So, what if you don't feel good yourself? What if, in spite of your active efforts to pursue your goals, everything seems to have gone wrong? We all have days like that. For example, one day I returned home from a successful week of business in New York to discover that I had made a mistake at the bank and twenty of my checks had bounced, while the money to cover them sat in another account. In addition, I found in the mailbox a $2,500 bill from my printer for a printing job I hadn't authorized yet because of a few errors I had noticed. Then, when I opened the door, I faced a sea of boxes, books, and suitcases—a graphic reminder that I had just moved.

But when things like this happen, you need to keep going, no matter how badly you feel at the moment, and act as if everything is going to be resolved for the best. Also, think about how you might learn from the experience. Then, soon, you will have worked out a way to solve the problem, at least for the present, and will feel good.

Acting "as if" is particularly important, because of the power of the subconscious, noted earlier. If you act "as if," your subconscious starts to think that this is so and acts accordingly. As a result, if you act as if you feel great, even if you do not feel this way at the time, soon you will start feeling good to match your actions. You must exercise your willpower to start the chain of action, but as your subconscious starts to act, you'll feel the way you want. Graphically, the process looks like this:

Your current feeling state
which you want to change
(feeling discouraged, depressed, etc.)
↓
Your mental thought about
how you would like to feel
(happy, positive, relaxed, etc.)
↓
Your act of will to start acting
in the way that you want to feel
(you *decide* you will act "as if" you are happy)
↓
Your action to appear
the way you want to be
(you cheerily smile at someone
and say you feel great!)
↓
You continue to act as if
you are this way to remind
your subconscious this is true
(you concentrate on your affirmations,
then enthusiastically make some calls
to invite people to an exciting meeting)
↓
You gradually start to feel
the way you want; or suddenly
you discover you feel this way
(you discover the problem that bothered you
no longer exists or is no longer as serious
as you thought. Or you decide you do not
need to be concerned with this now. Thus,
you suddenly feel relieved and happy)

The process works because your thoughts control your actions. You are—or soon become—what you think. As a result, when you learn to control your thoughts, you control your actions and the feelings related to those actions, too.

THINGS TO DO
TO FEEL POSITIVE AGAIN

There are a number of specific actions you can take to help you feel up again. Since different actions work for different people, use the ones that feel most suitable for you.

- Put up positive reminders around your house and take a walk around your house to feel better. For example, you might make up some posters that say something like this:

> WINNERS NEVER QUIT . . .
> AND QUITTERS NEVER WIN

> WHEN YOU'RE DOWN YOU'RE NOT OUT
> UNLESS YOU THINK YOU ARE

> THERE ARE NO FAILURES . . .
> JUST TEMPORARY DEFEATS

- Review your affirmations or goals. Visualize yourself attaining them now.
- Take a break from whatever you are doing, and do something you usually like to do (for example, play tennis, go to a movie, call a friend).
- Read an inspiring book (such as a book on how someone became successful).

• Participate in an exercise designed to make you feel positive.

Here are two possibilities.

1. *A Meditation Exercise*: Sit down in a comfortable position; then visualize a column of positive energy flowing into your feet and up your legs to the bottom of your spine. Then, see it flowing up your spine. At the same time, visualize a second column of positive energy flowing in through your forehead and down your head and neck to the top of your spine. Then, this energy starts swirling around your spine and goes down. Notice the two columns of energy swirling about—one swirling up your spine, the other down, until they meet in the center to form a positive, vibrating ball of energy. Experience that feeling for several minutes, and then, feeling infused by this energy, open your eyes, get up, and direct your energy into any activity you want to engage in now.

2. *A Physical Exercise*: Stand up with your feet solidly on the ground. Then rapidly lift your right arm (or left arm if you are left-handed) up and down, and each time your arm comes down, say with conviction, "I am positive . . . I am positive . . . I am positive." Or say, "I feel joy . . . I feel joy . . . I feel joy." Or something like that.

AND REMEMBER . . .
PERSIST, PERSIST, PERSIST

Just know that if you stay on the path, you will eventually make it. In the real estate business, salespeople know that about 90 to 95 percent of their leads will say no. But it's that 5 to 10 percent who say yes who produce thousands in commissions.

Other studies have shown that the average salesperson gets seven no's for every yes. Unfortunately, most quit before getting that yes. They give up on a particular prospect, and someone else makes the sale.

It's true for marketing any kind of product or service. The people who are making fantastic incomes did not let no's get them down. Sure they suffered temporary defeats. Some were broke at one time. But they didn't let that discourage them. They had a conviction and a commitment, and kept on pushing.

So persist, persist, persist. Most people quit when the going gets hard, since it's easier and seems more logical to stop. But if you've got that conviction—that burning desire to gain success—stay on the path.

The temptations to get off it will be many—friends and family members who urge you to quit; unsuccessful people who urge you to commiserate with them; problems and obstacles that get you down. But if you keep your conviction, stay positive, stay around positive, successful people, and keep working toward your goal, you'll make it. Just know it in your heart. Live it. Breathe it. And you will!

AND IF YOU STILL HAVE ANY RESISTANCES AND FEARS, WORK ON OVERCOMING THEM

Sometimes the idea of selling and promoting anything can be scary, and sometimes people resist becoming successful because it involves changing a variety of things in their life (friends, life-styles, daily activities). Or you may have specific fears, such as being rejected when someone says no, spending time doing something that turns out to be less productive than you thought, and so on.

We all typically have fears about something. One key to success is to work on getting rid of those fears that stand in the way of what you want to do.

Sometimes it works just to notice you have a fear and say to yourself, "I'm not going to let that bother me." Then, if you say that enough and do whatever you fear, the problem goes away after a while, because you realize it's not something to be afraid of. (For example, a friend used to be afraid of flying. But since it was increasingly inconvenient to have this fear, she forced herself to fly anyway. Then, after numerous successful flights, she suddenly realized she wasn't afraid to fly anymore.)

You can do that, too. Just do what you fear, or if it's a really big fear, work up to it by doing smaller things. For instance, if you are afraid of speaking to big groups, speak in small groups first, then in larger and larger groups, until you are no longer afraid of speaking.

Also, it helps to write out your fears and decide how to overcome each one. Use the accompanying chart (Chart 7) to do this. Then, as you get rid of each fear, cross it off, and perhaps give yourself a reward for achieving that goal.

CHART 7: A CHECKLIST FOR OVERCOMING MY FEARS

One of My Fears Is: _____

Why Do I Have This Fear? _____

_____

Gini Graham Scott

CHART 7: A CHECKLIST FOR OVERCOMING
MY FEARS (continued)

What I Need to Do to Overcome This Fear:

Specific Actions I Must Take: Attitudes and Feelings
I Must Change:

_____   _____

_____   _____

_____   _____

_____   _____

_____   _____

One of My Fears Is: _____

Why Do I Have This Fear? _____

_____

What I Need to Do to Overcome This Fear:

Specific Actions I Must Take: Attitudes and Feelings
I Must Change:

_____   _____

_____   _____

_____   _____

_____   _____

Chapter 5

SETTING YOUR GOALS
FOR SUCCESS

To succeed, you need a clear picture of where you are going and what you need to do to get there. Napoleon Hill, who specialized in studying success, has stated that "a definite purpose is the starting point of all achievement," and that's true in any kind of marketing. *You have to know what you want and how you're going to get it.*

But you must do more than just imagine it in general terms. You must do the following:

- Form a very specific, clear picture of what you want
- Determine what you need to get there
- Develop a plan of action
- Obtain the tools, techniques, or personnel you need to put that plan in action
- Set the date for achieving it
- Begin at once

You should be flexible, so you can modify the plan as needed. But always keep your purpose in mind.

Let's see how Napoleon Hill's basic principles of goal setting apply to success in marketing your own product or service. He states six basic steps:

1. *Fix in your mind your definite purpose or goal.* This way you have something concrete to work for. But also, determine your higher purpose, which represents your overall direction or reason for being. It's your rationale for wanting to achieve the goals you do, and it helps you put your goals in perspective. Also, knowing your purpose helps you keep on the path to achieving your goals. For example, your higher purpose might be something like, "I want to be in a position to contribute to the betterment of society," or "I want to develop a way to express my creative abilities." Your major goal then becomes a means to achieving this higher end.

2. *Determine what you are willing to give up to achieve your goal.* Everything in life has its price, and achieving success does, too. You may have to take time from your friends and family, take courses to learn key techniques, give up activities you enjoy to have the time to work on your goal. Whatever it takes, you must be willing to pay the price, and you must be clear what this price is for you.

3. *Establish a definite date when you want to achieve your goal.* If necessary, give yourself more time, but establish a date now. This sparks you with a sense of urgency. You're not just dreaming about some far-off idea. But you know you have to go after it now.

4. *Create a definite plan to go after your major purpose, and begin at once, even if you don't feel ready.* Your plan should list the specific steps you expect to take and when. Your goal may be long-term—for example: "I want to have a sales volume of $50,000 and be earning $5,000 a month by

January 1986." But you must figure out how you are going to develop the necessary sales organization and keep your people motivated to produce the product volume you need to achieve those earnings.

5. *Write out a clear statement of what you want and your plan for achieving it.* You should put all of the steps of your plan in writing, as described in the next section. Also, include in your plan some way to measure your progress, so you can see how well you are doing as you go along.

6. *Read your written statement aloud in the morning and before you go to bed, and as you say it, see yourself in possession of that goal.* This way you remind yourself of your goal and experience yourself having achieved it, so your goal and your hope of achieving it seem real. As Emile Coué once said: "What the mind can conceive, the mind can achieve." So imagine repeatedly what you want, to make it real, and your active imagination will attract to you what you need.

CREATING YOUR ACTION PLAN TO ACHIEVE YOUR GOALS

Now let's turn the above principles into action. Most of these principles apply whether you are marketing a product direct yourself or building a sales group to work with you.

1. *To determine your definite major purpose or goal, if you're not sure yet, write down all of your goals; then establish your priorities.* Start by brainstorming. Let your creative processes go, and write down whatever comes. List where you want to live, the kind of car you want, and the amount of money you would like to make, and be very clear why you want that much money. The amount should be related to the

life-style you want to live, so you need to make that much.

When you brainstorm, don't feel restricted by your current situation. Remember, you can change this. What you have done in the past has created your present situation. By the same token, your actions now can change what happens in the future.

The more concrete you make your future goals, the more likely you can realize them. Thus, when you list where you want to live or the kind of car you want, be specific. Visualize how the house looks, the kind of furniture in it, and see yourself living there. Imagine the car in the driveway. Notice its color. And so on. Some people use illustrations or cut-out magazine pictures to make their goals especially vivid and concrete.

Then, rate your goals in terms of priorities to pick your most important goal. Or if two or more goals seem related, group them together to form an overall goal. For example, you can link your house, car, boat, and fur coat together as part of the new $100,000-a-year life-style you envision. Or if you want a $100,000 grand retirement vacation, that's fine, too. Just be clear what you want. (You can use Chart 8.)

2. *Set a tentative date to realize this goal and go backward from there to determine what you need to do to achieve this goal.* For example, if you are selling the product direct yourself, ask yourself questions like: How many products do I need to sell personally to achieve a sales volume of $25,000 a month? How many products do I need to sell personally each week to meet this goal? How many customers must I contact each week to sell this many products? How many per day?

Or, if you are creating a sales network to market a product, ask yourself questions like the following: What kind of product volume do I need to earn $100,000? How many people do I need in my organization to get this kind of volume? How many people do I need to recruit to get this many active people in my organization? How many people do I need to contact in order to get this many recruits?

You have to estimate about how many contacts will become active distributors and how much volume these active people

CHART 8: MY GOALS AND DEFINITE MAJOR PURPOSE

My Current Goals (list in any order)	How I Rate My Current Goals (rate from 1—least important—to 10—most important)
1.	1.
2.	2.
3.	3.
4.	4.
5.	5.
6.	6.
7.	7.
8.	8.
9.	9.
10.	10.

CHART 8: MY GOALS AND DEFINITE MAJOR PURPOSE (continued)

My Overall Goals (combine two or more individual goals listed above to form an overall goal)	How I Rate My Overall Goals (rate from 1—least important to 5—most important)
1.	1.
2.	2.
3.	3.
4.	4.
5.	5.

will produce on the average. Start with an educated guess at first, and as you gain experience, modify the formula.

For example, in most businesses, according to Gerald Oliver, who wrote *How to Create a Fortune Sponsoring Distributors*, one out of three persons contacted will be interested, and one out of three who come to a meeting will get more involved. Then perhaps one-fifth to one-third of these become active. So you may need as many as twenty-seven to forty-five contacts to get one active salesperson. Or you may need to make more or fewer contacts in your own situation. As you start making contacts and getting people interested, keep track of the response and make adjustments accordingly.

3. *If you are creating a sales team, work out the numbers to illustrate the relationship between the number of active*

persons in your group, their average product volume, the effort needed to recruit them, and the time needed to build up your organization to a desired level. And if you find these numbers are too great, perhaps you need to scale down your goals, extend your time frame for accomplishing them, or step up the amount of effort you intend to invest.

For example, suppose you answer these questions as follows:

Amount of product volume needed to earn $50,000 a year = 500,000

Number of active persons needed to produce the volume = 1,000

Number of persons I or others on my team need to sign up to gain 1,000 active people = 5,000

Number of interested persons I and my team members need to talk to to get 5,000 sign-ups = 15,000

Number of persons I and my team members need to contact personally to obtain 15,000 interested people = 45,000

Number of persons I and my team members need to contact personally for each active person = 45 (45,000/1,000)

Length of time needed to contact 45 persons = two weeks

Length of time needed to build up an organization with 1,000 or more people, assuming I and my active distributors get 1 new active person every two weeks (45 contacts) = twenty-two weeks.

You can see how these assumptions translate into recruiting patterns for a sales group that has several levels in Chart 9. Many involved in creating such a network use a shorthand formula that suggests an organization will double every few weeks, using the assumption of regular recruiting. For example, the following kind of table—found in many books and pamphlets about this network or multi-level marketing approach—uses various time periods depending on how fast people are expected to recruit (for example, one new person a week, every two weeks, every month). Here, to correspond with Chart 9, the same assumption of one new active recruit every two weeks is used.

YOU

Week 1–2	=	1
Week 3–4	=	2
Week 5–6	=	4
Week 7–8	=	8
Week 9–10	=	16
Week 11–12	=	32
Week 13–14	=	64
Week 15–16	=	128
Week 17–18	=	256
Week 19–20	=	512
Week 21–22	=	1,024

However, if you'll notice in Chart 9, your organization more than doubles for the first few weeks, and then growth slows down somewhat in subsequent weeks, since the people on the bottom level of your organization (level five in the example) do not recruit additional people into your group, and you don't have any people on this level in your first few weeks.

In any event, if these assumptions hold, you could be right on target in about twenty-two weeks, or just under five months. But, you will find, things won't happen exactly as you plan. You may find that you need more than forty-five contacts over a two-week period to get your one serious person. And others in your organization may have that experience, too. Or you may find that members of your organization become less motivated as time goes on. Conversely, you may have a really

CHART 9: RATE OF GROWTH IN A SALES NETWORK, ASSUMING YOU AND YOUR ACTIVE DISTRIBUTORS EACH RECRUIT ONE NEW ACTIVE DISTRIBUTOR EVERY TWO WEEKS

Weeks	You Recruit	Cumulative Total Level #1	Level #1 Persons Recruit	Cumulative Total Level #2	Level #2 Persons Recruit	Cumulative Total Level #3	Level #3 Persons Recruit	Cumulative Total Level #4	Level #4 Persons Recruit	Cumulative Total Level #5	Total Persons Whole Group
1–2	1	1	–	–	–	–	–	–	–	–	1
3–4	1	2	1	1	–	–	–	–	–	–	3
5–6	1	3	2	3	1	1	–	–	–	–	7
7–8	1	4	3	6	3	4	1	1	–	–	15
9–10	1	5	4	10	6	10	4	5	1	1	31
11–12	1	6	5	15	10	20	10	15	5	6	62
13–14	1	7	6	21	15	35	20	35	15	21	119
15–16	1	8	7	28	21	56	35	70	35	56	218
17–18	1	9	8	36	28	84	56	126	70	126	381
19–20	1	10	9	45	36	120	84	210	126	252	637
21–22	1	11	10	55	45	165	120	330	210	462	1023
23–24	1	12	11	66	55	220	165	495	330	792	1585

dynamic group and meet your organizational goal more quickly. Thus, you must continually revise your plans as you gain more experience and feedback on what works and how.

4. *Turn your overall numbers about product volume and the number of those you want to recruit into smaller manageable chunks you can work with on a daily, weekly, and monthly basis.*

Your yearly plan gives you the big picture. But when you break it down into daily, weekly, or monthly goals, you have a clearer, more understandable target to shoot for, so you know better where you are going in the here and now, as well as where you are. Then, you can readily assess your progress as you go along and decide if your goals are realistic. If not, you can modify them.

You will still need to move the same amount of product personally or have the same number of people in your sales team to achieve your daily, weekly, or monthly target as you do to reach your yearly goals. But breaking these time periods down to smaller ones makes it easier to understand exactly what you must do immediately to make your sales target.

For example, if your earnings goal is $50,000 a year, that's about $4,000 a month in earnings or $40,000 a month in product volume, assuming a one-to-ten earnings-to-product-volume ratio. That means you must personally move $40,000 in product a month, or, if you have 100 active salespeople in your organization, each one must move an average $400 a month in product for you to gain these earnings. Now, that's an easier goal to work for than $480,000 in volume a year.

Similarly, when you break that monthly goal down to a weekly product-volume amount (say $10,000 personal or $100 for each person in your group), that's an even more immediate goal.

CALCULATING YOUR SUCCESS IN ACHIEVING YOUR GOALS

Whether you are setting yearly, monthly, weekly, or daily goals or are figuring out your success in achieving these goals, you need to use certain basic procedures. The process is more complex if you are not only selling a product but building a sales team, so many of the illustrations deal with this.

Ask two questions to determine how much you have to produce yourself or how many persons you need in your sales group to produce this amount:

1. How much product must I or my group move to earn a commission of _____ for a (year, month, week)? To figure this out, take the average ratio of product volume to commission earnings and multiply this by the commission you want to earn. For example, if the ratio is ten to one, you need to move $30,000 worth of product to earn $3,000 in commissions. The formula for this procedure is as follows:

Product Volume/ Commission Ratio (10)	×	Desired Commission ($3,000)	=	Product Volume Required ($30,000)

2. If I am working with a sales team, how many do I need in my group to move this much product? To figure this out, divide the desired total product volume by the average purchase volume of your active salespeople or distributors. Obviously, the higher each individual's purchase volume, the fewer persons you need. For example, if you need to gain a product volume of $30,000 in your total organization and each active distributor moves about $150 in product each month, you need 200 active persons in your organization.

69

The formula to obtain this answer is as follows:

$$\frac{\text{Total Product Volume Desired (\$30,000)}}{\text{Average Purchase Volume of Active Distributors (\$150)}} = \begin{array}{c}\text{Number of Distributors}\\ \text{(200) Needed}\end{array}$$

Next, if you are building a sales team, figure out how much time you need to get that many people in your group. To do this, determine how long it takes you on the average to recruit your active leaders and assume they will each do about the same as you. To figure out your own success rate over time, break down the sponsoring process into three phases:

- *The Initial Contact Phase*, when you make calls, place ads, and respond to them
- *The Presentation Phase*, when you make presentations or take interested prospects to meetings
- *The Training Phase*, when you assist your new distributors to become active themselves

To determine your average time to recruit and train each active distributor, determine approximately how many you contact in each phase and how much time you spend with them.

The process is not as awesome as it sounds. You can keep simple records using the forms on the following pages, and these will tell you how you are doing each month.

But first, let's see how this process might work in practice. For example, say that every third person you contact about being in your sales team is interested in going to a meeting, and that out of every three who go to a meeting, one signs up. Then, about a fifth of these become active. That means (1) You must contact three persons to get one interested person; (2) You must work with three interested persons to get one to sign up; (3) You must get five to sign up to get one active distributor.

These figures, in turn, translate into contacting nine persons to get one to sign up (three times three); and you must contact forty-five persons to get an active distributor (three times three times five). If the contacts are already interested, you need to work with only fifteen of them to get one active distributor (three times five).

Then, you need to attach hours to the average amount of time you spend with each person you deal with in each phase. For example, say you spend an average of five minutes on the phone or in casual conversation with each person you contact about setting up an appointment; an average of one hour for each presentation (including any travel and set-up time); and an average of four hours training each new distributor. Your time to get that one active distributor would be about thirty-nine hours, as follows:

Initial Contacts: 45 @ 5 minutes each	= 4	hours
Presentations: 15 @ 1 hour each	= 15	hours
Training New Distributor: 5 @ 4 hours each	= 20	hours
Total:	39	hours

Now, assuming you are involved in marketing your product or service on a part-time basis, spending about twenty hours a week, that means you will average one new active distributor every two weeks. And if you make the same assumptions about your active distributors, they will do the same.

As noted earlier, these assumptions are only that, because those in your sales group may be more or less active than you, and their level of activity may change over time, just as yours may. So you need to revise your figures and projections accordingly.

The following charts (Charts 10–18) are designed to give you a general picture of how you are doing. But remember, your results are only as good as your assumptions and data. Be ready to change your assumptions as you gather more information about your performance.

DESIGNING YOUR WEEKLY PLAN OF ACTION

To establish your weekly plans, look at your overall goals and monthly program and break down these figures into what you need to do each week.

Planning for Direct Retail Sales

To develop your plans for marketing a product directly, you need to determine the number of sales calls and presentations required to make so many sales. And you have to figure out how much time you need to do this, whether you are selling through party plan or direct to individual customers.

For instance, say you are involved in party plan selling and are seeking prospects who will put on a sales party for you. Also, suppose you have to make about ten initial contacts to get three persons who want to have a personal presentation; you must give three presentations to get one person who would like to arrange a party. Now if you attach times and results to this, you may find that it takes you about one hour to make the first contacts by phone; another three hours to make presentations to interested people to get one commitment; and then perhaps another three hours to work with the host on the arrangements for actually putting on the party. That means, on the average, you are spending about seven hours to arrange and put on each party. If your average sales party produces about $300 in sales and nets you a commission of $140, that's about $20 an hour.

As you recruit others to do the same thing, you will increase your earnings through overrides on the sales made by those in your sales organization. But the first stage is direct selling yourself—so you should know on the average how much you can expect to earn and how much time you need to invest to earn this.

Charts 10–13 on the following pages will help you to keep track of this.

Planning for Building a Sales Network

If you are building a sales network, you must break down your activities to include recruitment and training activities, too. Using the previous example about building a group, suppose you need to contact about one hundred persons a month or forty-five every two weeks and make presentations to those who are interested, to get one active distributor. Also, you need to work with your currently active distributors to motivate them and teach them to do the same.

Thus, on a weekly basis, you need to make about twenty contacts and invite about a third of these to meetings, and your distributors must do this, too.

Now, suppose it takes you about two hours to make calls or otherwise contact people who are interested in meeting with you to learn more. Then, you have to allow about one hour per meeting. So, you know you have to spend about ten hours per week in prospecting (two hours to set up meetings; eight hours for the meetings themselves). At the same time, you have to spend about two hours working with your active first-level distributors—say you have five—so allocate another ten hours for that.

Then, over the week, observe how well your plan is working. Are you contacting about as many persons as planned in the time allotted? On the average, are you getting the positive response you expect? If you are selling direct, approximately what percentage of those you contact are becoming customers

CHART 10: DAILY CONTACT SHEET AND TIME LOG FOR DIRECT RETAIL SALES

Month _____

Week # _____ Date _____

Day of Week	New People Contacted about Products or Sales Party		Presentations to Interested People		Arranging and Giving Sales Party		Number of People Making Purchases and Amount of Sales		
	No. Contacted	Time Spent	No. Contacted	Time Spent	No. at Party	Time Spent	No.	Gross Sales	Commission
Monday									
Tuesday									
Wednesday									
Thursday									
Friday									

Saturday									
Sunday									
Total									
Monday									
Tuesday									
Wednesday									
Thursday									
Friday									
Saturday									
Sunday									
Total									

CHART 11: MONTHLY SUMMARY OF PEOPLE CONTACTED, TIME SPENT, AND MONEY EARNED IN MAKING DIRECT RETAIL SALES

Month _____

Week	New People Contacted about Products or Sales Party		Presentations to Interested People		Arranging and Giving Sales Party		Number of People Making Purchases and Amount of Sales		
	No. Contacted	Time Spent	No. Contacted	Time Spent	No. at Party	Time Spent	No.	Gross Sales	Commission
Week 1									
Week 2									
Week 3									
Week 4									
Week 5									
Monthly Total									

CHART 12: NUMBER OF CONTACTS TO SET UP A SALES PARTY AND AVERAGE EARNINGS

Data Taken from Monthly Summary for _____

1. Average Number of New Persons Contacted to Get One Interested Person:

$$\frac{\text{Number of Persons Contacted}}{\text{Number of Persons Indicating Interest}} = \underline{\quad\quad}$$

2. Average Number of Interested Persons Needed to Arrange One Sales Party:

$$\frac{\text{Number of Persons Indicating Interest}}{\substack{\text{Number of Persons Agreeing} \\ \text{to Host a Party}}} = \underline{\quad\quad}$$

3. Average Number of Persons at Party:

$$\frac{\text{Number of Persons at Parties}}{\text{Number of Parties Given}} = \underline{\quad\quad}$$

4. Average Amount Sold Per Party:

$$\frac{\text{Total Amount Sold}}{\text{Number of Parties Given}} = \underline{\quad\quad}$$

5. Average Commission Earnings on Sales Per Party:

Average Amount Sold Per Party $\times$ Commission $=$

Example: Monthly Totals from Monthly Summary of Persons Contacted and Time Spent

77

CHART 12: NUMBER OF CONTACTS TO SET UP A SALES PARTY AND AVERAGE EARNINGS (continued)

No. of New Persons Contacted = 36
No. Interested in Hearing More = 12
No. Agreeing to Host a Party = 4
No. at Parties = 48
No. Making a Purchase = 24

1. $\dfrac{\text{No. Contacted}}{\text{No. Interested}} = \dfrac{36}{12} = 3$

2. $\dfrac{\text{No. Interested}}{\text{No. Hosting Party}} = \dfrac{12}{4} = 3$

3. $\dfrac{\text{No. at Party}}{\text{No. Parties Given}} = \dfrac{48}{4} = 12$

4. $\dfrac{\text{Total Amount Sold}}{\text{No. Parties Given}} = \dfrac{\$1200}{4} = \$300$

5. Amount Sold × Commission = $300 × 0.45 = $135

and how much are they buying? Or if you are working on developing a group, what percentage of those you contact are signing in and becoming active? Is this as you estimated?

Then, as necessary, modify your projections or change your activities. For example, if your projections are on target, but you want to increase the number of customers or the number of new salespeople signing, then increase the time you spend contacting and meeting new persons. Or if people aren't responding as enthusiastically as you expected, increase the amount of time you spend selling or recruiting—or perhaps improve your sales and recruiting techniques.

Similarly, assess the amount of time you need to spend with your customers or distributors. Do they need more help and therefore more of your time? Or are your people fine as they are? Find out what they need and plan your time accordingly. Then, advise your salespeople to do the same with their own distributors. You can use Charts 14–18 for keeping track.

CHART 13: AVERAGE TIME AND EARNINGS IN PUTTING ON SALES PARTIES

Data Taken from Monthly Summary for _____

1. Average Time Spent Contacting New Persons:

    $$\frac{\text{Total Time Contacting New Persons}}{\text{Number of New Persons Contacted}} = \text{_____}$$

2. Average Time Spent Giving Presentations to Interested Persons:

    $$\frac{\text{Total Time Giving Presentations}}{\text{Number of Interested Persons}} = \text{_____}$$

3. Average Time Spent Arranging and Giving Party:

    $$\frac{\text{Total Time Arranging and Giving Parties}}{\text{Number of Parties Given}} = \text{_____}$$

4. Average Time Spent in All Activities Involved in Putting on Parties:

    $$\frac{\text{Total Time Contacting, Presenting, and Putting on Parties}}{\text{Number of Parties Given}} = \text{_____}$$

5. Average Amount of Earnings Per Hour Spent:

    $$\frac{\text{Average Commission Earnings Per Party}}{\text{Average Time Spent Per Party}} = \text{_____}$$

Example: Monthly Totals from Monthly Summary of Persons Contacted, Time Spent, and Average Earnings

CHART 13: AVERAGE TIME AND EARNINGS IN PUTTING ON SALES PARTIES (continued)

Total Time Contacting New Persons = 4 hours
Total Time Giving Presentations = 12 hours
Total Time Arranging and Putting on Parties = 12 hours
Total Time Contacting, Presenting,
   and Putting on Parties = 28 hours
Average Earnings Per Party = $140

1. $\dfrac{\text{Time Contacting Persons}}{\text{No. Contacted}} = \dfrac{4 \text{ hrs}}{40} = \dfrac{240 \text{ min}}{40} = 6 \text{ min}$

2. $\dfrac{\text{Time Giving Presentations}}{\text{No. Interested}} = \dfrac{12 \text{ hrs}}{12} = 1 \text{ hr}$

3. $\dfrac{\text{Time Arranging and Putting on Parties}}{\text{No. of Parties}} = \dfrac{12 \text{ hrs}}{4} = 3 \text{ hrs}$

4. $\dfrac{\text{Time Contacting, Presenting, and Putting on Parties}}{\text{No. of Parties}} = \dfrac{28 \text{ hrs}}{4} = 7 \text{ hrs}$

5. $\dfrac{\text{Average Earnings Per Party}}{\text{Average No. of Hours Spent Per Party}} = \dfrac{\$140}{7 \text{ hrs}} = \$20 \text{ per hr}$

WORKING OUT YOUR DAILY SCHEDULE

With your weekly plans as a guide, set your schedule for each day. Say you are concerned with personal sales only and you know you have to spend about seven hours for each sales party you organize. If you want to put on two parties a week, that means about fourteen hours, or about three hours a day. Or if you are selling a big-ticket item direct, you can likewise plan how much time you need to spend on the average for each sale.

Similarly, if you are building a sales network, you must plan how much time to devote to that. For example, you know that to attain your goal of one active distributor every two weeks, you have to spend ten hours a week prospecting and ten hours a week working with your active distributors. That averages out to approximately two hours a day prospecting and two hours a day working with active distributors. You can vary the exact amount per day; but to achieve your long-term goals, you know you must spend about four hours working each day.

Thus, at the beginning of each week, whatever your particular marketing approach, sketch out your overall schedule. Then, before you go to bed each night, write out your "to-do list" for the following day, and indicate your priorities by numbering each item from one (very important) to five (not very important). Also, note the estimated time you need to perform each task, and roughly schedule when you plan to do what, in addition to your scheduled appointments.

If you can't do everything, you will be able to accomplish the most important activities first, and can transfer what you haven't done to a subsequent day, or perhaps drop an item entirely. When you do complete each activity, check it off.

This daily planning system is not only ideal for keeping you organized and on target; you also can use it as a record for tax purposes to show how much time you have spent on various business activities. (More about this in chapter 31, "Keeping Records.")

There are some excellent calendars for keeping track of your schedules and writing up your to-do list. (For example, Day Timers, Allentown, Pennsylvania 18001, has an excellent system. And many swear by a comprehensive time management program called the *Personal Resource System*, sold direct by a network of distributors.) Or use Chart 19 to create your own to-do list. I make up these to-do lists and carry them with me in my appointment calendar so I can readily refer to them.

CHART 14: DAILY CONTACT SHEET AND TIME LOG FOR BUILDING A SALES ORGANIZATION

Month _____

Week # _____   Date _____

Day of Week	New Persons Contacted about Sales Group		Presentations to Interested Persons		Training New Distributors		Number of Sign-Ups Becoming Active Distributors
	No. Contacted	Time Spent	No. Interested	Time Spent	No. Sign-Ups	Time Spent	
Monday							
Tuesday							
Wednesday							
Thursday							
Friday							

Saturday											
Sunday											
Total											
Monday											
Tuesday											
Wednesday											
Thursday											
Friday											
Saturday											
Sunday											
Total											

CHART 15: MONTHLY SUMMARY OF PERSONS CONTACTED AND TIME SPENT IN BUILDING A SALES ORGANIZATION

Month _____

Week	New Persons Contacted about Sales Group		Presentations to Interested Persons		Training New Distributors		Number of Sign-Ups Becoming Active Distributors
	No. Contacted	Time Spent	No. Interested	Time Spent	No. Sign-Ups	Time Spent	
Week 1							
Week 2							
Week 3							
Week 4							
Week 5							
Monthly Total							

CHART 16: NUMBER OF CONTACTS TO OBTAIN ACTIVE DISTRIBUTORS FOR SALES ORGANIZATION

Data Taken from Monthly Summary for _____

1. Average Number of New Persons
   Contacted to Get One Interested Person

   $$\frac{\text{Number of Persons Contacted}}{\text{Number of Persons Indicating Interest}} = \text{_____}$$

2. Average Number of Interested Persons
   Needed to Get One Sign-Up

   $$\frac{\text{Number of Persons Indicating Interest}}{\text{Number of Persons Signing Up}} = \text{_____}$$

3. Average Number of Sign-Ups
   Needed to Get One Active Distributor

   $$\frac{\text{Number of Persons Signing Up}}{\text{Number of Active Distributors}} = \text{_____}$$

4. Average Number of Contacts Needed
   to Obtain One Active Distributor

   $$\frac{\text{Number of Persons Contacted}}{\text{Number of Active Distributors}} = \text{_____}$$

   Or Multiply the Results of #1 $\times$ #2 $\times$ #3 = _____

Example: Monthly Totals from Monthly Summary of Persons
          Contacted and Time Spent

   No. of New Persons Contacted = 45
   No. Interested in a Meeting = 15

CHART 16: NUMBER OF CONTACTS
TO OBTAIN ACTIVE DISTRIBUTORS
FOR SALES ORGANIZATION (continued)

No. Signing Up = 5
No. of Sign-Ups Becoming Active Distributors = 1

1. $\dfrac{\text{No. Contacted}}{\text{No. Interested}} = \dfrac{45}{15} = 3$

2. $\dfrac{\text{No. Interested}}{\text{No. Signing Up}} = \dfrac{15}{5} = 3$

3. $\dfrac{\text{No. Signing Up}}{\text{No. Active}} = \dfrac{5}{1} = 5$

4. $\dfrac{\text{No. Contacted}}{\text{No. Active}} = \dfrac{45}{1} = 45$

Or #1 × #2 × #3 = 3 × 3 × 5 = 45

CHART 17: AVERAGE TIME SPENT
TO OBTAIN ACTIVE DISTRIBUTORS
FOR SALES ORGANIZATION

Data Taken from Monthly Summary for _____

1. Average Time Spent Contacting New Persons

   $\dfrac{\text{Total Time Contacting New Persons}}{\text{Number of New Persons Contacted}} =$ _____

2. Average Time Spent Giving Presentations to Interested Persons

   $\dfrac{\text{Total Time Giving Presentations}}{\text{Number of Interested Persons}} =$ _____

3. Average Time Spent Training New Distributors Signing Up

$$\frac{\text{Total Time Training New Distributors}}{\text{Number of New Distributors}} = \underline{\hspace{2cm}}$$

4. Average Time Spent in All Activites with Each Person

$$\frac{\text{Total Time Contacting, Presenting, Training}}{\text{Number of New People Contacted}} = \underline{\hspace{1cm}}$$

Example: Monthly Totals from Monthly Summary of Persons Contacted and Time Spent

Total Time Contacting New Persons = 3.75 hours
Total Time Giving Presentations = 15 hours
Total Time Training New Distributors = 20 hours
Total Time Contacting, Presenting, Training = 38.75 hours

1. Time
$$\frac{\text{Contacting Persons}}{\text{No. Contacted}} = \frac{3.75 \text{ hrs}}{45} = \frac{225 \text{ min}}{45} = 5 \text{ min}$$

2. $$\frac{\text{Time Giving Presentations}}{\text{No. Interested}} = \frac{15 \text{ hrs}}{15} = 1 \text{ hr}$$

3. $$\frac{\text{Time Training Distributors}}{\text{No. New Distributors}} = \frac{20 \text{ hrs}}{5} = 4 \text{ hrs}$$

4. Time Contacting, Presenting, Training
$$\frac{\text{Each Distributor}}{\text{No. of New Persons Contacted}} = \frac{38.75 \text{ hrs}}{45} = \frac{2325 \text{ min}}{45} = 52 \text{ min}$$

CHART 18: ESTIMATING YOUR OWN RATE OF ORGANIZATIONAL GROWTH
(ASSUMING YOU AND YOUR ACTIVE DISTRIBUTORS RECRUIT A GIVEN NUMBER OF NEW ACTIVE DISTRIBUTORS EACH TIME PERIOD)

Time Period	You Recruit	Cumulative Total Level #1	Level #1 Persons Recruit	Cumulative Total Level #2	Level #2 Persons Recruit	Cumulative Total Level #3	Level #3 Persons Recruit	Cumulative Total Level #4	Level #4 Persons Recruit	Cumulative Total Level #5	Total Persons Whole Group

Key: **Time Period**—Indicate whether weekly, biweekly, monthly, etc.

You Recruit—Indicate the average number of new active distributors you recruit in that period.

Cumulative Total Level #1—Make a running cumulative total of your new recruits as of that period.

Level #1 Persons Recruit—Assume that your Level #1 recruits do not become active until the next time period. Then write down the total number in Cumulative Level #1 for each time period in the column: Level #2 Persons Recruit for the following time period.

Cumulative Total Level #2—Make a running cumulative total of your Level #1s' recruits.

Level #2 Persons Recruit—Assume that your Level #2 recruits do not become active until the next time period. Then write down the total number in Cumulative Level #2 for each time period in the next column: Level #3 Persons Recruit for the following time period.

Continue this procedure for all levels in your organization down to level 5. *See Chart 9 for an example.*

CHART 19: THINGS TO DO LIST

Day of Week _____

Date _____

Things to Do... (Rate importance from 1–5)	Estimate of Time Needed

ASSESSING YOUR PROGRESS

You should review your progress and modify your goals or efforts to achieve them as needed on an ongoing basis. Mini-reviews are fine on a daily or weekly basis. And ideally, plan a more comprehensive review once a month.

Time Spent and Results

When you make your review, find out how much time you are spending for what results. Ask yourself the following questions, using the charts just described (Charts 10–19) to get the data you need.

My Progress in Direct Retail Sales

On the average, how many prospects do I need to contact to make a sale or set up a sales party?

In general, how much time am I spending for each sale I make or each sales party I put on?

My Progress in Building a Sales Group

On the average, how many contacts do I need and how many distributors do I need to sign up to find an active distributor?

How much time am I spending on the various phases of the recruiting-sponsoring process—making initial contacts and making presentations or taking prospects to meetings?

How much time am I devoting to training my distributors?

Overall, how much time do I need to sponsor and train one active distributor?

Financial Returns

Then, look at your financial returns for your personal sales and, if you have one, for your sales group as a whole.

Financial Returns from My Direct Retail Sales

Assessing your own financial returns is relatively simple, based on asking yourself these key questions: On the average, how much product volume am I moving personally? Each month? Each week? What is my total commission on these sales? On the average, how much am I earning relative to the time I am spending (that is, approximately what is my average return per hour)?

You can use Chart 20 to fill in the answers.

CHART 20: EARNINGS FROM MY DIRECT RETAIL SALES

Month _____

My Total Product Volume _____

My Total Commission on Sales _____

Number of Hours Spent on Direct Personal Sales _____

Average Earnings Per Hour:

$$\frac{\text{Commission}}{\text{No. of Hours}} = \underline{\hspace{4cm}}$$

Financial Returns from My Sales Group

To figure out these returns is a bit more complicated, since you don't have all the data yourself. If you can, get some information directly from your first-line distributors on their product volume, and where possible, request them to report on how their own immediate distributors are doing (though don't be pushy about this; only ask as you feel your distributors will be willing to share this information). You should also be able to get specific product volume data from your company's monthly statement, but getting it from your distributors gives you some advance information. Also, this is a way of checking the accuracy of your printout. (Yes, computers sometimes goof up!)

Using the data, ask yourself: What is the total product volume of the distributors in my group? How much product volume is each distributor moving on the average? How are my first- and second-level distributors doing compared to their distributors in my organization? What is my total commission on this amount of product volume? What is my average commission per distributor?

You can figure out the answers using Chart 21: Earnings from My Distributor Group.

Then, knowing your average commission per active distributor, you can estimate how your earnings are likely to grow as you increase the number of active distributors in your organization. Also, since you know how much time it takes to find an active distributor, you can estimate how long it will take to increase your earnings to a certain level.

For example, say it takes you an average of forty hours to find one active distributor and each active distributor brings you an average commission of $100 a month. Therefore, to increase your earnings by $500, you need to find five additional distributors—or spend about two hundred hours in recruiting, making presentations, and training. Of course, as these distributors bring in other active distributors, that will increase your income even more.

To estimate how much time you will need to sponsor the distributors for your group to achieve a desired level of earnings, just plug the appropriate figures into the formulas on Chart 22: An Estimate of Earnings and Distributors Needed.

CHART 21: EARNINGS FROM MY DISTRIBUTOR GROUP
(Get information from company's monthly statement)

Month _____

Total Product Volume _____   Total Distributors _____

Product Volume Per Level: Distributors Per Level:

1 _____   1 _____

2 _____   2 _____

3 _____   3 _____

4 _____   4 _____

5 _____   5 _____

Average Product Volume:

$$\frac{\text{Total Product Volume}}{\text{Number of Distributors}} = \underline{\hspace{2cm}}$$

Average Product Volume Per Level:

$$\frac{\text{Product Volume on Level \#}}{\text{Number of Distributors Level \#}} = \underline{\hspace{2cm}}$$

Total Commission: _____   Per Level (if available):

1 _____ 2 _____ 3 _____

4 _____ 5 _____

Average Rate of Commission:

$$\frac{\text{Total Commission}}{\text{Total Product Volume}} = \underline{\hspace{2cm}}$$

Average Rate of Commission Per Level:

$$\frac{\text{Commission from Level \#}}{\text{Product Volume Level \#}} = \underline{\hspace{2cm}}$$

Average Commission Per Distributor:

$$\frac{\text{Total Commission}}{\text{Total Distributors}} = \underline{\hspace{2cm}}$$

$$\frac{\text{Commission from Level \#}}{\text{Distributors on Level \#}} = \underline{\hspace{2cm}}$$

CHART 22: AN ESTIMATE OF EARNINGS AND DISTRIBUTORS NEEDED
(Get information from Earnings from My Distributor Group Chart)

Month _____

Total Commission = Average Commission Per Active Distributor × Total Number of Active Distributors

_____ = _____ × _____

Number of Active Distributors Needed to Achieve Desired Earnings = $\dfrac{\text{Desired Commission Earnings}}{\text{Average Commission Per Active Distributor}}$

_____ = _____

95

CHART 22: AN ESTIMATE OF EARNINGS AND DISTRIBUTORS NEEDED (continued)

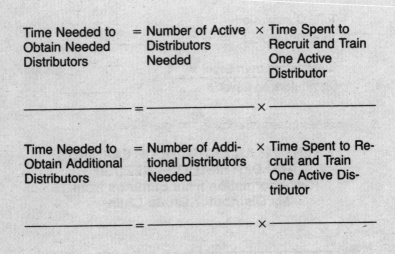

Time Needed to Obtain Needed Distributors = Number of Active Distributors Needed × Time Spent to Recruit and Train One Active Distributor

———————— = ———————— × ————————

Time Needed to Obtain Additional Distributors = Number of Additional Distributors Needed × Time Spent to Recruit and Train One Active Distributor

———————— = ———————— × ————————

    Finally, in light of your assessment of your progress to date, review your overall goals. What are your current goals? Your most important goals? Do you want to change any goals? What is your time line for achieving these goals and what must you do?

    If you have previously reviewed your goals, you can make a comparison between your past goals and your goals now. What kind of changes have occurred, if any? A form you can use for this process is Chart 23.

CHART 23: ASSESSING MY GOALS FOR SUCCESS

Date: _____

1. What are my current goals? How important are they to me?
    (list all your goals; then rate them on their importance to you from 1–10)

2. What is my most important goal?
    (it can be a single goal or an overall goal combining several listed above)

3. When do I want to achieve this goal? Date:

4. What must I do to achieve this goal?
    (work backward and list the steps)

5. What must I do each week, starting now, to get where I want to be?

    Week 1

    Week 2

    Week 3

    Week 4

    Week 5

Part III

CHOOSING THE RIGHT PRODUCTS OR PROGRAM FOR YOU

Chapter 6

SELECTING A GOOD
PRODUCT OR SERVICE

A major key to success in any kind of marketing is selecting the right products, services, or program to market ... and, most importantly, choosing a program that's right for you. If you are purchasing products wholesale from a supplier and marketing them yourself under your own company name or plan to do this, you can skip ahead to the discussion on testing your market. But if you are thinking of representing a direct sales or multi-level company, read on.

You need to be very careful in making your choice of a company; too many people hear about a "hot" item or company and jump on board because they think everyone else is doing so. But they haven't asked the right questions to assess properly the product or the company. Thus, after a big flurry of activity, they end up holding the bag because the company goes broke ... or because after they recruit a large sales team, they discover no one is buying the product, for the average consumer doesn't like it.

I know many people who had this experience, and as a

result they are burned out on direct sales or MLM, have lost their credibility with others, or a combination of both.

In one case, dozens of people gave their all to launch a new company, which I'll call the XYZ Corporation. They devoted long hours to marketing and strategy sessions; some gave up well-paying jobs. Unfortunately, the founders of the company were not ethical. They gave a great sales pitch about how they were giving everyone a great opportunity for financial freedom, and they soon had a thriving organization of a few hundred people in California. Here and there, a few people checked them out with the Chamber of Commerce in their home state, and they managed to talk their way out of the few complaints reported. Everyone so wanted to believe in their vision! But after a few months, when promised checks bounced and a planned newsletter did not appear, when referrals from shared advertising did not materialize, and when the company moved to another state, people finally realized they had been taken. Some are even suing the company. Good luck!

In another case, about 35,000 people signed up in a three-month frenzy of activity. The hype was incredible. There were stories about one distributor for the company getting 2,000 persons in his sales organization in six days, about another group getting 3,500 in two weeks; but, in fact, the distributors had merely purchased large quantities of membership kits. One distributor took out a full-page ad in a local newspaper claiming the new program was the greatest pyramid scheme yet. And others gave rousing meetings where they told people they didn't have to use the program if they didn't want to—they could just think about how much money they would make. Soon several attorney generals were investigating the company.

The problem was that nobody signing up bothered to check through the hype to assess the company's program and marketing plan or the founders' track record. If they had, they would have seen clear danger signals. For example, when the program was in operation in a few localities, only 10 percent of the sign-ups were actually using it. Also, the founders hadn't done their homework in checking state laws, with the result that the company's marketing plan was found illegal in a half-dozen states. So the company ended up changing its plan, fighting to lift restraining orders, and seeking new funding sources to handle the legal battle and cover the added expenses due to program changes. Finally, after a series of changes— so many that distributors were wryly calling it "the plan of the week"—the company folded, leaving a network of furious, hurt, and embittered distributors. They thought they were in on the greatest ground-floor opportunity yet, only to have it turn to dust.

In other cases, a company is undercapitalized and is likely to go under, because a company normally can't depend on the sales network to bring in the funds it needs to operate fast enough. For example, one natural foods company signed up over five hundred distributors, but they didn't buy enough product. So after a few months of operation and $6,000 in bills, the owner of the company said "enough" and closed the doors.

Some companies have been shut down or have run the risk of this happening because their products or programs came up against various regulations and laws, and no one in the company took care of the necessary product tests or marketing plan reviews. For example, a health or drug product may run into problems with the Food and Drug Administration if it hasn't passed the appropriate research tests, no matter what the sales hype claims. Also, a company may have problems if it is paying commissions for membership sign-ups, since this policy runs afoul of illegal pyramid laws in some states, and the attorney general may act. Or, if the company prints up hypothetical earnings in its literature and makes outrageous claims, the post office can shut it down.

Thus, it is absolutely essential to check out carefully any program you consider getting involved in and to ask questions, until you are sure the product and the company are solid; for if the company goes out of business, you do, too!

The new program should pass the test in four critical areas.

THE PRODUCT OR SERVICE SHOULD BE OF GOOD QUALITY AND SOMETHING PEOPLE NEED AND WANT

The product or service should have broad appeal either to the overall market or to a certain market segment within it (for example, singles, homeowners, women). Also, the product should have a long-term market potential and not just be a fad item.

The product should be one you believe in and are proud to represent. You personally should know that the products actually perform and are priced competitively. Also, preferably, you personally should use or want to use these products, so that you can give a sincere testimonial about them to potential consumers and distributors. Too, the products should be backed by a guarantee of customer satisfaction.

Ideally, the product line should be consumable, so you get repeat sales. Or alternatively, the company should have a full line of products and should be continually coming out with new products, so you have something to sell the same customer again and again.

Although some one-product companies do well when they have something unique (such as an unusual toothbrush or mouthwash) and make it easy for the distributor to sell their product by handing out a brochure, one-product companies usually don't last for long. The reason is that the distributors generally find it takes more effort than it is worth to continually find new customers for a one-shot sale. So they soon lose their motivation. Instead it's usually better to work in a program where you can build up a network of customers and distributors who will use the company's products on an ongoing basis.

The claims the company makes for the product should be in line with government regulations. If not, the company is likely to run into problems with governmental agencies, and when that happens, that often means disaster.

People should have a reason to get the product from you, either because it is not available at a local retailer or because you offer a service to help consumers use a product they can't normally get elsewhere. For example, some computer and software products are sold both retail and through direct sales, but direct sales distributors can still compete because they offer additional personal support.

THE COMPANY SHOULD BE SOLID AND REPUTABLE

The company should appear as if it is going to be around a long time. You are building a business, not joining a "get-rich scheme" in which people get in and out fast, and the only ones who get rich are those who get in soon enough. Thus, any company you represent should be one that is planning for a long-term future, rather than for deriving a quick profit by rapidly building up a sales network through a surge of initial emotional excitement.

If the company has been around for a year or more, it should have a good performance record. To meet this test, ask yourself questions such as the following: How has it done in previous years? How much product has been sold? How many distributors have joined? Is the company expanding its product line? What kind of growth is the company experiencing in its sales volume and distributor force? How does the company's growth compare to the competition? Does the company have a good record of paying commission checks correctly and on time? Does the company ship its product promptly?

If the company is fairly new, a "ground-floor" opportunity, the management team should be solid, so the potentials of the new venture outweigh the risks of starting up. In any start-up situation, there are always more risks, as well as a tremendous potential if the venture goes well. This potential depends heavily on the management team and founding distributors behind the company. So ask some hard questions about who is involved.

What is the background of the company founders?

What other ventures have they started and how successful have they been?

What sort of experts or advisers are involved in the design of the product?

What sort of support does the company have from researchers, scientists, trade associations, or industry leaders and spokesmen?

Whether the company is old or new, it should have the appropriate credentials. Some of the questions to ask are these.

Is the company listed and well respected by local business organizations such as the Chamber of Commerce or Better Business Bureau?

Has the company taken care of the necessary legal procedures, so it is authorized to operate in a particular state?

Does the company check out positively with various trade, regulatory, and protection agencies, such as the state attorney general, consumer protection agency, or direct sales association?

Do the company founders have a solid business background?

Has the company hired experts in the area of management,

finance, product development, motivation, and training? Does it have the necessary experts or advisers to assist, either as officers, employees, or consultants?

The company should be willing to provide information about its track record or officers. The company should include this information in its literature. And if you ask, company officers should be willing to talk about this. As long as a company is good and solid, its people should be delighted and proud to say so; if not, you should wonder why not.

THE COMPANY SHOULD PROVIDE ITS DISTRIBUTORS WITH GOOD PROFESSIONAL SUPPORT

The company should have a good professional image. In today's media-conscious age, a good professional image is a must for any company, and that means attractive, well-written literature, professionally prepared tapes and cassettes, and dynamic video or slide-sound presentations. Your company must not only *be* good and solid, but it must *look* good and solid, too.

The company should provide enough material so you can readily tell its story. Such material not only informs, but it gives the company credibility. People are more likely to believe what they see, and they respond emotionally when they see a program presented well.

The company's material should be top-notch and professional. Ideally, brochures should be colorful and on slick glossy paper. There should be color photos showing the product or company. Any written material should be clear, interesting, and to the point.

Also, the literature should make no wild, misleading claims about fabulous income potential. And if you discover typos, bad grammar, or unclear writing—watch out—that's a sign of an unprofessional, badly managed company.

Ideally, the company should have audio and video cassettes, as well as printed materials available. The more dynamic material the company can provide you, the more it helps you in building your business.

Ideally, the company will send out its officers or other staff members into the field to assist with training and meetings. This way the company provides additional leadership and motivation to its people in the field. And meetings with company officials make the company seem more credible.

The company should appropriately recognize the accomplishments of its successful distributors. The company should do this through occasional rallies, award ceremonies, reports in a newsletter, and so on. Not only does this make the successful distributors feel good about what they have done for the company, but it motivates the other distributors to emulate the examples of success.

THE COMPANY SHOULD HAVE A GOOD COMMISSION PROGRAM OR MARKETING PLAN

You should be able to get started with a limited personal investment—generally less than $100. You typically need a sales kit and an introductory supply of product to get started, and you should be able to start with a small amount.

If the company is a direct sales company, its commissions and bonus plan should enable you to earn a good income in return for your time and effort.

If the company is a multi-level company, its marketing plan should include certain additional features.

A multi-level marketing plan should comply with generally

accepted legal requirements. These criteria differ widely from state to state, but in general, the plan should have these elements to protect the company from problems with the postal authorities and state attorney generals: (1) The company should not have any minimum purchase requirements to become a distributor, although the company can require distributors to attain a minimal level of activity as an incentive to receive bonuses. (2) The company only pays commissions and bonuses on the sale of its product, not for recruiting. (3) The company does not make any unrealistic claims about potential earnings. (4) The company provides its distributors with training materials and sales literature at cost, since a company cannot make a profit on these items.

An MLM company's marketing plan should both pay the distributor well and enable the company to make money. Every plan is different, but when you add up the percentages, companies commonly pay out about 35–45 percent of the retail price. If a company pays out too little—less than 30 percent—this is unfair to the distributor, although some companies have been successful paying out as little as 20–25 percent. Conversely, if a company pays out too much—over 55 percent—the company is apt to have problems staying profitable as it grows, or it may be charging too much for its merchandise.

Whatever the particulars, work out the payouts to determine the full percentage the company is paying out. Initially, the company won't pay out the full amount, because there aren't people on all levels of the plan; typically, it takes a company about a year to get up to speed and make a full payout. But once it does, the percentages should be ones the company can live with, or, with success, the company will go bust!

A multi-level marketing plan should provide an incentive for distributors both to make direct sales and to work with their downline (lower-level distributors). The distributor should be able to earn enough making direct sales to consumers to make this worthwhile. At the same time, the plan should encourage the distributor to build an organization, by providing sufficient bonuses and overrides on group production.

A multi-level marketing plan should emphasize personal consumption of the product and retailing to consumers, not just recruiting. Accordingly, commissions should be paid only on products sold, not on recruits. If not, the plan is illegal.

Watch out for multi-level marketing plans with balloon commissions. In these plans, the company pays a small commission on your first few levels and then a large commission on your third, fourth, or fifth levels. These plans look great on paper, since it seems as if you can make an enormous amount of money as your organization grows. But in reality, most people don't create sales networks that go down that far. So the company pays out very little commission, and these plans are quite misleading.

Other attractive MLM features to look for: (1) The company pays bonuses directly and allows its distributors to order directly from the company. (2) The marketing plan is completely computerized, so the distributor only has to take care of his or her own bookkeeping activities and does not have to handle paying commissions to downline members. (3) The plan protects the distributor from permanently losing someone he or she sponsors if he or she is temporarily unable to participate in the program.

Once a direct sales or multi-level program passes this four-point test, you must do three more things to fully market-research the program and make a final decision on whether to market it and how far to go with it.

DO A MARKET TEST OF THE PRODUCT OR SERVICE TO SEE HOW WELL PROSPECTIVE CONSUMERS AND DISTRIBUTORS RESPOND

You may need to sign into the program to get the product or necessary support for an adequate test. But before you do sign up, if you must, or go full blast with the program, check out the market.

You may think this is the greatest product; the person who presents it may claim that everyone is jumping at the opportunity to buy it or distribute it. But even so, check it out. People say all sorts of things at sales meetings—much of it rumor or exaggeration. Plus, it's often easy to get people marketing one product to jump at new business opportunity.

But the real test comes with the consumer. There may be over five million direct sales and MLM distributors today. But there are over two hundred million other people in the United States, and most of them are not involved in this kind of marketing. So you need to learn if your product appeals to people generally, not just people interested in marketing. Then, too, different products do well in different areas, because lifestyles, interests, and personal wants differ.

Thus, do a small market test. Show the product or describe the service to prospective buyers. You can start with relatives and friends, but since most of your customers and distributors are likely to be strangers, it's better to try the product out on people you don't know well. And strangers can be more objective with you anyway.

You can try out your product in numerous ways. Bring some samples to a party or meeting. Set up a stand at a fair or flea market. Arrange a mini-study at a shopping center, as some

111

big companies do when they test their product. You can give out samples, ask people to fill out a short questionnaire with their reactions, and find out if anyone wants to buy it.

Then, you have a better idea of what the response to the product is likely to be, and if you decide to go with the company, you can use the results of your test to inform and motivate your sales team.

DETERMINE YOUR TARGET MARKET

Different types of people like different types of products, so take this into consideration in deciding both whether you want to market a program and *how* to market it.

Being aware of different markets is particularly important if you are already marketing one product or service and are thinking about adding another line. Some people keep their marketing efforts for different products separate. But it makes good sense to combine products which appeal to the same market. For about the same amount of effort, you can sell two programs to the same people. Thus, if you are already selling a weight loss program, it may make sense to add a low-calorie food product, because both appeal to the health-conscious individual. On the other hand, if you try to market to different target groups, you may find yourself getting fragmented.

In any event, whether you are distributing one product or several, you need to know your market, and it may not always be the market you think. For example, video games are primarily marketed to the eighteen and under market; but increasingly, adults are playing video games, too.

So, make a list of the various markets for your product, and think in terms of some of the following categories:

Age
Sex
Marital Status
Race or Ethnic Group
Income Level
Geographic Region

Also, list any special groups that might be especially interested, such as:

Business Groups
Companies
Health Clubs
Church Groups
Singles Clubs

Then, try out your program on the people who you feel are your prime market, and emphasize the feature of your product you think might appeal to them most. For example, in marketing a health product to singles, emphasize how they will look and feel better, and therefore find it easier to meet other people.

After your test, evaluate how well you do. Are the people you expect to like the product responding? If not, why not? Is it your approach or the product? If it's your approach that's the problem, change it. If it's the product, maybe you're not targeting your product to the right group. Then, either try another market, or perhaps consider marketing another product or service to the same group.

DECIDE IF THE PRODUCT OR PROGRAM IS RIGHT FOR YOU

After you have carefully assessed the product, the company, and the market, your involvement ultimately depends on the key question: Is the product or program right for me? Every other test can come up positive. But you still need that gut-level intuitive feeling that says: This is the program for me.

In short, you must be committed; you must really want to work with that product or program. Otherwise, your lack of commitment and sincere involvement will show. And if you're not 100 percent behind what you are doing, you won't have the necessary motivation and drive to achieve success.

There are over 1,500 direct sales and MLM programs, and tens of thousands of other products or services you can market. Potentially, you can make a good income and perhaps get wealthy marketing almost anything. But you need to choose one or a few programs that work for you.

There are four personal factors to consider in making your choice.

Do You Use This Product or Service? Many distributors promote a product or service they don't use, and some do it quite successfully. Others find it is much more personally satisfying and more convincing to consumers when they promote a product they use. One advantage of being a user is that you can give personal examples of experiences with the product, and people put a great deal of faith in such personal testimonials—more so than they do just hearing claims about a product.

Do You Feel 100 Percent behind Promoting the Product? Even if you use the product, you still need a desire to promote it. A critical question here is: Does that product fit your image of the business you'd like to be in? For example, you may be using a great soap or mouthwash, but you don't feel comfortable selling household or dental care products. Instead, you'd rather promote travel, meeting people, and fun.

So, don't just pick a program because it's hot, but pick a good program you can really relate to. And if you have expertise in some field, perhaps choose a product related to that. For example, if you're a doctor or nurse, choose health products; if you've been a travel agent, try travel. You don't need expertise to be successful, but if you already have special training, a product line in your field is a natural for you.

Do You Want to Work Closely with the People Promoting the Product? Since marketing is a people business, liking and relating well to the people you work with can make all the difference. If a direct sales or MLM program is new in your area and you'll be kicking off the program, this may not be a major issue, since you will be creating the local sales network yourself.

But if the program is established, you will be connecting up with a network of already active distributors—through your sponsor in the case of an MLM program. Since this network puts on meetings, seminars, and other activities you can attend, an important question to ask yourself is whether you want to work closely with these people on an ongoing basis. Can you identify with them and see yourself readily fitting into the network? Is your sponsor someone you want to work closely with?

As you get more active in the program, this network will become much more than a group with whom to conduct business, for these people will become your friends and supporters, too. So it's critical that you feel good about the people you'll be working with.

If you do, plunge in and go to work. But if not, perhaps you should reconsider. Maybe you'd do better with another program, where you could feel closer to the people involved. In MLM or any direct sales program, being in tune with the people you associate with is critical; whatever you want to call it—"energy . . . vibes . . . a sense of attunement"—you become successful by working together as a team. And that means you have to truly want to be part of that team.

Do You Want to Work with an Established Program or Help Launch a Start-Up? Some marketing people like the security of promoting an established program with a proven track record. They like becoming part of an already organized network of people involved in the program. Others like the excitement of developing something new. They accept—even enjoy—the risks associated with a ground-floor opportunity, and are willing to adapt to the sometimes frequent changes of course and marketing plan as the company gets off the ground. They feel there is more potential for big money with a successful new venture if it makes it, and they would rather take their chances. You have to decide what's right for you: a brand-new company; a company that's a few months to a year old; a company that's been in business over a year or longer; or creating your own marketing company from scratch.

If all signs are go, get behind the product or program. But otherwise, think again. It may not be a good product or program . . . or maybe it's just not right for you!

The keys to selecting a good program are summarized in Chart 24. If you are having trouble deciding on a direct sales or MLM program, you can use the rating form in Chart 25 to rate each program on the considerations discussed in this chapter.

CHART 24: THE KEYS TO SELECTING A GOOD PRODUCT OR SERVICE TO MARKET

The Four Basics for Choosing a Company to Represent

1. A good quality product or service which people need and want

2. A solid and reputable company

3. Good professional support from the company

4. A good commission program or marketing plan

Other Major Considerations for Marketing Any Product or Service

1. Your success in market testing the product or service in your area

2. The type of target market to whom the product or service appeals

3. Your personal feeling that the program is right for you

   a. It helps to use the product or service, though this isn't necessary.

   b. You should feel 100 percent committed to promoting this particular product or service.

   c. You should want to work closely with the people involved in the program.

   d. The length of time in business—as start-up, new company, or established company—suits your personal style. Or you have what it takes to start your own company from scratch.

117

CHART 25: RATING A DIRECT SALES
OR MULTI-LEVEL PROGRAM

To use this chart:
1) Rate the importance of each consideration from 1 to 5.
2) Rate how well the program does with respect to each consideration from −5 (very poorly) to +5 (very positively). If you're not sure, don't know, or feel neutral, rate it "zero." In other words, you are using a rating scale that looks like this:

−5	−4	−3	−2	−1	0	+1	+2	+3	+4	+5
very poorly					neutral					very positively

3) Multiply your importance rating by your positive or negative rating to determine how you rate the overall value of the program on that consideration.
4) Add up your overall rating for each category (1, 2, 3, and so on) and then for all of the categories.
5) Now you can use the total for comparisons with other program ratings to help you make a decision.

NAME OF PROGRAM: _____

Important Considerations	Importance of Issue (Rate 1–5)	How Program Rates on Issue (Rate −5 to +5)	Overall Value of Program (Multiply Ratings)
1. *The Company's Products and Services*			

STRIKE IT RICH IN PERSONAL SELLING

Important Considerations	Importance of Issue (Rate 1–5)	How Program Rates on Issue (Rate −5 to +5)	Overall Value of Program (Multiply Ratings)
Does this product or service have broad appeal?			
How much do people need and want this product or service?			
How good is the quality of this product or service?			
Is the product one I truly want to represent?			
Is the product consumable?			
Does the company have a full line of products?			
Is the company continually coming out with new products (or are there renewals)?			

CHART 25: RATING A DIRECT SALES
OR MULTI-LEVEL PROGRAM (continued)

NAME OF PROGRAM: _____

Important Considerations	Importance of Issue (Rate 1–5)	How Program Rates on Issue (Rate −5 to +5)	Overall Value of Program (Multiply Ratings)
Do people have a reason to get the product through me? (For example, it's not available retail; I can offer extra service.)			
Total Category Rating:			
2. *The Company's Stability and Reputation*			
How solid and reputable is the company?			
Does the company look as if it will be around for a long time?			

STRIKE IT RICH IN PERSONAL SELLING

Important Considerations	Importance of Issue (Rate 1–5)	How Program Rates on Issue (Rate −5 to +5)	Overall Value of Program (Multiply Ratings)
Does the company have the necessary credentials?			
Does the company have good support from experts, advisers, or leaders in the industry?			
How experienced are the company's officers?			
Does the company have a good track record?			
How does the company's growth rate or product compare to the competition?			
Total Category Rating			

CHART 25: RATING A DIRECT SALES
OR MULTI-LEVEL PROGRAM (continued)

NAME OF PROGRAM: _____

Important Considerations	Importance of Issue (Rate 1–5)	How Program Rates on Issue (Rate −5 to +5)	Overall Value of Program (Multiply Ratings)
3. *The Company's Commission Program or Marketing Plan*			
If it's a direct sales or non-MLM company, does the company have a good commission and bonus plan?			
Can you get started for a limited personal investment (generally less than $100)?			
If it's an MLM company, does its marketing plan seem to meet the major legal requirements?			

STRIKE IT RICH IN PERSONAL SELLING

Important Considerations	Importance of Issue (Rate 1–5)	How Program Rates on Issue (Rate −5 to +5)	Overall Value of Program (Multiply Ratings)
Is the MLM plan generous to distributors?			
Does the MLM plan permit sufficient profits to the company?			
Are the MLM payout arrangements for each level designed both to motivate people to make direct sales and to help their downline?			
Does the MLM company pay bonuses directly to the distributor?			
Can all MLM distributors order direct from the company?			

CHART 25: RATING A DIRECT SALES
OR MULTI-LEVEL PROGRAM (continued)

NAME OF PROGRAM: _____

Important Considerations	Importance of Issue (Rate 1–5)	How Program Rates on Issue (Rate −5 to +5)	Overall Value of Program (Multiply Ratings)
Is the MLM plan completely computerized to minimize the distributor's bookkeeping activity?			
Total Category Rating:			
4. The Quality of Support Provided by the Company			
Does the company have a good professional image?			
How good is the quality of the company's literature and sales aids?			

STRIKE IT RICH IN PERSONAL SELLING

Important Considerations	Importance of Issue (Rate 1–5)	How Program Rates on Issue (Rate −5 to +5)	Overall Value of Program (Multiply Ratings)
Does the company provide enough materials?			
Does the company offer good support in the field (for example, send officers or staff members to put on meetings)?			
Total Category Rating:			
5. *Market Test Results*			
How well do prospective consumers like the product or service?			
How likely are prospective consumers to buy it?			
Total Category Rating:			

CHART 25: RATING A DIRECT SALES
OR MULTI-LEVEL PROGRAM (continued)

NAME OF PROGRAM: _____

Important Considerations	Importance of Issue (Rate 1–5)	How Program Rates on Issue (Rate −5 to +5)	Overall Value of Program (Multiply Ratings)
6. *Target Market*			
Do I want to market to the target market for this product?			
Does this product line appeal to a market I am already selling to?			
Total Category Rating:			
7. *Personal Considerations*			
Do I use this product or service?			

Important Considerations	Importance of Issue (Rate 1–5)	How Program Rates on Issue (Rate −5 to +5)	Overall Value of Program (Multiply Ratings)
Am I 100 percent behind promoting this product?			
Do I want to work closely with the people who are now promoting this product?			
How do I feel about how long the company has been in business? (Or about starting my own company?)			
Total Category Rating:			
Total for All Categories:			

SELECTING ONE PRODUCT LINE OR MANY?

One big issue that comes up in selecting a product or services to market is the question of marketing the products from more than one company. You'll hear arguments on both sides, and the controversy is far from settled. Should you join one program, a few, or many?

Traditionally, the old-line direct sales companies like Amway and Shaklee have stressed loyalty to the company and have offered their distributors a large line of products so they can make a living selling only these products.

But in the last few years, many new companies have emerged that are small and offer only a few products, so many distributors have begun promoting several product lines. When *Multi-Level Marketing News* magazine, an industry publication with about 15,000 readers, surveyed its readers, they found these distributors were each involved in an average of 3.8 companies.

On the other hand, some of the most successful distributors argue that it is best to focus on one company at a time. They claim that it is best to concentrate your energy and build a sales network in depth. If you do too many programs, you can get scattered, they say.

At the same time, many distributors believe it works well to do two or even three compatible programs together, or to launch a second or third program after the first one is solidly established. They see this as a way of selling more to the same market.

Others argue for doing several companies at a time, because there is a great deal of flux in the direct sales and multi-level industry. Then, they say, if one company has problems or goes under, you still have other programs to market. So, "don't put all your eggs in one basket," they say.

In any case, most distributors agree you don't want to become a direct sales or multi-level marketing junkie, who signs up in everything and then does practically nothing with anything, because he or she is so scattered, he or she can't focus on anything.

So what should you do? Basically, you must assess your own needs. How much time do you want to devote to marketing? And how experienced are you in this field?

If you are new and/or have only a limited amount of time, it's probably best to focus on one product or program and learn to do it well. Then, as you gain experience or have more time, perhaps add another line. But make sure you are comfortable with handling two product lines and make sure they are compatible. (For example, a diet and low-calorie food product might work well together; but two diet programs would compete with each other, while a diet program and convenience food line might pull you into two different markets.)

In some cases, distributors see themselves much like department stores—offering a variety of products, but only through direct sales. Or they may see themselves as MLM brokers, turning people on to a variety of MLM programs. Such a broad-based approach may work for some people who have wide marketing experience and are able aggressively to market several lines themselves or to attract strong distributors into their organization.

But, in general, focusing your efforts works best, and in multi-level marketing this focus works especially well, because the key to success in MLM is building a strong organization, not just moving a lot of product yourself. If you try to do too much, not only will you be fragmented, but your group members may become confused and therefore less productive.

So choose carefully and choose well. Then, you can confidently concentrate your efforts, because you have chosen a
good, solid company with good products you are proud to
represent.

Chapter 7

CHOOSING A GOOD SALES LEADER OR SPONSOR

Choosing a sponsor is an issue if the product or service you are marketing comes from a multi-level company. If you are a sales rep for a direct sales company working with a local or company sales manager or have put together your own sales package with products or services you buy wholesale, you can skip this section. In a direct sales situation you will typically be working with the manager assigned to your territory, so you have no choice. And when you create your own sales program, you're on your own.

Once you have found a good network marketing or multi-level program, your next step is choosing a good sales leader or sponsor. Commonly, people sign up under the first person who tells them about the program, and that can be fine, depending on your own needs and what this person offers as a sponsor. For example, if the person is someone you know, like, or can readily work with, and that person is actively working the program, it makes perfect sense to sign up and work together.

But *you don't have to sign up with the first person who tells you about a program!* Some people may tell you that the ethics of multi-level are that you should, but you are not just joining a fun social club. You are making a business decision and becoming part of a business organization, unless you want to be a consumer only, and then, if you deal direct with the company, it may not matter who your sponsor is.

The reason for choosing your sponsor carefully is that the organization you join plays a crucial part in whether or not you are successful. Also, as an active distributor, you will be making the people in that group a lot of money. So look at how effectively that organization will help you. If you have any reservations, take a little time to shop around. See what other organizations working the program are doing, and seriously weigh the pros and cons of each one. Of course, there may be personal or political reasons for getting involved in a group when someone you know asks to sponsor you. But recognize that these are not the only considerations, and weigh them along with the rest.

Taking this time to make your decision carefully is important if you truly want to be successful, because all too often, in MLM, someone simply tells you or sends you a letter about a great new program. But, then, he or she is mainly interested in signing you up, or is involved in so many programs or has signed up so many people that he or she doesn't have time to really support you. So you are effectively on your own.

For self-starters, working alone can be fine. But most individuals need to work closely with someone for a few weeks or months until they really feel solid about working the program. And the assistance of a good team leader or sponsor who is in touch with the latest program developments is an important ingredient of success for anyone.

Thus, after you hear about a program and decide it may be right for you, consider whether you really do want the person who told you to be your sponsor. All things being equal, that's the most natural decision. But if not, realize you can choose someone else . . . and perhaps you should!

Some key issues to consider in making your decision:

- Do I know and like my prospective sponsor? Is this someone I would like to work with?
- Does my prospective sponsor seem to be sincere and honest?
- What kind of organization is my prospective sponsor part of or has he or she built up? Are these people I would enjoy working with? Would I feel comfortable introducing them to my personal friends?
- Is my prospective sponsor sincerely committed to the program, and is he or she someone who is likely to remain committed despite adversity, so I won't be abandoned?
- How actively is my prospective sponsor promoting the program? Is this a primary focus or one of many programs he or she is promoting?
- What kind of support will my prospective sponsor offer me personally? Is he or she willing to work closely with me to train me?
- Does my sponsor seem sincerely willing to assist me in achieving my own financial success, not just his or her own?
- What kind of activities, training tools, seminars, etc., can my prospective sponsor provide me with to help me be successful?
- How knowledgeable is my sponsor about multi-level marketing generally? To what extent is he or she in touch with the latest developments in the field? Does the sponsor continually educate himself about the MLM business?
- If my prospective sponsor lives in another area, is he or she able and willing to provide the ongoing assistance I need?

In fact, ask your prospective sponsor these kinds of questions. The sponsor should be willing and able to explain how he or she will support you.

If you aren't sure whether to go with a particular sponsor, or if you have several options, it helps to list the advantages or disadvantages of choosing each sponsor. You can use Chart 26 to help you choose. I've listed some major issues, and you should add your own considerations. Decide how important different issues are, rate the pros and cons, total them up, and use the results to help you decide.

Certainly, trust your intuition or gut-level feeling. But use this list to help you make your decision rationally, too!

CHART 26: RATING MY PROSPECTIVE SPONSOR

To use this chart:
1) Rate the importance of each consideration from 1 to 5.
2) Rate the pros and cons of your prospective sponsor with respect to each consideration using a rating scale from −5 (very negative) to +5 (very positive). If you're not sure, don't know, or feel neutral, your rating is "zero." In other words, you are using a rating scale that looks like this:

−5	−4	−3	−2	−1	0	+1	+2	+3	+4	+5
very negative					neutral					very positive

3) Multiply your importance rating by your positive/negative rating to determine your overall rating for your prospective sponsor on that issue.
4) Add up your overall value rating for all considerations.
5) Now you can use this total to help you make a decision.

134

NAME OF PROSPECTIVE SPONSOR _____

Important Considerations for Me	Importance of Issue (Rate 1–5)	How Sponsor Rates on Issue (Rate −5 to +5)	Overall Rating (Multiply Ratings)
How well do I know or like my prospective sponsor? How well would I like to work with him or her?			
Does my prospective sponsor seem sincere and honest?			
Is my prospective sponsor part of an active organization I would enjoy working with?			
Is my prospective sponsor sincerely committed to the program?			
How actively is my prospective sponsor promoting the program?			

CHART 26: RATING MY PROSPECTIVE SPONSOR
(continued)

NAME OF PROSPECTIVE SPONSOR _____

Important Considerations for Me	Importance of Issue (Rate 1–5)	How Sponsor Rates on Issue (Rate −5 to +5)	Overall Rating (Multiply Ratings)
How much support and training will my prospective sponsor offer me?			
Does my sponsor offer various kinds of activities, like seminars or classes, or has he or she developed training tools to help members of his or her downline?			
How knowledgeable is my prospective sponsor about MLM generally? How well is he or she in touch with the latest in the field? What kind of track record does he or she have?			

STRIKE IT RICH IN PERSONAL SELLING

Important Considerations for Me	Importance of Issue (Rate 1–5)	How Sponsor Rates on Issue (Rate −5 to +5)	Overall Rating (Multiply Ratings)
Does my prospective sponsor live in the area? Or if not, can he or she still provide the assistance I need?			
TOTAL RATING:			

Chapter 8

GETTING PREPARED

Okay. You've chosen the products or services you want to represent, you are convinced they are good, and you're ready to turn on the world.

Your next step is to thoroughly know your product and your company. Also, if you not only are selling to consumers but are seeking people for your sales team, you need to be completely knowledgeable about the company's marketing plan. In either case, you want to be able to give a solid, professional presentation and answer any questions that are likely to come up. And you want to have the necessary sales literature on hand to buttress what you say.

Learn as much as you can in the beginning to get started on the right foot. Then, keep learning all you can as you go along. The more knowledgeable you are, the more professional your presentation, the more effective you will be.

To get this information, read all you can about the product and the company. Sit down with your direct sales manager or MLM sponsor and ask him or her to go into the program in depth. And go to at least one, or preferably more, product demonstrations or opportunity meetings, so you feel really solid about the program. Also, these activities will connect you with others marketing the product and will help you feel motivated, excited, and inspired to get on out there and market it. You should be prepared to give information in three main areas and have the necessary sales literature to back you up. These three areas are (1) product information, (2) company information, and if you are recruiting a sales group, (3) marketing plan information.

KNOWING YOUR PRODUCT

You must know much more about the product than if you were just a user, and you must be able to translate this knowledge into a brief product description that makes the product appeal to what the potential customer wants and needs.

To be convincing and persuasive, you must fully understand and stress three main points about the product: (1) its major selling *features*; (2) the *benefits* of purchasing the product based on these features; (3) the *advantages* of this product over the competition.

Also, you need to know this information for each product in the line and be able to talk about the features, benefits, and competitive advantages of the product line as a whole. If you can speak about these points from your own experience of using the products, this certainly helps.

But whether you use the products or not, think about their unique features and how these benefit the user. These features include product characteristics such as

- the nature of the product and what it does (for example, tastes better, looks better, works better)
- the price of the product (for example, lower cost)
- the quality of the materials used (such as higher quality)
- the service offered with the product (for example, better maintenance, special training in using the product)

Now think about how these product features translate into user benefits. For example, a diet product will make you thinner and healthier and give you a better, younger appearance.

Also, acquire the back-up technical knowledge you need to explain why the product works as it does or has other features and benefits. This information is particularly important if you are marketing a line of high-technology products, food, diet programs, or drug products, where people are likely to ask questions. It's not just good enough to say, "I started using this product, and I lost five pounds and never felt better." This may satisfy some people. But you have to be able to explain about the ingredients, if someone asks.

Finally, become familiar with the competition. Try out some of your competitor's products to learn how they are similar and different and how their features and benefits compare. Perhaps sit in on one of your competitor's product demonstrations or opportunity meetings to see what their sales reps or distributors say.

Sometimes your company, sales manager, or sponsor may be reluctant to have you investigate the competition, because they are afraid you may get recruited away. However, if your product is good or better that shouldn't happen. Also, when you know about the competition you have made an informed choice in deciding to promote your product or service, which helps to give you credibility when you market it. You have made your choice based on a full knowledge of the field, and you can knowledgeably tell others about the differences.

Even if there are relatively few product differences, you have other reasons for selecting that product (such as liking the company better or more local support). When you are informed, you can most effectively pitch these advantages, because you know what your product offers relative to the competition.

KNOWING YOUR COMPANY

You should also be knowledgeable about any company you represent. You should have gained some of this information when you were deciding what products or services to market, and now you should make yourself even more familiar with the company so you can convincingly talk about it to others.

You can get much of this information from company literature, but if you truly get serious about the product line, a visit to company headquarters might be in order. Meet the officers personally and look over their offices. Take a tour through their factory. You'll feel more solid about the company, and you will convey this confidence to your customers and to anyone on your sales team.

Some of the key areas to investigate include:

- Who are the company officers? What kind of professional background do they have? What is their track record in other business ventures, if any?
- How long has the company been in business?
- What is the company's sales volume? How fast is its sales volume growing?
- How many distributors does the company have now? How fast is its distributor network growing?
- How prepared is the company to handle growth?
- How open is the company to making available information about itself and its officers?
- Is the company a member of professional or trade associations in its field? Is it listed with local business agencies, such as the Chamber of Commerce and Better Business Bureau, and if so, what is its record?
- Has the company filed the necessary business and legal

documents to do business in the states where it is operating?

- How has the company arranged to handle its computer records? (Some use a computer service; some keep track of computer records internally.) Does the company have a good record for paying out commissions accurately and on time?

KNOWING YOUR MARKETING PLAN

If you are seeking others to join your sales network, be fully familiar with your company's marketing plan, so you can convincingly present the business opportunity. First, study the descriptive material offered by your company and perhaps by your sponsor or others marketing the product line. Know what the commissions and bonuses are on sales by you and others in your sales network, and know if your company has purchase volumes, minimum requirements, breakaway bonuses, or other special payment incentives.

Then work out some scenarios about what you and your sales group are likely to make, given certain assumptions about your success in recruiting new active distributors and the amount of product moved by each distributor. Sometimes your sales group leader or sponsor may already have developed some projections, but you may have to work out these scenarios yourself.

Due to current postal regulations and various state laws, companies are not permitted to create such projections, since the authorities have ruled it is misleading to suggest hypothetical earnings. Companies can only publish the average earnings of an average distributor. But if you are dynamic and promote the product line successfully, you will make much more.

So think about the possibilities, and write out or review these projections to gain a firmer sense of how you will make money with your product and how much you can make. To avoid any legal problems, don't mail this material to prospective recruits. But you can use it to go over the program with people on a one-on-one basis. Still, be sure to emphasize that any projections are only hypothetical.

Some key points to know about your marketing plan include the following:

- What is the commission for direct sales? What are the commissions, bonuses, or overrides at each level?
- What kind of purchase volumes or minimums are necessary each month to get a bonus? To stay an active distributor?
- How many first-line distributors are necessary to get a commission from your group's efforts? (Some companies require a certain number of people at your first level or require you to recruit one new person a month until your group has grown to a certain point, for you to get bonuses.)
- How large must your organization be before you qualify for extra commissions or leadership bonuses? How much volume must your sales organizations do before the company pays out extra commissions or leadership bonuses?
- How much commission money is the company paying out to its sales force, assuming it pays out commissions to active distributors on all levels?

You may be able to find some of these answers from company literature or from your group leader or sponsor. If not, work out the answers yourself. Some answers may not be that easy to find, since some marketing plans are extremely complex and hard to decipher, so you may need a computer to understand what is being paid out to whom. But do what you can to get the full picture.

This way, you not only can give a more knowledgeable, convincing presentation, but you have a better idea of what to do to achieve a certain income goal. (For example, to make $3,000 a month, you realize you need about three hundred distributors in your sales group doing a volume of about $100 a month each.) Also, you better understand how to work with your organization because you know how the payouts for sales are distributed.

Since companies distribute the percentages paid out in commissions and bonuses in very different ways, these differences suggest different ways to proceed. For example, if you are marketing products for a company with a simple 7 percent down five levels plan, the earnings picture is relatively straightforward, and the earnings potential of each distributor for you is about the same. But if your company offers 1 percent on the first level, 33 percent on the second level, and 12 percent, 6 percent, and 3 percent respectively on the third, fourth, and fifth levels, as one company has, this encourages distributors to put new recruits under their first-level sign-ups.

It is also important to understand the marketing plan fully, so you can field questions like: How does the company make money? If the company seems to be paying out too much, people tend to get suspicious, and the company may be on shaky ground eventually, too.

Remember, when a company with a network or MLM sales program is new, it will only be paying out about 25 percent of its compensation plan, since its first distributors are only starting to build their organizations. But as the company grows and its distributor ranks fill out, it starts to pay out more—probably 50 percent by the end of its first six months to a year, and then perhaps 75 percent or so after that. Since most distributor networks do not fill out completely, the company will never make full payouts.

In any event, the company's marketing plan should be realistic, and you should be able to show others how this is so. So work out the percentages to indicate how much your company pays under various conditions, or get this information from your group leader or sponsor. Normally, companies pay out about 35–55 percent to their sales force, and if the company appears to be paying any more or less, you should be able to explain this.

Finally, be able to answer questions about how the company's marketing plan complies with local and federal laws that affect direct sales or multi-level marketing. You want to be able to assure people knowledgeably that the plan is A-okay.

OBTAINING SALES LITERATURE

Make sure you have the necessary sales literature to back you up. Most good companies provide good quality literature, including full-color brochures. Or if you are launching your own product line, write your own. It is important to have this kind of material if you want to present your product or service in a good light and show that the company behind it is a successful, quality organization, too.

When a company is first starting, there may be some delays in getting this literature, and you may want to improvise by developing your own or getting some distributor-produced literature from your group leader or sponsor (though be careful to conform to company guidelines when you get creative). Normally, though, the company will produce its own basic literature supply, and some companies do not allow distributors to produce their own material, unless approved by the company, to avoid misstatements and inappropriate claims.

In any case, if a company is slow in providing literature or if the quality is not good, that's cause for concern. Today, when everyone is so visually oriented and gets so much information from visual communications like TV, the image a company presents in its material is crucial. Its graphic and written imagery must present the company in its best light.

The first company I represented didn't recognize the importance of this point, and it paid many times over. When the company first started—very much on a shoestring—its first brochure was an instant-printed flyer. And the most important benefits of the program were written last!

It took the company months to get its first color brochures, and in the meantime, many distributors found potential consumers were skeptical and didn't join, because the benefits the company offered—primarily consumer discounts—seemed so nebulous without written information to back up the company's claim.

Some distributors tried to remedy the problem by designing their own descriptive flyers. But unfortunately, some of the information was wrong and provoked some prospects to call their county district attorney. The result was a series of frantic meetings between the president of the company and some local D.A.s to assure them all was in order.

Then, when the company finally introduced its own training and procedures manual, the book was filled with typos and grammatical mistakes. Also, the company kept promising a slick, glossy newsletter—it was coming for about four months—and when it finally appeared, it was merely a double-sided legal-sized flyer.

Now, after numerous defections from distributors who once had held high hopes, the company is defunct.

To be sure, the company was beset with numerous other problems, including mismanagement and a lack of integrity. But its lack of good literature played a major part in its decline.

Instead of putting money into quality literature, the company president spent most of his money on trips around the country, so he could entertain and enthuse the troops. But these efforts created only a temporary upsurge of enthusiasm. Then, when the distributors returned home, they still did not have sufficient support materials to present the program adequately.

As a result, gradually many distributors grew dispirited, new recruits failed to materialize, and the company had a much slower growth rate than anticipated, accompanied by the inevitable financial woes. The company had appeared with a burst of initial excitement, because so many people liked the concept. But the company failed, because it never came through with the necessary professional support.

In short, you need good sales materials to present your message, and you should look to the company you are representing to provide these ... unless you are starting your own sales venture from scratch. Then, as necessary, supplement this literature with materials from your group leader or sponsor or with materials you develop yourself.

Part IV

GETTING CUSTOMERS AND SPONSORING DISTRIBUTORS

INTRODUCTION TO PART IV

In some sales programs, where your customer may also become a distributor, the process of selling customers and recruiting members of your sales network can be combined. But in effect, they are two separate processes—in the first, you are selling the individual on becoming a user or consumer. In the other, you are seeking to enlist sales associates who will sell the product or service to someone else, whether that person becomes a consumer or not.

In some direct sales programs, you are only interested in selling customers; in others—the network sales and multi-level programs—you are seeking members for your sales team, too.

Since the two processes are often linked together, I have discussed them together in this section. Use what is appropriate for your own approach. If you are only interested in selling to customers yourself, skip the material on recruiting sales associates or distributors. But if you are creating a sales group as well as seeking customers, everything applies.

Chapter 9

BASIC SALES PRINCIPLES

MULTI-LEVEL MARKETING
AND SELLING

Whenever you are marketing your product or service through
direct sales or multi-level marketing, you are essentially selling, as well as sharing and informing others. Whether you are
talking to people in person, calling them, placing ads, passing
out brochures, or sending letters, you are selling something.

Frequently, those in direct sales or MLM try to downplay
this sales aspect, since, to many, selling has a bad name. They
think of the hustler trying to sell something someone doesn't
want or can't afford. Or they try to avoid calling what they
are doing sales, since many persons think they can't sell anything. Thus, you'll frequently hear someone describe a marketing program this way: "Oh, it's just sharing. You just tell
a few people about the product, and they share it with others,
and that's all there is to it."

Well, sharing and telling others is certainly part of the process. But don't be fooled. *Direct sales and MLM do involve
selling, too*. Perhaps you may not want to call it that, to appease

the sensibilities of those who might become active distributors
if you don't call what they will be doing selling, at first. But
any form of direct marketing is still selling, and to be successful, you need to recognize the basic sales principles whenever you "share" or inform others about the product or service.
For selling involves more than telling—it involves persuading
others to take some action, too. And if you don't motivate
them to do that, you don't move any product.

Furthermore, you must be convinced yourself that there is
absolutely nothing wrong with selling. Basically, selling involves facilitating the exchange of goods and services for other
goods, services, or money, and this exchange can be of mutual
benefit to all parties. To be sure, the process can be misused
when someone sells you something which you don't want or
something which isn't of value. But the true salesperson seeks
to learn your needs and wants, in order to show you how a
valuable product or service can offer you benefits to satisfy
these desires.

In turn, the value of selling is shown by the fact that successful salespeople make very good incomes. In fact, as marketing consultant Debbie Ballard notes in her book *Secrets of
Multi-Level Fortune Building*, selling is one of the most highly
paid professions in the world, and top salespeople make more
than many high-income professionals such as doctors and lawyers. She observes, "There are more people in sales today
making over $100,000 a year than there are in the medical,
legal, and engineering professions."

THE BASIC PRINCIPLES OF SELLING

The basic principles of selling have been widely noted in
books dealing with sales techniques. There are five basic steps:
(1) attracting the prospect's attention; (2) getting and keeping
the prospect's *interest*; (3) conveying the *conviction* that this

is a beneficial product; (4) stimulating the prospect's *desire* to obtain that product or service; and (5) making a successful *close*, so the prospect takes the desired action: buying a product or service, signing up as a distributor, or otherwise agreeing to participate further.

Salespeople are also aware of and use the key motivators to promote attention, interest, conviction, and desire, and to close the sale. These motivators have been variously described as self-preservation, protection, or security; comfort and ease; romance, love, and affection; recognition or pride; and financial gain or profit.

In a widely quoted theory, Abraham Maslow suggests that these basic motives or needs can be organized in a hierarchy, in that a person seeks to satisfy a lower-order need first. Then as he or she fulfills that need, he or she becomes interested in achieving a higher-order motivation. According to Maslow, beginning with the most basic, these needs are:

1. The need for survival or self-preservation (which would include attaining a basic financial livelihood)
2. The need for safety and security (including a desire for comfort and ease)
3. The need for belonging (and romance, love, and affection)
4. The need for self-esteem (and recognition, pride, and financial achievement to show self-worth)
5. The need for self-actualization (through creative expression and setting and accomplishing goals, which could include attaining financial wealth)

Although financial gain or profit is not a primary goal in Maslow's list, it is actually intermixed at every level, since one's income is instrumental to achieving each of these other goals. You need money to survive; it gives you security; it helps you find acceptance and love; it is a source of self-esteem; and it gives you the wherewithal to pursue creative expression.

DIRECTING YOUR MESSAGE TO YOUR PROSPECT'S WANTS AND NEEDS

The key to successfully selling anything is appealing to the wants and needs that motivate a person, and recognizing that wants and needs can be quite different. Whereas a want is something a person desires, sometimes very intensely, sometimes not, a need is something a person requires to function well. While an intense desire can turn into a need, a person also can intensely want what he or she needs. But the two are not the same. For example, a person may *want* a beautiful car and house, but he or she *doesn't need* them to survive. Conversely, a person may *need* to lose weight for health reasons, but he or she *may not want* to make the effort to do so.

While some wants and needs are very common (such as the desire for a good income, nice house, and freedom and independence), people have particular motivations that are especially appealing to them, and they have different priorities in attaining these desires. Therefore, successful salespeople learn to listen and probe to find out what motivates a certain person—they search for his or her "hot button."

You can easily recognize five different types of people as you talk—each one responding most strongly to one of the five basic needs.

People Who Want Security: These people don't care that much about being rich. Mainly, they want enough to take care of their monthly bills and give them a secure retirement. Frequently, they have low or below-average incomes, and their main concern is making it.

People Who Want Comfort and Ease: These people are satisfied to be comfortable and want to take it easy and relax. They want to do more than just "make it" and pay the bills. They want an easy, comfortable life, with perhaps a nice home in the suburbs, a car, and the usual conveniences. Occasional vacations are nice, too. Frequently, these people are blue-collar workers and office workers with middle-level jobs who are satisfied or resigned to being where they are.

People Who Seek Romance, Love, and Affection: These people are especially interested in being with other people and in living an exciting, interesting life. They crave travel, adventure, and a circle of fun, interesting friends. They are not primarily interested in money for itself, but because it enables them to achieve their goal of having fun and meeting interesting people.

People Who Seek Recognition: These people want power, prestige, and respect from others. They want to prove their self-worth through their success. Typically, you'll find such people among the strivers who are trying very hard to make it in some field or among those who have already attained a position of power in business, politics, or the arts. Sure, they may want a high income, because money is a measure of success in our society. But primarily, they enjoy achievement for its own sake and for the power and prestige that comes with it.

People Who Seek Financial Gain: These people are especially interested in the trappings of success and the status associated with it. They have or want fancy cars, big homes, furs, diamonds. And when they travel, they go first class. While some may pursue the same life-style as the people who seek recognition, their primary motivation is money and status rather than power, prestige, and accomplishment. In fact, they typically want more money than they have—no matter how much they have—because acquiring money is a kind of game in which they want more and more.

THE BASIC PROCEDURES FOR MAKING A SALE

Before you make your pitch, determine if your product or service will meet your prospect's needs by asking questions and listening to what your prospect wants. Then, judge for yourself if your product is appropriate, and if so, go on. Otherwise, why bother? Your prospect will respect you more if you say you don't think the product is right for him or her—and when you approach the person again with something he or she really does need, the person will be much more receptive.

Next, talk about your product and show how its features provide benefits that will satisfy the person's needs. As much as possible, involve your prospect by letting him or her experience the product through as many senses as possible. For example, besides talking about and showing the product, so the person *sees* and *hears* about it, let him or her *touch* the product, and if appropriate, *smell* and *taste* it. And let him or her *use* the product if possible, too.

Have a rough outline in your mind of the major points you want to cover. But let the presentation flow spontaneously to suit the person you are with. This way, your pitch won't sound canned.

And don't be concerned if you forget anything. Your prospect will probably never know, since you're the expert on the product. Besides, most people only recall about 10 to 20 percent of what you say—experts claim we forget about 80 percent of everything we hear in a day and about 90 percent in a week. So if you try to fit in everything, your prospect probably won't remember it anyway. Instead, it's usually more effective to repeat your main points a few times, because people learn through reinforcement (which is why the same commercials run again and again).

If time allows, spice up your presentation with some anecdotes, testimonials, demonstrations, photographs, color brochures—anything to make it more vivid and convincing.

Allow some time for questions—either during your presentation or afterward—but don't let too many questions disrupt the flow of your presentation or get you bogged down in details. If there seem to be too many, ask your prospect (or prospects) to hold questions till later and cover any minor points quickly.

Then, press for the conclusion of the sale. If your prospect wants to think about it, try to overcome any questions or objections on the spot to push for a decision. But if your prospect still wants time to consider, set up another meeting if you can.

Sometimes, emphasizing that you are offering a money-back guarantee helps to convince the person to try it now. He or she feels there is nothing to lose. Also, it's better to use this than the approach that offers a free sample, because this way a person has invested something in using the product. It's easy to say yes to a free offer and not really care about the product being offered. But when a person puts in money, even with a money-back guarantee, that person has an added incentive to try what he or she has bought.

Finally, ask for referrals. When you do, it's best to mention categories of people who might be interested in your product or service. This helps people think of names and phone numbers more easily than if you ask vaguely, "Is there anyone you know that . . . ?" For example, ask if they have any neighbors, people at work, members of groups they belong to that might be interested. And after you mention each group, pause to give them a chance to think. Then, when people offer suggestions, ask them to get you the addresses and phone numbers at that time. Otherwise, it's too easy to forget. Or they may be busy later.

If someone does give you a referral and you are building a sales network, this can be a good time to mention the advantage of being part of this network, for then the referral could become the person's own customer instead of yours. If the prospect wants to know more, you can talk about the business opportunity . . . or suggest a follow-up meeting to go into that.

Once you conclude the sale, explain how to place additional orders, if these are likely. Indicate if reorders are direct from the company. Or, if you will be supplying your customers, invite the person to call you, or indicate that you will call at a certain time.

These major steps to making a sale can be summarized as follows:

1. Ask your prospect questions and listen to find out what he or she needs.
2. Determine if your product or service will meet these needs.
3. If you feel there is a good fit between needs and benefits, describe your product or service and show how its benefits will satisfy your prospect's needs.
4. Have a general idea of what you want to say, but be spontaneous, and use whatever techniques you can to make your presentation more vivid and convincing.
5. Invite the prospect to ask questions, and answer them.
6. If the prospect needs to think about things, press for a decision now, and if that doesn't work, try to set up another meeting.
7. Ask for referrals, and if appropriate, suggest that the prospect can make money by contacting these people

him- or herself. Also, he or she can save money by buying wholesale.

8. If you expect reorders, explain how the prospect can do this.

HOW TO MAKE THE FIVE KEYS TO SUCCESSFUL SALES WORK FOR YOU

Once you determine that a person is a likely prospect, your sales presentation should include the five key sales elements described earlier—getting a prospect to (1) pay attention, (2) be interested, (3) develop a conviction, (4) have a desire, and (5) take action. Here are some techniques to achieve these results.

Gaining Attention

When you know how to use the five motivators effectively, gaining someone's attention becomes easy. Avoid the trite overly general opener, such as, "Can I help you?" Usually, the person will say no.

Instead, say something interesting and attention getting, such as, "How would you like to earn twice what you do now, work with a fun group of people, take that trip you've always wanted, and use your creative abilities to achieve this end?"

Notice that in a few words you have introduced most of the motivators, which should make the prospect perk up and listen to what you have to say next. Other possibilities are short to-the-point statements and questions such as, "Are you the weight you would like to be now?" Or, "This is the number-one diet in the United States today."

Have a few opening lines prepared, and use them as appropriate. Note that your initial approach is extremely important. You have about four to ten seconds to make your first impression and get the person's attention. Then, in this short time, your prospect decides if he or she wants to listen to what you have to say next. Also, he or she develops a mental set about how to receive what you say. When you make the right approach, the person will be receptive; if not, he or she will tune you out, or may listen with a kind of prove-it-to-me attitude, even while seeming to listen to you respectfully. So, if the person is willing to hear you at all, you have to struggle to reverse that first impression.

Thus, it's critical to gain attention from the beginning the right way.

Building Interest

To build interest, stress the product benefits that appeal to the five major motivations. Thus, don't just explain how a product works and why, but describe the benefits these features offer. *Stress benefits, not product functions*.

For example, in promoting a health product say something like:

You'll be able to lose five to ten pounds a week. You get all the nutrients you need, because this formula contains all the essential amino acids, vitamins, and minerals doctors recommend.

Not:

This product has been tested, and contains eight amino acids, fifteen vitamins, and twenty minerals.

Also, to be effective in sales, find out about the person's particular motives and interests, so you can relate the benefits of the product to these. Thus, ask questions, listen, find out what the person wants. In addition, drawing the person out is valuable for another reason—it gets him or her involved in the conversation, and this involvement builds interest.

Yet, while you invite the prospect to speak, keep control of the conversation, and encourage him or her to say only so much. Then, if the person starts asking too many questions or shifts the presentation off track, bring it back again to the main points you want to make. By the same token, when you make a call to arrange a meeting, keep the conversation short and cut off any attempts to draw it out.

Developing Conviction

In this phase of the presentation, you want to convince the person you have a good, valuable product and you are someone worth listening to. *So, besides selling the product, you are selling yourself.*

The first impression you make starts the process. During the rest of the presentation, continue to back that up.

For example, start off with a good professional appearance. You want to look the part of success. That means dressing stylishly, keeping your clothes freshly cleaned and pressed, having your shoes shined, and carrying any sales material in an appropriately professional way (such as having a leather binder or carrying case). Also, pick a meeting place that is nicely furnished to convey a success image (no seedy coffee shops, please). And if you drive to a meeting, make sure your car will make a good impression, or if not (say you're just starting out), park a few blocks away. Since people judge you initially by the symbols of success, outfit yourself accordingly to acquire the credibility you need.

Then, add to this first impression your own conviction, belief, and enthusiasm that the product is good and you are sure that it is. To be convincing, you must appear confident of yourself and of your product. And to *appear* confident, you must *believe* in your own worth and in the worth of your product. You may need to act *as if* to develop this belief and confidence, as discussed in chapter 3, "Thinking Success." But however you do it, you need to acquire these qualities to sell yourself and your product, for your faith and conviction will inspire others to develop this conviction and confidence in you and the product, too. Confidence and conviction are contagious.

Encouraging Desire

Desire springs from interest and conviction and involves an appeal to the emotions. You can make a person interested or convince someone of the product's merit by appealing to the intellect. But to make a person truly desire something, you must engage the emotions, too.

Successful salespeople do this in many ways. One is by painting a very attractive picture, so the person can literally see, taste, smell, or otherwise experience possessing the product. Or they make the person feel a sense of loss or of not being "with it" if he or she doesn't have the item. ("Everyone is getting it . . . it's the latest fad.")

Also, salespeople appeal to the person's feeling of self-importance or self-image. ("You'll be the first one to get this, and everyone else will want one, too.") Or they appeal to the person's desire for financial wealth. ("Just think. If you get in now, you're getting in on the ground floor. So you'll have the potential to make much more than if you wait.")

Making a Close

The final step is making the close, where you ask your prospect to do something. Of course, you have to be sensitive that the person *is ready* to act, so you must watch for the appropriate "buy signals" indicating that the person has been sold on you and the product. Then, when the person seems ready to respond (for example, by making comments like "Boy, this really sounds good" or "You're right, I think this would be a good program for me"), it's time to close by asking for some action.

You can ask for this action directly. For example: "Why don't we take care of signing you up now?" "Would you like to order a case of product?"

Or, for a more subtle finale, many salespeople prefer an assumptive close in which they act as if the customer has already agreed to buy or sign up, and they are just affirming that. For example: "Okay [pulling out an order form], where would you like your first order and distributor kit to be sent?" "Would you prefer to start with one case of product or two?"

USING YOUR PROSPECT'S WAY OF TAKING IN INFORMATION IN YOUR SALES PRESENTATION

Successful salespersons recognize that people respond to presentations in different ways, regardless of the particular things that motivate them, because they perceive and receive information differently. Some people are more visual and like to see pictures and details. Others are more auditory and prefer to take in information by hearing it. Still others tend to react on a feeling or gut level and respond based on their actual or imagined experience of something. Finally, some people tend to listen to their inner voice in reacting or making decisions.

I once belonged to a group that divided people with these different perceptions into four personality types—the visionary (who is visually oriented), the intuitive (who is auditorially oriented), the feeler (who is feeling oriented), and the prophet (who is attuned to the inner voice). At many meetings, the group leader would seat people according to their personality type, and when people responded to questions and related experiences, you could see the differences dramatically in the way people experienced and described things. The visual people painted pictures; the feelers talked about how things felt to them, and so forth.

Thus, when you talk to people about your product or business opportunity, come in on their wavelength, as in the following examples.

With the *visual* person, paint a vivid picture. "When you drink our health drink, you'll see those pounds melt away." Or, "With all the money you'll save on this program, just imagine all the things you can buy that you want. You can redecorate the house with some beautiful drapes. And imagine giving your next party there. Your guests will love it."

With the *auditory* person, use auditory references. "You'll love this travel program. Just think about being on our tour to Peru now. You're lying in your tent listening to the gurgle of the brook near you. You can hear the singing of musicians, accompanied by flutes."

With the *feeling* person, emphasize how he or she will feel as a result of the experience. "You'll really feel great when you try our new vitamins. You'll feel extra energy and you'll just charge through the chores you have to do each day." Or, "The trip will be an experience you'll never forget. You'll experience the excitement of traveling through the wilderness and discovering new plants and animals. Then, at night, you'll experience a marvelous tranquillity, when the moon rises and the whole world around you seems absolutely still."

With people who respond to the *inner voice*, suggest that they can experience knowing the product or program is right for them. "When I heard about this health program, I knew instantly it was right for me. And that's the way it is for many people. There are many diets. But when they hear about this one, they experience the magic. They know instantly, This is the program for me."

OTHER KEYS TO
SUCCESSFUL SELLING

Be Aware of Every Opportunity to Tell Your Story. Wherever you are, whomever you are with, look for an opportunity to talk about your product or business and how it has helped you. For example, someone mentions a problem (such as being tired), and you offer a solution (try your product). But don't make what you say sound like a sales pitch. Simply share about the value of the product or the company, and how either has improved your life.

Drop Teasers about Your Product or Business. Then let others *ask* you for more information. The advantage of this approach is that people get intrigued and reach out to you for information, instead of your having to persuade them to do something. As a result, they don't think you are trying to sell them something and get defensive.

This strategy is particularly good with friends, who might be sensitive to your using their friendship to make them act. But you can employ this approach with anyone. Just dangle out some information—such as how your new business helped you save on taxes or get a new car—and see if people bite. Then, like a good fisherman, let out plenty of line, and if people pull on it, reel them in.

Avoid the Canned Sales Pitch. Speak with sincerity and from the heart about how your product has helped you and how it might benefit others. Have the key points you want to mention in mind, but adapt your presentation to your listener's interests, wants, and needs.

Sell Your Prospect on YOU First. To make people respond more positively to your product or business opportunity, sell them on *you* first. You may have an easier time with people you know, because they are already sold on you, though some may still have to be convinced. However, the people you don't know need even more reassurance.

So take time to get to know your prospect (if you don't already) and let that person get to know you. Show you care. For example, ask about his or her family, job, or recreational interests. Then, only after you have sold yourself should you try to sell your product or opportunity.

Use Yourself as an Example. Tell people how using a product has changed you or how well you have done in finding others to join your sales team to market the product. Or let the way you have changed speak for itself with people you know. For example, suppose you have lost twenty pounds or have gotten a new car. People will notice. And when people see your success, they will start asking how they can have what you have, too.

So, as a sales opener, use *you*! Your own actions and success are more powerful than anything you might say. They not only grab attention, but they have the power to convince, too.

Get As Much Information As You Can about Your Prospect in Advance. This way you can find out who your prospect is and what motivates him or her before you make your pitch. Gerald Oliver, an MLM consultant on selling and recruiting, calls this the "pre-approach." Your purpose in gathering information is to find out the person's primary motives. What does she want out of life? What does he need? Then, you can show how your product will fill the bill.

Also, gaining advance information has several other advantages. You avoid mistakes, such as telling someone about a great vacation plan when he or she has just lost a job. You avoid wasting time contacting or making a presentation to people who are not likely to be interested. Also, you can make your pitch with more confidence, because you know more about what your prospect wants. And having extra information gives you an advantage over your competition.

There are two main ways to get this information: (1) Ask people who know the prospect about his interests and needs, or observe for yourself when you are with this person, or at his home (for example, you can get insights from the way a person's home is furnished, or the books he reads); (2) Ask your prospect what he wants or needs, or how he thinks any problems he has might be solved.

Qualify Your Prospect at the Outset. Determine if your prospect really might be interested in your product or business opportunity in the beginning of your discussion or presentation. You don't want to spend a lot of time explaining something to someone who doesn't qualify or already has what you are selling. After all, you don't want to sell snow to Eskimoes.

So qualify your prospect by asking a few leading questions. These can also be excellent attention-getters, too.

Follow Up. Frequently, one contact—whether by phone, letter, or in person—is not enough. After you set up an appointment, you need to call back to reconfirm or even set it again. If you send a letter, you need a call a few days afterward to find out the response—or even to remind the person to read it. Likewise, after a presentation, if a person wants to think it over, you need to contact that person in a few days to help him or her make a positive decision.

And when you follow up, do it quickly—while your initial contact or presentation is still fresh in people's minds. This is when they are most interested. Don't give them a chance to cool off.

Employ the Principles of Good Communication. Know what you want to say. Be clear about the purpose of your message and the ideas you want to present.

Know who your audience is and orient your message to that person or persons.

Consider the interests, needs, and wants of your listeners, and appeal to these.

Talk about things people can readily identify with, to develop rapport with your audience. (For example, make your point by telling a story or sharing a joke.)

Use simple, concrete words to promote understanding.

Communicate only a small amount at a time so people can readily follow your message. Then you don't overwhelm and confuse your listeners with too many points or too much detail.

Use repetition and associations with familiar ideas to promote retention of your message. That means, say the same thing several times in several ways so people remember it!

Use the appropriate tone, manner, and gestures in presenting your message, because these are part of your message, along with your content. In fact, the *way* you say something can be more influential than *what* you say, because people react on an emotional, feeling level.

Emphasize the areas where you and your listeners are in agreement. This promotes rapport. Then, if you want to promote change or the acceptance of new ideas, start where your prospect is at; gradually, you can work toward a shift.

Get feedback by asking questions and listening.

Anticipate the objections that might come up and learn how to overcome them.

Chapter 10

ANSWERING OBJECTIONS

Inevitably, in selling, you are going to encounter objections, and you need to be ready to respond. Often an objection is a request for more information, and then you need to have the appropriate information on hand. Other times persons raise objections because they are seeking reassurance, and you must be able to reassure them so they feel more confident about your product, your company, or you.

As long as an objection exists, it stands as a barrier between you and your making a successful sale. So you need to know how to answer and eliminate objections to proceed to a successful close.

One key to answering objections effectively is knowing that objections are likely to come up and being prepared in advance to answer them. Or if you are just starting to contact people, take notes as objections arise, so you will be more prepared to respond next time.

A good way to answer objections is to acknowledge the objection respectfully but then do one of the following: turn the objection around to show how it is really an advantage; pass over that objection to stress a benefit that outweighs it; or ask why the person feels that way (if you feel this is not a strongly held objection or is based on incorrect facts which you can correct).

You also need to respond calmly and confidently, without getting nervous and flustered, and being prepared will help you do this.

Be aware, too, that some people raise objections or say they are not interested when you first approach them, simply to test you. How much do *you* believe in the product? How persuasive and convincing are you? Then, if you persist, they quickly cave in.

While some objections will be specific to your product, company, or industry, many come up when you describe any direct sales, network marketing, or multi-level program. Commonly, they fall in certain categories:

    concerns about selling
    concerns about having enough time
    concerns about the legitimacy of the company or about
      MLM as a sales method
    concerns about the amount of investment involved
    concerns about using or marketing the product
    concerns about being successful
    concerns about conflicts because of other marketing
      commitments
    general feelings of uncertainty

Here are some of the most common objections in each category, along with some responses you can use when they come up.

Concerns about Selling

I'm not sure I can really sell; I don't like selling.
    "You're not really selling. You're really sharing information about the program with a few other people."

"There's nothing wrong with selling. Many people have a misconception about what selling is. They think it involves hard sell or convincing someone to buy something they didn't want or need. But selling really involves conveying information to people and showing them how something you have to offer can benefit them. It's learning about and understanding other people's needs and figuring out how to satisfy them."

"The most successful individuals in network (personal, multilevel, and so on) programs are not salespeople. Rather, they are people who want to help and teach each other. Salespeople often want to sell someone right away and move on to the next person, so this kind of selling doesn't work for them. By contrast, teachers are usually very successful, since they know how to teach others, and they have learned how to be patient in working with people."

I don't know many people; I'm new in the area and don't have many contacts.

"You don't have to contact only people you know. We can show you how to contact many people you don't know. Our organization has all sorts of aids to help you, including sample letters, phone scripts, and ads. And we'll teach you how to use these effectively."

"You really know more people than you think. You know the people you deal with every day, such as the clerks where you shop and the postman who delivers your mail. And you know the tellers at your bank, the gas station attendant down the street. And if you go to any group meetings, you'll get to know people there, too."

"You don't have to know many people to be successful in a network (multi-level) marketing business. You just need to share with a few people; then they will tell others about the program. And these people will tell others. Then, all of these people become part of your network. So you only need to know a few people."

Concerns about Having Enough Time

I'm very busy; I don't have much time.
   "You have more time than you think. Even if you're a very busy professional person, you'll find you have some extra hours each week. So let's see how you spend your time by calculating how much time you spend working, eating, engaging in leisure activities, and with your family. Also, let's see how much time you spend relaxing and not doing much at all. Now think about your priorities. You could take an hour or two a day and find you have about five to ten extra hours a week you could devote to this project."
   "You don't have to spend much time in a network (multi-level) marketing program to make money. You only need to work with a few people."

I like to spend my free time with my family and friends.
   "You can in this program. That's the beauty of it. Many families participate together in a direct sales or network marketing program, because you can work the program right out of your home. And when people in a family share the work together, that lightens the load for everyone. Plus, it will bring you closer together."
   "You can involve your friends in this program, too, and you'll all work together as a group. In fact, you can plan social activities together as part of promoting the program."

Concerns about the Amount of Investment Involved

The distributor fee is too expensive; the sales kit costs too much.
   "It's not really that much when you think about it. If we

break the fee down, you'll see that it only costs a few dollars a month or a few pennies a day."

"You should think of this fee as an investment in yourself."

"This fee is really very little when you consider that you are getting an opportunity for yourself. And there are very few businesses which you can start for less than a hundred dollars. Most businesses cost several thousand dollars, maybe more, to start. And when you consider the fantastic earnings potential in this business, you'll realize the distributor fee is not that much."

I can't afford to get involved right now; I need a job and don't have enough money.

"You don't have to give up your present income. That's the beauty of a direct sales (network marketing, MLM) business. You can do it part-time and choose your own hours. So you can keep working on your regular job until you have enough money from your business and you don't need to work for anyone else."

"If you only think about getting a job and working for someone else, you'll never become really successful. The only way to really succeed and attain financial independence is to be in business for yourself. And this business requires only a minimal investment in return for the potential of earning a large income. What other business can you enter for so little? Then, think of the high income that is possible for you in the future when you start now."

"But can you afford not to get involved? Just think how much you will save and all the benefits you will get by buying this product. And think of the chance you have to make a good monthly income, too, if you act now."

Concerns about Using or Marketing the Product

I don't think I would use the product; it's not a product for me.

"It helps if you use the product. But you don't have to use it to market it, as long as you agree it's a good product. If you see this as a good business opportunity, you can simply promote the program."

"Some very successful distributors (sales reps) don't use the product themselves. But they actively promote it to people who do use it."

I'm not interested in marketing the program.

"That's fine. You can simply be a consumer."

"You don't have to market an MLM (network marketing) program when you become a distributor. You can be as active or inactive as you want. But if you are going to be using the product regularly, being a distributor gives you a chance to purchase the product at wholesale. So you can save a lot of money that way."

Concerns about Being Successful

I'd like to see how you do first in an MLM (network marketing) program.

"Fine. I'll be glad to get back to you later. But right now you have a chance to get in on the ground floor and help build the program in this area. If you wait until you see that I'm successful, you won't have as much opportunity, because the area will already be developed and many others will be involved."

"The people who are extremely successful in multi-level

177

(network sales) are those who get in on the ground floor of a fast-growing program. If you wait, you may find the opportunity has passed you by, because most of the persons you know will be involved by then, and you'll have to work harder to find other people to sponsor into your sales group."

"I'm inviting you to be one of the individuals who can help make it happen. There are three kinds of people—those who make it happen, those who wait for it to happen, and those who don't know what's happening. That's why I decided to get involved—to make it happen—and that's why I'm inviting you to join me now."

"Okay. I'll contact you later."

I'm not sure if I will be successful; I don't know if this program will work for me.

"It will work for you if you believe it will. It already has worked for thousands of people in other areas. But if you don't believe this is the program for you, it won't work. It's up to you. You have to recognize this is a good program for you and put your energies behind making it work. Then, it will."

"I'll do everything I can to support you in making it work, if you join my sales group. But you have to be committed to making it work for yourself, too."

"Is there anything I can do to help you become more certain? Would you like more information on the company, the product, the management, what our group will do to support you?"

"Okay. Maybe it won't. This program isn't for everybody. Think about it and let me know. I'll check back with you in a few days. If you decide you want to get involved, we'll do everything we can to help you become successful."

General Feelings of Uncertainty

I'll think it over; I can't make a decision right now.

"What do you need to think over? Is there some objection

you have? For example, do you have any reservations about the company? About its management? About the product? Do you feel the membership fee is too high? Do you want to discuss this with your spouse?"

(The point of asking questions is to find out exactly what is holding the person back. Frequently persons express general uncertainty when they still have some objection, but do not want to come right out and say it for several reasons. They may feel embarrassed to tell you they don't have enough money. They may not want to admit they must talk to someone else before making a decision. Or they may not be exactly sure what the objection is. But if you guide the person to raise specific objections, you then know what they are, and so may be able to overcome them.)

"Okay, if you really must think it over, I'll get back to you in a day or two to find out what you decide."

Concerns about the Legitimacy of the Company or MLM

How do I know this is a legitimate program? I'd like to check it out first.

"The company is listed with the Better Business Bureau and Chamber of Commerce. The company also has a full description of its management in its literature, and I'm truly impressed with their background."

"The company already has several thousand distributors marketing its product, and the company is well funded. The company describes its financial backing in its literature."

The MLM company sounds like an illegal pyramid.

"Multi-level is very different from an illegal pyramid because..." (Then describe the differences explained in chapter 2.)

"Many people have been incorrectly using the name 'multi-level' to refer to illegal pyramids and chain letter schemes. But, in fact, multi-level marketing is a competely legal form of marketing, since it moves a valuable product or service, whereas an illegal pyramid involves only the movement of money, and people get hurt. There are many important differences which include..." (Then describe them.)

I've already been burned in a multi-level (network marketing) program; I was with another organization and didn't make any money.

"Every multi-level program is different. Some programs are not as good as others. And sometimes there are other reasons why a program doesn't work for you, such as a sponsor who doesn't help you enough or a product people don't like that much. I think this program is very good and *will* work for you because..." (Then go into the specifics.)

"That doesn't mean you should give up on multi-level. If you get a bad apple once, that doesn't mean you should give up on eating apples. Or if you have a car accident, that doesn't mean you should stop driving. It's the same in multi-level. You can learn from the first experience, and when you have the right program and work it right, it can really work for you."

I don't believe people in MLM (network marketing) can really make that much; I can't believe I'll really make that much money.

"But it's true. People do make incredibly large amounts in a successful multi-level (network marketing) program when they get in on the ground floor and build a large organization. For example, there are people in Amway who are getting checks for five hundred thousand and seven hundred fifty thousand dollars. People in Cambridge have gotten checks for over two hundred thousand dollars a month. Most distributors don't make that kind of money, but it's possible."

"You have to realize that you can make a high income and you will. You won't overnight. It takes about six to twelve months of hard work to build up your business in an MLM (network marketing) program. But if you build a strong organization, you can be earning several thousand a month in the near future, and then increase your business even more."

"Your income grows by the principle of multiplication of effort in MLM, so as your organization multiplies in size, your incomes does too. It takes time to build an organization in depth—perhaps four to six months before you start seeing a large income develop. But if you work at it, in two or three years, sometimes sooner, you can be earning a very substantial income. In some programs, some distributors have started earning fifty thousand dollars a month after eight or nine months."

"You have to believe you will keep working toward this goal. Many persons get stuck in believing they will keep earning what they are earning now. But if you start imagining yourself making these big amounts you'll find your thinking will help you change. So you'll become the prosperous person you want to be."

Concerns about Conflicts because of Other Marketing Commitments

I've already heard about the program from someone else; I'm already in another MLM (network marketing) downline.

"Just because you heard about the program from someone else doesn't mean you have to join that person's sales group. You should consider how much support you will get from your sponsor or sales leader. You may find that our organization gives you much more help and support if you are really serious about marketing this program."

"Our organization can offer you a great deal of support that you won't get from most other groups marketing this product or service. For example, we offer special trainings, sales literature we prepare ourselves, and regular presentations. We will put on some individual presentations for you when you get started. Also, we have meetings all over the area, which you and your guests can attend. Plus, we send out a regular newsletter to keep you informed."

"If you already have a commitment to another person and can't change downlines or switch sales groups, perhaps we can still arrange to support you if you aren't getting enough support from the group you are in. For example, you can have another member of your family sponsor into or join our group, or perhaps a friend can sponsor in or join for you."

"We'd like to work with you, but like many distributors, we follow a policy of working only with the people in our downline or sales group. The reason is that we do all we can to make you successful. But if you are in another downline or sales group, we are just building up our competition. After all . . . does Macy's tell Gimbel's? However, if things change so you can join us, please let me know, and we'll be glad to work with you then."

I'm already in another MLM (network marketing) company; I don't want to confuse the people in my organization with another product.

"There is no reason you can't be involved in two or more marketing programs at the same time, as long as they are compatible. Many distributors (or sales reps) today handle several products."

"Being in another marketing program will help you sell this. You already have a downline or sales group you can start with, and this program will supplement the product line you already have. Besides, if you don't contact the people in your organization, someone else probably will, and many of your people may join under this person, since many distributors (or sales reps) are involved in several programs."

"Some people in MLM (network marketing) handle two programs, but keep their downlines (or sales teams) separate. Now that you've got a solid organization in one program, you could build another organization with this new program and market it to completely different people."

And If You Get a No . . . How to Handle Rejection

Whenever you are selling anything, you're going to get some no's. No matter how terrific your presentation, no matter if you've done everything right—you'll still get them.

So you have to accept this. The no's come with the territory, and you need to learn how to handle rejection when it occurs.

First, regard every rejection as an opportunity to learn something. Review your presentation or approach. Was there anything you might have done to make it better? How can you improve for next time? Or perhaps the person you contacted would not have been interested regardless of what you said. If so, what can you do to better assess and qualify a prospect in advance, so you can better target whom you spend your time with?

Secondly, remind yourself that direct sales, network, or multi-level marketing, like any forms of sales, are numbers games, and a certain percentage of the people contacted are going to say no. You can't hope to bat 100 percent every time. You can increase your batting score by improving your presentation and your assessment of people. But still, some people are going to say no. So think in terms of percentages, and remember if a certain percent say no, a certain percent will say yes. Thus, every time you get a no, you are that much closer to getting a yes next time.

Finally, do not take the no's as a personal rejection and get upset. Instead, look at the no's as part of the sales game. Sometimes you win; sometimes you lose. And the no's are merely strikes—but not outs. So keep going up to bat . . . and eventually, your strikes will turn into home runs.

Chapter 11

HOW TO START
PROSPECTING

DIFFERENT APPROACHES FOR
DIFFERENT PROGRAMS

Your approach to prospecting will vary depending on whether you are just seeking customers to sell to directly, or are also seeking distributors or sales reps to join a sales team. In the first case, your only concern is with potential purchasers for the product or service; in the second case, you will want eventually to recruit or sponsor new people into your organization who may or may not be consumers, too.

In this chapter we'll focus on what to look for if you are building a sales team, since you should be aware of what to look for in prospects as you market the product yourself. So if you're only seeking customers, you can skip most of this chapter.

Gini Graham Scott

PUTTING YOUR EMPHASIS IN THE RIGHT PLACE—ON PRODUCT SALES

Whether you are selling to the ultimate customers or building a sales team, too, always *emphasize product sales*.

This statement may seem self-evident when you are selling direct yourself. But some people lose sight of this principle when they are involved in building an organization of distributors in MLM or network marketing programs, since the big success in these programs comes from building a large group. So, they focus almost exclusively on creating such a group.

But, initially, whatever kind of program you are marketing, you need to work on promoting and selling the product itself. Then, if you want to create a sales team, look for some key distributors to market and promote the product, too.

The reason for this emphasis is that whether you personally sell the product or have a sales team working with you, you have to move product, and it helps if you or your people actually like and consume the product. Some distributors are very effective who are interested only in the business opportunity and see a large market for the product among other people. But one risk of going after distributors who are mainly interested in business is that you may build up a big organization but not move much product.

So *emphasize product sales*, whether you are appealing to prospects as consumers, as business opportunity seekers, or both.

DIFFERENT STYLES OF
PROSPECTING FOR A SALES GROUP

You will find that some successful MLM and network marketing people only go after distributors seeking a business opportunity. For example, Gerald Oliver, who wrote *How to Create a Fortune Sponsoring Distributors*, built a large sales organization by asking personal contacts two questions: Do you want to make more money? and Are you willing to trade at least five to ten hours per week for it? Then, he would invite his contact to meet for coffee or to get together in his home without telling the person what the business opportunity involved. His rationale was that he wanted to find people who were looking for an opportunity and willing to follow him. He didn't want people who wanted to know the details or think over the opportunity first. They had to be not only interested in making more money but willing to meet him to discuss the opportunity, no questions asked.

Now that approach may work for some. And perhaps it may have been more effective in the past when only a few giant direct sales and multi-level companies like Amway and Shaklee offered such business opportunities. But now, when there are over 1,500 direct sales programs, people want to know up-front what the product or company is, and some people are downright hostile to the "mysterious business opportunity" approach. In fact, some people have told me stories of broken friendships because they were enticed to come to a gathering to meet a wonderful group of people and then found themselves in the midst of a sales presentation.

Other people are very successful getting prospects to be consumers first and then turning them into distributors of that product. Since many more people are potential consumers than

187

distributors (typically out of every ten to twenty consumers, you'll find one active distributor), this approach can really pay off.

Don Failla, who wrote the best-selling *How to Build a Large Successful Multi-Level Marketing Organization*, looks for distributors and consumers at the same time, while emphasizing the principle of *sharing* the opportunity and the product, rather than *selling*. He lets people know there is a business opportunity if they are interested, and then talks product.

So you can employ different styles of prospecting, depending on what feels right for you. Or choose the style that's most appropriate for your prospect.

LOOKING FOR LEADS
FOR DISTRIBUTORS

Whatever style you use, once you are ready to go with a program your first task is prospecting for consumers and, if you are in an MLM or network program, prospective distributors, too. If you are going to be seeking distributors, do this as soon as possible to increase the chances of your contacts joining your downline, for if you wait, someone else may contact them before you, and you may find your hot prospects already signed up under someone else when you call.

The first stage of prospecting is developing and contacting leads. One common approach is to list all the persons you know and contact them first. In fact, some very successful distributors recruit only those they know—an approach used and described by Jim Sweeney in his book, *M.L.M.: A Shortcut to Financial Freedom*. But many other successful distributors go outside their circle of friends and sponsor mostly strangers, as Debbie Ballard discusses in *Secrets of Multi-Level Fortune Building*.

So either strategy will work. It depends on your circle of

friends and acquaintances. If you know a large number of people who have been in sales, business, or promotional work, you may be able to recruit easily from your own network. But if your contacts have limited business experience or come from fields that are traditionally far afield from business, such as the arts or academia, you will probably have to reach out much farther.

The key is to decide what works for you. Some people don't have to go beyond their own network for active distributors. But most do.

Thus, it's likely that most of your customers and distributors will be strangers. And often these strangers will be more receptive to your message, whereas the people you know may be the most skeptical—since they already have an image of you as one kind of person. So when you start marketing a new program and changing your life, initially they may be dubious or wait to see what happens. But then, after you start to succeed, they will come around.

So, of course, contact the people you know first—some may be your most ardent supporters and most loyal distributors. But if some are critical or ridicule what you are doing, don't let that discourage you. Just go on to someone else who is more receptive, and let the skeptics come around when they are ready.

GETTING YOUR FIRST FRONT-LINE DISTRIBUTORS

Eventually, in multi-level or network marketing, you want to narrow down your focus to work with a handful of front-line distributors—usually a maximum of five to ten at first—and teach them what to do. But, as must be emphasized, *you typically have to go through many prospects to find those effective, committed distributors and train them.*

For finding them is like a numbers game. In most businesses involving outside sales, salespeople know that only one person out of every three or four they call will be interested in an appointment to learn more, and perhaps only one out of three or four will be interested in participating in the program. And of these perhaps only one out of three or four will become extremely active—a leader in the program.

So, to get one distributor, you may have to make nine to sixteen calls, and to find that star leader, maybe twenty-seven to sixty-four calls. But in the long run, that kind of persistence pays off. And as you get better in the prospecting game, you'll be able to recruit with much less effort.

So, don't get discouraged. As they say in sales, *the more no's you get, the closer you are to getting a yes*.

HOW TO FIND YOUR STAR RECRUITS

Initially, after you target your market (discussed in the next section), be open to contacting everyone who might be interested as a consumer or business opportunity seeker, because you never know where you will find that person who will really catch fire and run with your program.

However, look for key qualities when you talk to people about joining your sales team, because people with certain characteristics or personality traits are most likely to be successful. Essentially, such a person has the right success attitudes, likes working with people, and is good in sales.

Gerald D. Oliver has identified seventeen success traits, which he describes in his book, *How to Create a Fortune Sponsoring Distributors*. He used these guidelines primarily in recruiting successful sales people in the insurance field and in creating an Amway organization, but these qualities are equally applicable to success in any multi-level or network sales program. When Oliver interviews people who may be interested in joining his organization, he asks key questions about what they did in the past, on the grounds that a person's actions in the future can be predicted from what he or she did in the past.

According to Oliver, a successful person will have shown these seventeen behavior patterns:

- Has *persisted* and isn't a quitter
- Has *paid the price* by working hard and doing more than expected
- Has *accepted* risks—both financial and career-related
- Has *organized him- or herself*, so he or she has goals and a plan to achieve them
- Has *responded to a challenge* and is willing to take on difficult tasks or to compete
- Has *improved or advanced him- or herself* through study and working hard to get ahead
- Has *offered service* by trying a little harder to do the job or by doing volunteer work for the community
- Has *learned quickly* in a wide range of areas
- Has *called on people* by actively going out to make contacts
- Has *worked diligently* by putting in long hours on productive work
- Has *coached or taught others* various skills or knowledge
- Has *achieved successful sales results*, and thus has a track record in outside selling
- Has *entered competitions and won*, indicating that he or she loves to compete and wants to win
- Has *taken care of details*, indicating that the person is able to follow through on any project from beginning to end
- Has *directed and managed people*, and is a natural leader whom others like and respect

- Has *initiated new ideas and activities*, and is thus highly creative
- Has *made and accumulated money* in other fields, including selling

Other qualities of the successful person are noted by Jim Sweeney in his book, *M.L.M.: A Shortcut to Financial Freedom*.

- *The person is hungry and is reaching higher.* Even a professional who is still reaching can fall in this category, although many people who haven't "made it" yet are especially likely to be hungry.
- *The person wants to do something about his or her hunger.* The person must be willing to work to change his or her place in life. Some people struggle to make it each month and wish for additional income, but they don't *work* for it. Successful people do!
- *The person must be a good listener.* You have to listen to other people's needs and problems in order to give them what they want. People who only try to sell don't do this, and they often leave their potential prospects puzzled, frustrated, or feeling hostile.
- *The person must be willing to be taught.* One must be willing to learn new information and new techniques for doing things. When people think they know everything, they usually don't and don't allow themselves to learn more. Then, when they have to perform, they soon fail and quickly drop by the wayside.
- *The person must be able to motivate people.* And this doesn't mean the person must be a top public speaker. Some people are great motivators by setting an inspiring example.
- *The person must like people.* One must be willing to help others, not just care about what can be earned

from them, because multi-level or network marketing is a "people" business, based on networking with other people.

The following chart (Chart 27) has been developed by drawing on these success behavior patterns noted by Oliver, Sweeney, and others. It lists the key qualities to look for and the kinds of questions to ask about a person's past activities.

CHART 27: THE QUALITIES TO LOOK FOR IN YOUR STAR RECRUITS

Qualities to Look For	Questions to Ask
1. *Persistence and Willingness to Work Hard*	
Has a strong desire to succeed	How much do you want to be successful?
Is willing to keep going, even when others give up	What are you willing to do to achieve this success?
Invests time in hard, but productive, work	How do you feel about working overtime? Are you willing to work weekends, give up vacations?
Is willing to work long hours and do more than expected to achieve a result	Have you worked on any project which others tried to get you to give up, but which you completed successfully?
Is future oriented	What are your goals for the future?

Gini Graham Scott

CHART 27: THE QUALITIES TO LOOK FOR IN YOUR STAR RECRUITS (continued)

Qualities to Look For	Questions to Ask
Tries a little harder to offer more than the competition	Do you have any side businesses now? How successful are they?
Volunteers time to worthwhile causes and community work	Do you do any volunteer work? Why did you choose the volunteer work you do?

2. *Well Organized and Goal Directed*

Has goals	What are your goals?
Has a plan to achieve these goals	How do you plan to achieve your goals? What have you done so far to achieve them?
Sets up an organized work schedule, and plans each day	Do you plan what you are going to do each day? How do you do this?
Is good on detail work	How do you like taking care of details? Have you managed an office?
Is able to coordinate projects so they run smoothly; follows through from the beginning to the end of a project	What kind of projects have you been in charge of? What kind of responsibilities have you had on these projects?

194

Qualities to Look For	Questions to Ask
3. *Interested in Learning and Self-Advancement*	
Likes to learn	What is your educational background?
Learns quickly and retains information easily	Do you learn fast? What are some examples of this?
Has taken special courses, such as home study, adult education, or correspondence courses, or has taught him- or herself some skill	What sort of courses and programs have you participated in during your free time?
Reads widely	What have you read recently? What kinds of books do you like to read?
Knows about a wide variety of subjects	What are your major interests? What do you like to do in your free time?
4. *Willing to Compete and Eager to Win*	
Has a competitive spirit	Are you active in sports? Have you been involved in any sports competitions? How did you do?
Eager to take on challenges	How do you like competition? Do you look for opportunities to compete?

CHART 27: THE QUALITIES TO LOOK FOR IN YOUR STAR RECRUITS (continued)

Qualities to Look For	Questions to Ask
Willing to take on difficult jobs that seem almost impossible and make them work (such as turning around a company that is losing money or helping a brand-new candidate win)	What is the most difficult job you ever did? What was the outcome? How do you account for your success? Have you ever taken on an almost impossible task? What was it, and why did you decide to do it?
Has a record of entering and winning in competitions	What kind of awards have you won?
Has a strong desire to win	How important is it to you to win?

5. *Works Well with People and Takes the Initiative in Working with Them*

Likes people and feels comfortable working with them	How do you like working with people?
Has previously made calls on people to get them to do something, such as vote or contribute to some cause	Have you been involved in any political or fund-raising campaigns? What did you do?

6. *Good at Teaching and Managing People*

STRIKE IT RICH IN PERSONAL SELLING

Qualities to Look For	Questions to Ask
Has been a coach, teacher, or group leader	What kind of experience have you had in leading groups? Have you done any teaching? What did you teach?
Is good at and enjoys imparting his or her knowledge or skill to others	How do you like leading groups or teaching?
Is a popular or well-respected leader of people (as a committee head, political leader, office manager, and so on)	What kind of managerial experience have you had? How many people did you supervise? How did you like being in management? How successful do you consider your experience managing others? Why? Have you ever run for a political or other office? What were the results?

7. *Has Creativity and Initiative*

Is very creative	What would you do if you were marketing this program?
Comes up with new ideas easily	What kind of innovations or changes have you introduced on previous jobs or projects? What was the response to them? What did you do to see that these changes were carried out?

197

CHART 27: THE QUALITIES TO LOOK FOR IN YOUR STAR RECRUITS (continued)

Qualities to Look For	Questions to Ask
Is receptive to change and seeks new ways of doing things	How do you feel when someone tells you to do something differently? What do you do? Do you like doing things the way others do them? Do you frequently think about doing something another way?

8. *A Previous Track Record of Success*

Qualities to Look For	Questions to Ask
Has been successful in an outside sales job (such as selling cars, insurance, or consumer products), where he or she went to the customer and was able to sell the product	What kind of experience have you had in direct sales? What kind of success did you have selling different products?
Has made and accumulated money in other fields, including selling	What business ventures have been especially successful for you? How did you measure your success?

Chapter 12

LOCATING LEADS
AND MAKING
YOUR FIRST CONTACTS

TARGETING YOUR MARKET

To locate potential consumers and/or distributors most efficiently, target your market. Even though a product has broad appeal, you will need to determine the best approach to reach the market.

Make a list of all the potential types of users. Then prioritize which categories of people would be best to contact first by rating them from one (least important) to five (most important). You can use Chart 28 to do this.

The chart is divided into two sections: types of individuals (for example, teenagers, children, mothers) and types of groups (such as health clubs, travel clubs, singles groups). Just think of as many types of individuals and groups as you can who might be interested; then rate them to indicate the most likely prospects.

For example, if you have a weight control product, your list might start off looking something like this:

Types of Individuals—overweight people, mothers, single people;

Types of Groups—health clubs, health stores (if you can contact stores), weight watcher groups, singles organizations, PTAs, MLM people in another diet program.

CHART 28: THE TARGET MARKET FOR MY PRODUCT OR SERVICE
(first list all the markets you can; then rate each market from one—least likely—to five—most likely)

Target Market	Rating	Comments
Types of Individuals Who Would Be Most Likely to Use the Product or Service		

Target Market	Rating	Comments
Types of Groups That Would Be Most Likely to Use the Product or Service		

SOURCES FOR LEADS

Leads are everywhere. Even if you start off with persons you know, you'll find you know many more people than you think. A *Reader's Digest* research survey once showed that the average American knows over four hundred people.

So start by systematically making a list of leads. The Target Market list will help you think of groups that might have a special interest. Also, go through your personal telephone books, business card files, membership lists of groups you

belong to, and combine all of these names together onto one
master list.

To help you think about whom to contact, list them by
category. Then, when you contact these people, be sure to ask
for referrals, if they don't want to purchase the product or
learn more about the business opportunity themselves. These
referrals will not only give you new leads, but they help open
the door when you call. On the other hand, if your contacts
do get involved in the program as distributors, help them make
their own contacts.

Some of the categories to contact include:

Relatives
Neighbors
Current friends
Old friends
School friends
Work associates
Members of groups you belong to—church groups, so-
    cial groups, interest groups, service clubs, and com-
    munity groups
Fellow commuters
Merchants or store clerks where you shop
People who have services you use, such as doctors, den-
    tists, hairdressers, postal carriers, repair people, gas
    station attendants
People you meet at parties
People you meet at classes, seminars, workshops
Referrals

Initially, list everyone. You never know who might be a
prospect until you ask. At the same time, maximize your ef-
ficiency by rating the people you plan to contact with a priority
system from one (maybes) to five (probably not prospects).
You can use Chart 29 to make your list and rate your prospects.

CHART 29: PERSONS I KNOW, TO CONTACT

Relatives
1. _____
2. _____
3. _____
4. _____
5. _____

Neighbors
1. _____
2. _____
3. _____
4. _____
5. _____

Current Friends
1. _____
2. _____
3. _____
4. _____
5. _____

Old Friends
1. _____
2. _____
3. _____
4. _____
5. _____

School Friends
1. _____
2. _____
3. _____
4. _____
5. _____

People in Groups I Belong To
1. _____
2. _____
3. _____
4. _____
5. _____

Fellow Commuters
1. _____
2. _____
3. _____
4. _____
5. _____

Merchants or Store Clerks
1. _____
2. _____
3. _____
4. _____
5. _____

People Who Serve Me
1. _____
2. _____
3. _____
4. _____
5. _____

People at Parties
1. _____
2. _____
3. _____
4. _____
5. _____

CHART 29: PERSONS I KNOW, TO CONTACT
(continued)

People at Work
1. _____
2. _____
3. _____
4. _____
5. _____

People from Classes, Seminars
1. _____
2. _____
3. _____
4. _____
5. _____

Friends at Church
1. _____
2. _____
3. _____
4. _____
5. _____

People I Play Sports With
1. _____
2. _____
3. _____
4. _____
5. _____

Although you should contact people as you meet them on a daily basis, making this list will remind you to make these contacts.

Also, make a list of special groups and types of individuals who would be especially interested in the program and are part of a large network of people. The heads of groups are especially good to contact, because they can turn their whole group onto the program, if they are interested.

Some of the groups and individuals with wide contact networks include:

Churches and temples (contact the minister, priest, or rabbi)

Religious or church groups

Community service clubs, such as the Lions, Rotarians, fraternal lodges, women's service groups

Youth groups, such as Boy Scouts, Girl Scouts, local youth center

Self-improvement groups, such as toastmasters, est
Entrepreneur groups
Local business networking groups
Homeowner associations
Tenant groups
Political groups, such as Young Republicans, Young
     Democrats, special interest organizations
Activity clubs, such as sports clubs, travel clubs
Singles groups
Senior citizen groups
Insurance and real estate agents
Schools
People in other MLM businesses (particularly if they are
     promoting a related product to the same market)
People looking for jobs

You can use Chart 30, Special Groups and Types of People
to Contact, to make your list. Or if you decide to focus on a
particular category (say churches or real estate agents), use
the Leads Contact Sheet (Chart 31).

Then, when you contact people, keep a record, either on a
single form like the Leads Contact Sheet or on an index card,
for each person or group. Or even better, use a computer if
you can to keep track of your records. A form you can use
for your index cards is on Chart 32.

When you are targeting particular categories of individuals
or groups, you can get special directories of members of that
group (for example, a list of all real estate agents who belong
to a local trade association). Or use your telephone Yellow
Pages and look under the appropriate heading to make your
list (for example, churches, real estate agents).

When someone refers you to someone else, indicate the
name of the person making the referral on your Leads Contact
Sheet or index card.

Keeping these records is very important, not only to give

you ideas about whom to contact, but to help you keep track of each contact, when, and the response. Then, you have a clear picture of who is or is not interested, and whom to contact again, when, and about what.

CHART 30: SPECIAL GROUPS AND TYPES OF PEOPLE TO CONTACT

Churches and Religious Groups
1. _____
2. _____
3. _____
4. _____
5. _____

Homeowner/Tenant Groups
1. _____
2. _____
3. _____
4. _____
5. _____

Community Service Clubs
1. _____
2. _____
3. _____
4. _____
5. _____

Political Groups
1. _____
2. _____
3. _____
4. _____
5. _____

Youth Groups
1. _____
2. _____
3. _____
4. _____
5. _____

Singles Groups
1. _____
2. _____
3. _____
4. _____
5. _____

Self-improvement Groups
1. _____
2. _____
3. _____
4. _____
5. _____

Activity Clubs
1. _____
2. _____
3. _____
4. _____
5. _____

Local Trade Associations	Senior Citizen Groups
1. _____	1. _____
2. _____	2. _____
3. _____	3. _____
4. _____	4. _____
5. _____	5. _____

Entrepreneur/Business Groups	Schools and School Groups
1. _____	1. _____
2. _____	2. _____
3. _____	3. _____
4. _____	4. _____
5. _____	5. _____

Real Estate/Insurance Agents	People in Other MLM Businesses
1. _____	1. _____
2. _____	2. _____
3. _____	3. _____
4. _____	4. _____
5. _____	5. _____

Instructions for Using Leads Contact Sheet and Card

Obtain and record the following information from your contact:

Date: Note dates of *any* contacts, and if you need to call again, the date when you are supposed to do so. When you do follow up, note that date, too.

Name, Address, Zip: Whenever you contact someone, always try to get that person's name and address.

Phone Number: Unless you are contacting a company representative, try to get the person's work and evening phone numbers, and indicate which is which. Note the best time to call (day, evenings, weekends).

Referred By: Note the original source of the referral—a person, newspaper ad, and so forth.

Interest: Indicate whether interested (*Y*) or not (*N*). If the person is uncertain, sense what direction they are leaning in and add a question mark (*Y?, N?*). If you're not sure, just put down a question mark (*?*).

Meeting: If the person is interested in meeting with you personally or coming to a general meeting note this (*Y*) and indicate the day the individual plans to come. Then, you can easily call to reconfirm the day before or the day of the meeting.

Attendance: Indicate if he or she attended (*Y*). If not (*N*), you may want to follow up to find out what happened. Or at least you have a record of the results.

Membership: Indicate if the person decided to join (*Y*) or not (*N*). If the person is still considering, note this for follow-up later.

Comments: This is the place to record your observations or reactions, such as "sounds like a hot prospect," "especially interested in fishing." Then, when you call again or meet together, you can orient your presentation accordingly.

GETTING REFERRALS

Whenever you talk to someone who is not interested, always ask for a referral to others who might be interested either in the product, the business opportunity, or both, as appropriate. Try to get at least three referrals, and note any special comments (such as "mention the boat trip"). Then, when you contact these persons, if they are not interested, ask for a referral, too. And so on. This way, you have an ever-expanding network of people to contact.

Later, if you build a sales group, you can refer these names

CHART 31: LEADS CONTACT SHEET

Date	Name, Address, Zip	Phone	Referred by	Interest Y/N	Meeting Y/N	Attend Y/N	Membership Y/N	Comments

CHART 32: LEADS CONTACT CARD

Name: _____

Address: _____

City, State, Zip: _____

Phone: _____

How Referred: _____

Program(s) Described: _____

Dates Contacted	About What	Interest Y/N	Meeting Y/N	Result Y/N	Comments
_____	_____	_____	_____	_____	_____
_____	_____	_____	_____	_____	_____
_____	_____	_____	_____	_____	_____
_____	_____	_____	_____	_____	_____

to people in your organization, so you don't do it all yourself and find that your growing file of names becomes unmanageable. But more about that later.

Getting referrals is extremely important, because when you mention a personal reference, the person you are contacting is much more willing to listen. So keep track of who referred

CHART 33: REFERRALS

Date	Name of Lead	Address and Zip	Phone	Person Making Referral	Comments

you to whom, and use these names to open doors when you make your first contact.

The preceding Referrals Chart (Chart 33) will help you keep track of these referrals. Then, when you contact someone who is interested, transfer his or her name to your list of active prospects.

SOME EASY WAYS TO GET STARTED

After targeting your potential market and thinking about leads, the next step is starting to contact potential consumers and distributors. An easy way to get started is to do things close to home and talk to others about the program as you go about your everyday business. Then, after you have some experience, you can gradually try other ways, such as advertising and contacting the leaders of groups.

Here are some things you can do with little or no effort or expense.

Invite a few friends and neighbors to a presentation at your house. If you feel comfortable, do the presentation yourself. Otherwise, ask the leader of your sales group or sponsor, who should be willing to do a few presentations to get you started.

Invite a few friends, neighbors, or business associates to a nearby meeting about your product or business opportunity. And take them there yourself. Otherwise, people often say they will meet you there and don't show up.

Tell the group leader or program chairman of an organization you belong to about your new program and offer to put on a free event for them (possibly your sales group leader or sponsor will do it).

Carry little packets of literature with you. These may include an introductory flyer on the program; a list of meeting locations, if available; your name and phone number; a small sample of the product, if feasible. Hand these packets out to the people you meet, suggesting they might like to try the product. Or, as appropriate, indicate that this is also a business opportunity, if they want to earn some extra money.

You can hand these materials out to almost anyone. Some possibilities are the tolltaker where you pay your toll, the gas station attendant who sells you gas, the waitress in a restaurant who serves you, the bartender who sells you a drink, the store clerk who sells you merchandise, the teller at your bank, the person you sit next to on a bus, train, or plane, a person you meet at a party or meeting, customers or exhibitors at trade shows and fairs, people waiting on line with you, people leaving an event that suggests they might be especially interested in your product (such as people at a health fair if you have a health product), and anybody else you meet as you go about your daily life.

Put up posters or flyers at places you go to, such as campus buildings and bulletin boards, churches and community centers, supermarkets, coin-op laundries, stores or restaurants that display posters and flyers.

Or leave flyers for display at parties, meetings and conferences, and your office or school.

If you can, make an announcement about your program at an event and then pass out flyers. Your announcement will focus attention on your message and give you more credibility. It suggests you have the support of the leader of the group.

START TALKING ABOUT YOUR PRODUCT OR PROGRAM WHEREVER YOU ARE

You can easily promote your product or business whatever you do—just bring it up casually in the conversation when you talk to friends, business associates, whomever you meet. Emphasize the benefits of the product or the business opportunity, as appropriate.

For example, if someone mentions having trouble losing weight and you are promoting a health program, that's a perfect opener to describe the products.

If you are starting to become successful, you can promote the business by bringing up some of the ways your life has changed (for example, a new car, a vacation to Hawaii) as you talk. If a friend observes that she wishes she could take some time off to travel, you can explain that you just took a great trip there—all made possible by your new business. Then, you can explain how she can get involved in this business, too.

Similarly, when you are at the post office buying stamps, you might comment, "You know, you've been seeing a lot of me these days, because of my new business. I have people writing to me from all over the country."

Or, when a friend mentions that he's saving for a new camera you might tell him, "Say, I'm in this terrific new program where you could earn that money by working a few extra hours a week."

LEARN HOW TO MARKET TO YOUR TARGET AUDIENCE

Since everyone you contact has different wants and needs, and certain groups or types of individuals have special interests you can identify, think how you can slant your presentation to appeal to different markets. This way you emphasize the features of your program that are likely to be of special interest to the particular individual or group you are contacting.

Most salespeople tend to vary their approach on an ad hoc basis as they contact people. But it helps to develop a systematic approach to different markets, particularly if you are going to be advertising, creating flyers, sending letters, or otherwise seriously promoting your program.

One way to systematically adapt your marketing approach to your target audience is to use the Target Market—Product Benefits Form (Chart 34) to help you determine what features might best be promoted to each group.

Use the matrix in this way:

1. List the key features or benefits of the program in Column 1.
2. List the groups you think might be most interested in the program across the top.
3. Go down each column, and for each group, place an X in the box if you think that group might be especially interested in that product feature.
4. Indicate how important you think each feature checked might be to members of that group by rating it from one (least important) to five (most important).
5. Tailor your advertising, flyers, letters, or other promotional efforts to emphasize the features with special appeal to that group.

CHART 34: TARGET MARKET—PRODUCT BENEFITS FORM
What Product Benefits Appeal to Different Target Markets

PRODUCT FEATURES AND BENEFITS
(List the key features or benefits of the program)

TARGET MARKET

(List the types of individuals or groups the program is most likely to appeal to; then go down the column and check off the features or benefits you think would have the most appeal to that group)

Chapter 13

ADVERTISING YOUR
PROGRAM EFFECTIVELY

Some distributors for products never advertise and only
contact people they already know; others use advertising extensively to go beyond their usual network of acquaintances.
The best approach for you depends on the type of product you
are marketing, your target market, and the receptivity of your
personal network to purchase or distribute the product. Some
people have contacts who would love the product or are business and sales oriented; others don't. So if your personal network is not very receptive to your product—or even if it is—
you may find advertising an excellent way to increase your
sales.

Advertising can be the basis of a mail order or direct mail
approach to marketing a product or to developing a national
network of distributors. A growing number of people are working direct sales programs this way, either to expand beyond
their locally based network or because they would prefer not
to have all the people contact of traditional MLM and network
sales.

However, mail order/direct mail marketing is a completely

different advertising approach from what I will be discussing here, and it is best left to experienced direct-sales people who already have built a local sales organization or downline and to people who want to focus on mail order/direct mail selling. It's an approach that deserves a book in itself.

Rather, I want to focus on advertising in your local area to develop leads—leads that you then follow up with personal contact through one-on-one meetings, small group gatherings at your home, or invitations to larger meetings in your area.

The approach can be extremely effective, if you

- Select the right media for your target market;
- Develop systematic procedures to keep track of your advertising sources and the results;
- Use the right approach in your ad to attract interest and motivate people to call;
- Use the right approach when people call, so they want to meet you and hear about your program.

At first, you may need to experiment to hit on the right formula; and you will probably need to repeat your message several times to build your audience, since repetition promotes familiarity, and familiarity builds your credibility and leads people to become curious about who you are. Then, when you work out the right formula, keep doing it; and if you have an organization of distributors, teach others what you have learned so they can start advertising effectively—perhaps instead of you.

CHOOSING THE RIGHT MEDIA

First, know the market you want to reach and pick the local newspapers, magazines, or other media directed to that market. For example, if you are marketing a health product, try a local publication that features articles on health and self-improvement; or if your product would be of special interest to singles, try a singles paper.

If you have a product with broad appeal, you can advertise almost anywhere. But be aware of the market for each media source you use, and direct your ads to that market.

Besides the most familiar media in your area, there are probably many you don't know about, such as special interest magazines and newsletters. So to explore further, check at your local library for guides listing publications and other media sources in your area. Some excellent sources include *Literary Marketplace*, a media guide for your state (for example, California has the *California Media Guide*), and *Bacon's Publicity Checker*. Ask your librarian for other suggestions.

The media you choose depend on your purpose. For example, if you are putting on a special event to promote your product or placing a help-wanted ad to find salespeople, your local newspaper, advertiser, or college paper may be a good place to advertise. However, if you are advertising the product or service, a special interest publication (like a publication for singles or money-conscious consumers) may be ideal.

The key is to choose your media to fit your target market and then use the right advertising approach to reach that market.

Chart 35 suggests the types of approaches to emphasize in different media.

DEVELOPING SYSTEMATIC PROCEDURES FOR PLACING ADS

To get the most mileage for your advertising dollar, be systematic in how you advertise and record the results. Keep

CHART 35: WHERE AND HOW TO ADVERTISE

Media Sources	Type of Approach to Emphasize			
	Help Wanted	Business Opportunity	Products Services	Special Event
City-Wide Newspaper	x	x		
Community Newspaper (usually a weekly)	x			x
Local Advertiser	x	x	x	x
College Newspaper	x			x
Singles-Oriented Publication			x	x
Consumer-Oriented Publication			x	
Business Networking Newsletter	x	x		
Other Special Interest Publication			x	x
Local Radio Show			x	x
Local TV Show			x	x

track of the schedules, costs, and procedures for placing ads in the particular media sources you are considering. Then, keep track of the response when the ad appears, to determine which media sources produce the best results—based on the rate of response and the percentage of responses which turn into consumers or distributors. Also, use this information to determine your approximate costs for each positive response.

Initially, do some research to build up a file of potential advertising sources. Call up potential sources and ask about the costs for classified and display advertising (that is, by the word, line, column inch), discounts for repeated ads, advertising deadlines, and specific requirements for placing an ad (for example, do you have to have camera-ready copy or can the publisher set your ad in type?). It helps to list the name of a contact person, too.

By knowing this information in advance, you can readily tailor your ads to suit each publisher's specifications. Also, you can plan an organized ad budget and allot so much for advertising in each media source. For ready access, keep all this information in one place (such as on Chart 36, the Advertising Placement Form).

In some cases, such as newspaper classifieds, you can call in your ad. But most publications require you to send in your ad copy with a check for payment. Sometimes, you can stop by the office with your copy, but other publishers prefer that you don't.

Also, ask about special sections, issues, or programs where you might advertise. Then, you may get a larger audience or more people from a particular group you want to reach. For example, if a local singles magazine is running a feature on health classes, this is an ideal time to advertise a health product.

When you do advertise, list the date (or dates) your ad is scheduled to run, and check that it does. While some publications will send you tear sheets with your ad, most don't.

When your ad runs, record the number of responses you

CHART 36: ADVERTISING PLACEMENT FORM

Name of Publication or Media Source; Name of Contact	Address, Zip, Phone No.	Ad Cost or Rate	Ad Specs Format	Deadline	Circulation Market and Comments	Date Run	Response — Calls	Response — Meetings	Response — Sign Up

receive for each ad and the number of callers who arrange to meet with you. Also, note how many of these subsequently become consumers and distributors. Your records will prove invaluable in helping you assess how you are doing and planning your next ad campaign.

USING THE RIGHT APPROACH TO ATTRACT INTEREST

The response to advertising can be unpredictable—a little like gambling in Las Vegas—but if you follow certain principles, you'll up your odds.

Don't say too much in a single ad. Zero in on the main point and possibly one or two subpoints, and feature these. Also, don't go into too much detail explaining. You mainly want to pique readers' interest enough so they will respond. Don't give away your whole story, so a person feels complete and moves on.

Emphasize the benefit or advantage to the consumer or business opportunity seeker. If you feel a certain group may be especially interested, play up that. For example, I know some distributors who were very effective in running ads in their local advertiser that began: "*Housewives*: Do you want to save money and obtain a substantial part-time monthly income? Work only a few hours a day at home."

Start off with an eye-catching headline and use sharp catchy copy. Keep your sentences short and simple to understand. Make your ad easy and interesting to read.

In a display ad, make your message stand out. Do this by leaving plenty of white space. Don't crowd your copy together. Use a picture or logo if you can. And vary the size of your headlines, if you have more than one. A sleek, professional-looking ad is appealing and impressive. But if your ad is a jumble of badly organized, badly written ideas, you'll t r a potential prospects away.

At the end of the ad, as in any form of sales, ask for some action. "Call for more information." "Act now!" "Take advantage of our special offer, which is good only until (use a specific date)."

Use your business name. Your ad will seem more professional. Don't just say, call "Al" or "Mary" or "Mr. Davis." You'll get more calls—and more serious ones—when you indicate you are a business. For example: "Contact United Business Associates and ask for Mr. Davis."

Plan to advertise a few times, because of the value of repetition. A single ad isn't always a fair test, since the power of advertising builds as your ad is repeated.

Experiment in the beginning to see what works best for you. Try changing one or two things each time. For example, change your headline or copy slightly to see which ad has the biggest draw. Or notice when an ad that has been drawing well starts to taper off. You may need to change your copy or advertise something new. Or perhaps it's time to stop advertising in that media outlet for a while because you have started to exhaust the market.

When you can, specify where you want your ad to go in a publication. And if the publication has several sections where your ad might fit, try experimenting with where your ad pulls best, and use different ad copy as appropriate. For example, suppose a publication has these four categories where you might run your ad: business opportunities, miscellaneous merchandise, notices, and help wanted. Why not try each one over a month or two and see which produces the best response?

Also, know the policies of the company you are promoting before you advertise. Some companies allow their distributors to advertise using the company name freely, as long as the advertiser states he or she is an independent distributor. But increasingly, companies have restrictive guidelines to keep a certain company image and to protect themselves from wild claims or misstatements from distributors. So you may need to check all advertising with your company first for its approval. On the other hand, some companies forbid you to use the company name, and some distributors prefer not to use it anyway, so they can develop their own company name and image. Thus, check ad policies first and advertise accordingly.

Using Different Advertising Approaches for the Same Program

It makes sense to separate your advertising for consumers and for job and business opportunity seekers. Many people who are involved in building a sales group try to do both in the same ad—for example, they try to reach health-conscious consumers with an ad like: "A fantastic weight control program ... and make money, too!"

The only problem with this kind of ad is that you confuse your appeal. On the one hand, you may turn off some potential consumers, since they view this "make money, too" message as an indication they are going to be confronted with some kind of a business pitch. Once they try the product and are sold on it, they may become receptive to the business opportunity, but they are initially interested in being consumers. On the other hand, a person who wants a business opportunity may feel this double program–make-money appeal suggests part-time rather than serious work.

So keep your ad message simple—either consumer oriented or business or job oriented, but not both.

Then, tailor your ad to your particular market, keeping these key points, previously noted, in mind:

Keep your copy short and to the point.
Focus on a benefit or advantage.

Make your copy catchy.
Make your ad eye-catching.
Ask for action.
Include your business name.

Sample Ads Using These Principles

The following ads illustrate how these principles are used in practice, when targeted to different groups of people. Each ad should end with your company name, contact person (maybe you), and a phone number.

Advertising Your Product to Consumers
Start off by showing how one of the features of your product or service can benefit the customer. For example:

Ad for a Discount Consumer Club:

SICK OF HIGH PRICES?
Learn how you can save on almost everything you buy now—discounts from about 20%–50%, sometimes more, on most items. Call now and start saving.

Ad for a Health Program:

DISCOVER YOUR PATH TO
TOTAL FITNESS AND WELL-BEING
with an exciting new health program designed just for you. Let one of our trained counselors show you how. The program includes a weight control diet, healthy gourmet foods you can prepare in minutes, an exercise program, and more. Start now. Call: _____

Advertising Joining Your Sales Group to Business Opportunity Seekers

Emphasize the business advantages and the earnings potential, but also include a little about the product. Too many business opportunity ads sound the same. "Make a fortune in your spare time." "Retire in two months with a substantial monthly income." "The greatest business opportunity yet." The problem with these vague ads is that they can easily sound like scams, and you don't give the reader a reason to respond to your ad rather than to any other.

So, be specific and briefly describe the type of product or service involved. Or, list the kinds of skills needed to run this business. For example:

Ad for a Discount Consumer Club:

MAKE MONEY SHOWING
PEOPLE HOW TO SAVE

Become a distributor for this fast-growing new program that enables consumers to save 20%–50% off on almost everything they buy. Find out how you can be in this lucrative business for less than $50. We train.

Ad for a Health Program:

SALES MANAGEMENT OPPORTUNITY
IN THE FAST-GROWING HEALTH FIELD

Market a popular new health program which combines weight control, nutrition, exercise, and attitude change into a single program backed by heavy promotion and sales training support. Invest less than $50 and get started now.

Another good business approach is to target a particular group that might be especially interested in this opportunity and direct your ad to them. For example:

Ad for a Discount Consumer Club:

TEACHERS! Discover a great opportunity to make money on the side, and potentially earn more than you do teaching. You let others know how they can save money buying what they normally buy every day. Use your teaching skills to inspire and train others.

Ad for a Health Program:

HOUSEWIVES: MAKE A FORTUNE
in your spare time showing friends and neighbors how they can control their weight and enjoy vibrant health with a brand-new health and fitness program. Easy work you can do from your home, and involve your whole family, too.

Advertising Joining Your Sales Group to Job Seekers

In these ads, emphasize the types of skills needed and the earnings potential. Many job seekers are thinking in terms of more traditional sales and marketing positions, but they can be shifted to realizing the advantages of going into business for themselves and using their skills in their own business.

So in your ads, emphasize the types of "job" functions they will be performing, such as marketing, distribution, sales, sales management, training, consulting, leading groups, speaking, and making presentations. Also, indicate the product or service they will be involved with when they use these skills. For example:

Ad for a Consumer Discount Club:

SALES MANAGEMENT

Exciting new consumer savings program. Use your sales and promotional skills to work with and direct a team of people in marketing this new club that offers everyone savings of 20%–50% on the products they buy every day. Call now about this terrific career opportunity.

Ad for a Health Program:

MARKETING/SALES

Promote a terrific new health program that combines weight control, nutritious foods, exercise, and self-help tapes. Earn a high commission. Unlimited potential if you're motivated to work hard and learn. We train.

Using the Right Approach When People Respond to Your Ad

We'll discuss some good responses when people call in more detail in the section on phone techniques, since people may call not only because of your advertising but because they learned about you from other sources, such as posters, leaflets, letters, and other persons. Yet regardless of how they happened to call, you should keep in mind several general pointers:

1. *When people respond to an ad, find out which one and note this*, so you can tabulate the results for each ad. Also, try to get names and phone numbers immediately, so you have them readily available for follow-up. A good way to do this is to introduce yourself first: "Hi. This is Dave Smith. And

your name is . . .? Also, let me get your phone number, in case we get interrupted and I need to call you back."

2. *Be prepared for calls and have a general idea of what you want to say.* It's helpful to use an outline or informal script at first, so you cover the major points. Also, by being prepared, you can keep control of the conversation and direct it.

3. *Very briefly and enthusiastically note the main features or benefits of the program.* This way you review, recap, and perhaps expand upon the main points noted in your ad. For example:

To Calls about Your Consumer Discount Program:

"Oh, yes, you're calling about our exciting new consumer discount program which saves consumers about twenty to fifty percent on everything they buy anyway. We're looking for some dynamic people who want to move into sales management to help us market this."

To Calls about Your Health Program:

"Yes, I'm glad you called about our exciting new health program, which provides a complete fitness package. It combines a diet program, nutritious foods you can prepare in minutes, an exercise program, and tapes that can help you change your bad habits to become healthier and happier. The program is growing rapidly, and we need people to help us expand even further."

4. *As soon as you can, turn the conversation back to your respondent* by asking a few questions about why he or she called and what he or she hopes to obtain from the product or business opportunity. This way, you find out about the person's wants and needs and can orient your approach accordingly.

STRIKE IT RICH IN PERSONAL SELLING

5. *Briefly point out how the product or business will suit each person's situation.* But again, don't tell too much. Just tell people enough to get them to want to meet you and find out more. Just as in your advertising, you want to pique their curiosity, but not satiate it by telling too much.

Thus, if people ask for detailed information, perhaps give them some sketchy hints, but point out that this is the kind of material you cover in depth when you meet with them personally to put on a meeting about the program. Indicate that you will be glad to give them the whole story then. But you can't do justice to the program over the phone, since you have materials to show or give them.

In some cases, people will ask to see something written, like a flyer or brochure. Depending on your own personal style, you can respond one of two ways:

The Be-Glad-to-Send-You-Information Approach:

"Sure. I'll be glad to send you a brochure. But this will only give you a brief taste of the program. After you see this, we can arrange a meeting and go over the program in more detail. I'll also have much more material to give you then. I'll call you in a few days to set something up."

The No-We-Don't-Send-Out-Information Approach:

"Gee, I wish I could send you something. But we've been flooded with calls and don't have time to send out materials before our first interview (or meeting). So I hope you can come in to take advantage of this marvelous opportunity right away." Then, if they are still unsure, you can add: "But if you do want to see some examples of our program first, I'll be glad to send you a brochure in a few days, as soon as things settle down."

231

6. *If people do pump you for more information than you want to give*, remember, *you are—and want to stay—in control of the conversation.* So politely, but firmly, explain that you can't go into that much detail on the phone, but you would like to meet with them to explain the program further.

Chapter 14

USING BROCHURES, FLYERS, AND POSTERS EFFECTIVELY

DISTRIBUTING YOUR MATERIALS

Brochures, flyers, and posters can be an extremely effective tool for inviting people to call you for individual presentations or to announce upcoming product demonstrations, sales parties, or opportunity meetings. In fact, you should carry some sales literature with you at all times. Then, as appropriate, hand someone a flyer or packet of materials, put up a poster, or give someone a stack of flyers or brochures to display.

Use the company's handouts, where available, or make your own, as needed. If you do create your own, you may need to get the company's approval if you use its name. (Check the company's policies and procedures.) But if you don't mention the company, you are relatively free to say what you want.

You can use these materials in a variety of ways to suit your own personal style. For example, one woman who belongs to a number of different groups regularly brings flyers and brochures to meetings and distributes them to participants. In some cases, she gives a brief presentation about the program at business networking meetings, and then invites everyone to take some of her materials.

Another man regularly takes flyers to parties and events and hands them out. Depending upon circumstances, he variously leaves them at the door (so people can pick them up as they arrive), scatters them at tables around the room (the refreshments area is particularly good for this purpose), or discreetly hands them out to people after talking to them briefly.

Another woman, who also gives out flyers at parties, finds a way to turn the conversation around to her program. Then, if the person seems interested, she pulls a flyer out of her purse, saying something like, "Well, since you're interested, here's a flyer describing the program in more depth and some of our upcoming events. I hope you can come." She does the same thing when she goes shopping or to a meeting.

The advantage of using these materials after a brief conversation about the program is that people have something tangible to look at, and that helps to make the program seem more solid. Also, it's a vivid reminder of your conversation.

How and Where to Distribute Materials

You can always give brochures or flyers to a few people after you talk awhile at any party or meeting. But if you want to do more, check with the host to see how much promotion you can do. In some cases, you may be pleasantly surprised, for the host will invite you to say a few words to the whole group. But other times, the host may not want any promotion at a purely social occasion. So be sure to ask first. You certainly don't want to create hard feelings—or worse, be asked to leave.

Other places you can hand out materials are lines for events.

Or you can give them to the people you contact as you do whatever you do every day.

Sometimes, you may be limited to only a few words of explanation. For instance, one friend passes out flyers to toll-booth collectors as she drives through, and has time to make only a brief remark, such as: "Here's a great way to save money," "Here's a way you can make more than you are making now." Yet, people do call. When she has more time, she says a little about the program first; then, if the person is interested, she hands out a flyer that reviews some of the key points she has already mentioned and lists upcoming meetings and activities guests can attend.

Also, you can put up flyers in key locations (such as at your local supermarket, copy service, or laundromat). If you can, put them in the windows of stores that have other flyers on display, or ask store clerks to put them on the counter so people can take them. You'll find that certain stores are particularly amenable to these displays—typically stores that are already distributing other materials, like free newspapers and magazines. (Commonly, these include record stores, bookstores, magazine and smoke shops, and health centers.)

Places where groups gather are another place to put up flyers, such as the bulletin board or display table in a church, youth center, or lodge meeting hall. School and college bulletin boards are ideal, too. You may also find car windshields a good place to put flyers when the cars are parked for a particular event related to your product (such as a health conference if you are promoting health products).

An easy way to distribute flyers is to take a few stacks with you when you do your usual errands and drop them off or post them, as appropriate. If you are working with a group of distributors, you can get others in your organization to help you. Another alternative is to hire a postering service, which distributes flyers from different groups to key distribution points. Or hire high school or college students.

Still another strategy is leafletting at selected locations. For example, hand out flyers on a food product to people leaving a supermarket. Or pass out leaflets on a health product near a health store. However, when you do leaflet, observe some common courtesies and comply with any legal restrictions. For instance, don't stand too close to a store, so that you don't seem to be working for the store and don't upset the owner, who may see you as a competitor. As long as you are not directly in front of a store and are on a public street, not on the store owner's territory, you can usually hand out flyers and samples freely. But do wait until people come out of a store—that way you don't appear to be discouraging them from going in.

If you are at a shopping center, the whole complex may have laws restricting the distribution of material. But it's probably easier to just go ahead and do it. Someone will tell you if you can't. And once you start doing something, people are more likely to let you keep doing it. Conversely, when you ask, people are more apt to say no, regardless of whether you are allowed to do something or not.

Trade shows and consumer events (including flea markets, county fairs, gift shows, arts and craft shows, and ethnic festivals) are also good distribution sites. However, be sure you don't run afoul of the people who have already paid for exhibit booths. So, it's best to talk to people first, and then hand out materials to those who express interest. Exhibitors with related products may be especially likely prospects. Or hand out flyers to those leaving the event.

You might also try distributing materials at the unemployment office, if you want to appeal to job seekers—though again, talk to people first or hand out flyers outside the office.

Chart 37 summarizes some of these key points about where to hand out flyers and brochures.

Also, you can keep track of the effectiveness of your distribution efforts by keeping a list of where you have distributed materials and the response. You can use Chart 38, Flyer and Poster Distribution List, for this purpose. When you receive calls, note on your list of inquiries (discussed in the section on phone techniques, chapter 16) that they heard about your program from a brochure, flyer, or poster, and where they saw this.

CREATING EFFECTIVE BROCHURES, FLYERS, AND POSTERS

In order for your brochures, flyers, and posters to be effective, they must look good. They must be eye-catching, inviting, and look as if a solid professional organization is behind them.

And you don't need big bucks or art talent to create professional-looking materials that will draw people to your meetings and events. You can do it yourself with a limited investment (under twenty-five dollars) and some graphic aids—tools anyone can use.

First, in writing and organizing your copy follow the same principles used in advertising.

- Don't try to say too much on the same brochure, flyer, or poster.
- Focus on a few key points.
- Use a different size or type of letter to highlight major ideas.
- Leave plenty of blank space around your copy, so it is easy to read.
- Break up your copy into brief paragraphs to encourage readability.
- Ask for some action, such as:
    Come to a particular event (list date, time, place, cost, and indicate if a reservation is necessary);

Call to ask for more details;
Call to attend a business opportunity meeting.

Second, use the basic principles of graphic design to create an attractive, inviting look. And if you're not an artist, use the graphic aids we'll discuss. You can get this professional look by doing the following:

- Use bold, eye-catching headlines that convey your key message in a few words.
- Use type or lettering that has the appropriate feel for your message. (For example, use solid, conventional lettering to describe a business opportunity, free-flowing unusual lettering to convey a feeling of fun.)
- Use a picture or two to make your flyer look more lively.
- Use a good-quality typewriter (preferably electric, and if you have proportional spacing or access to a word processor, so much the better).

The following materials are graphic aids that will make it really simple for anyone to get this quality look.

Rub-On Letters. You simply press them on paper to create instant headlines. There are many brands, which come in hundreds of different sizes and type styles: Letraset, Prestype, Instantype, Better Letter, and so on. Just ask to see a type book and choose. About five to eight dollars a sheet.

A Burnisher. For rubbing on the letters. You can also use the end of a pencil or pen, although a burnisher—a pencil-shaped instrument with a rounded point—has a nice feel and is made for this purpose. About four dollars.

A Rubber Stamp Catalogue or Book of Clip Art. Great for illustrations. Simply cut out the pictures you like and paste them in position on the layout for your flyer. About three to five dollars.

A Ruler. Preferably a metal one. Use it to make sure your layout is both centered and straight. About one to five dollars.

A Light Blue Pencil. Use this to rule lines for your headlines. It's light blue because this color won't show in copies. About one dollar.

Spray Glue. Get the kind that allows you to reposition. Spray it on the back of your copy or artwork and place this wherever you want on your layout. About six to eight dollars.

Plain White Paper. Good bond typing paper will do. Use this for creating your layout. About four to eight dollars a ream.

Ko•Rec•Type or White-Out. Use this to clean up your final layout. About one dollar.

Now, you are ready to go to work.

1. Type up a rough draft of your copy. As much as you can, use the same spacing you plan to use on your final flyer.

2. Lay out your copy on an 8½ by 11–inch sheet. Feel free to cut, paste, and move the typed copy around on the flyer until you like the layout. Then, type up the final draft, and make sure there are no typos.

3. Visualize where your headlines and pictures might go.

4. To create your headlines, take your ruler and blue pencil and draw one or more light blue lines. Then, using your burnisher or other implement, rub on the letters to create your headline above the line you have just ruled. Use your judgment to properly space the letters into words and phrases. Choose the size and style of lettering to fit the space and present the image or reinforce the message you want to convey.

5. Cut out the headlines, and position them, along with your final copy, on your layout. Use your blue pencil to mark

where everything should go. Then, place each item in turn facedown on some newsprint or paper, spray-glue it, and place it as indicated on your flyer. Use your ruler to make sure the headlines and copy are centered and straight.

6. Now find a picture or two you like from the rubber stamp catalogue or book of clip art. Use a picture that fits your message. For example, for a travel-party flyer, use a picture with an outline of a palm tree on a small South Pacific–style island. For a dance party, use a picture of a couple dancing and perhaps a picture of a messenger announcing the event.

7. Then, cut out the picture (if you may want to use it again, make a copy first) and spray-glue it on your flyer, just as you did the headline and copy. But now you don't need to use the ruler. Just eyeball it, and place the picture or pictures wherever it feels right to you.

8. Finally, check over your layout and copy for any errors, smudges, spots, etcetera, and use the White-Out or Ko•Rec•Type to remove these.

9. Choose an appropriate color for your flyer. (I like having several stacks of different colored paper around so it's easier to choose. But if you prefer, get the colored paper you need from your printer. The per-copy cost is greater, but you don't have to invest money in stock.)

You can use certain colors to convey traditional associations—for example, green suggests money, yellow or orange suggests kitchens and food. Or choose a color that fits your personal style.

10. Now you are ready to make as many copies of your flyer as you want. The least expensive way is to take your master layout to your local instant copy center—and *voilà*— your flyer can be ready in minutes or overnight.

But one caution. Make a master copy from your original, or have your copy center make one. The reason for this is that the rub-on letters sometimes flake when kept for a while, leaving you with awful-looking, raggedy letters when you go to print more. But if you have a master, you can use this. It's better to use the original as long as you can, since it always gives you a sharper image. But if you can't, you have always got the copy.

11. If you wish, make extra copies of your artwork for others in your organization. Then, they can change any necessary details, such as the name and address of the person to contact, to print their own flyers.

Chart 39 summarizes the step-by-step procedures just described for creating flyers. Following this are some examples of flyers I created, using these techniques, to attract dozens of people to meetings and events.

For posters, simply use larger headline lettering throughout. And keep your copy very short and sweet—around twenty-five words or less is best.

Choose a poster board of the appropriate color. You can get precut boards at your local art supply store. Usually, these are cut to twenty-two by twenty-eight inches.

Use a ruler and pencil (a T-square is ideal if you have one), and lightly draw the number of lines you need for your copy. Then, measure the space you need for each word (or eyeball it if you are good at this), and rub on the letters. When you are done, use a soft rubber eraser to erase the lines. And presto—almost instant posters.

CHART 37: PLACES TO DISTRIBUTE BROCHURES, FLYERS, AND POSTERS

Good Places to Hand Out Flyers
  At Meetings
  At Parties
  At Events
  On Lines
  To People You See Every Day

Good Places to Display Flyers
  Stores and Centers
    Supermarket
    Laundromat
    Copy Service
    Record Stores
    Bookstores
    Magazine Shops
    Smoke Shops
    Health Centers
    Other Store Windows and Counters
  Places Where Groups Gather
    Churches
    Youth Centers
    Lodge Meeting Halls
    Schools and Colleges
  Car Windshields (of cars parked at selected events)

Good Places to Leaflet
  At Stores
  At a Shopping Center
  At Trade Shows
  At Consumer Events
    Flea Markets
    County Fairs
    Gift Shows
    Arts and Crafts Shows
    Ethnic Festivals
  At the Unemployment Office

CHART 38: FLYER AND POSTER
DISTRIBUTION LIST

Date	Location	No. Left	Name of Contact Phone No. if any

CHART 39: HOW TO CREATE
AN EFFECTIVE FLYER

1. Type up a rough draft of your copy.

2. Lay out your rough draft.

3. Plot out where your headlines and pictures might go.

4. Create your headlines.

5. Position your copy and headlines on your flyer and glue them on.

6. Choose some pictures.

7. Cut out the pictures and glue them on your flyer.

8. Check your layout and copy for any errors or smudges and clean it up with White-Out or Ko•Rec•Type.

9. Select the color paper you want to print on.

10. Make as many copies of your flyer as you want.

11. If you wish, make extra copies of your artwork for others in your organization.

Travel Party

Join us to hear about a great new travel club, TRAVEL 800, that enables you to go anywhere in the world you want and get a 50% rebate on the agent's commission.

Also, you get rental car discounts, members only tours at wholesale prices, featured tours of the month, and a regular newsletter keeping you up-to-date on current travel news.

Plus, you have an opportunity to make money by letting others know about the club. Some major corporations have already signed up for their employees. So why not...

TRAVEL ANYWHERE & PAY LESS!!!

Then, after you hear this exciting presentation, join us for a Gala Party, which includes:

> No host bar
> Entertainment
> Hors D'Oeuvres
> Getting-to-Know You Games by GAMEWORLD

TRAVEL PRESENTATION: 7-8:30 p.m. (NO CHARGE)

PARTY: 8:30-11 p.m. ($5-10 depending on where we go)

WHERE: At the BUSINESS OPPORTUNITY CENTER
2412 14th Avenue, SF (near Taraval)

WHEN: PARTIES IN APRIL:

Tuesday, April 26

To make your reservation:

GAMEWORLD (415) 658-2747

Fun, Fitness & Travel Party

From 6:30-8:00 p.m....

Join us for a fun evening featuring a dinner catered with foods from a new company promoting total health and fitness. (These foods include chocolate, vanilla, and strawberry nutritional drinks, low calorie gourmet foods which are ready in minutes -- chicken cacciatore, cod n'sauce, sweet 'n sour chicken, beef stew, pasta 'n beef in tomato sauce, and chicken chowder -- plus nutritional snack bars). Then, hear about this company's total weight control and fitness program, developed by a top medical staff at a health and wellness center in California, which includes an exercise program and behavioral modification tapes, besides these foods. The program is designed to be tailored to your own lifestyle. Also, learn about the fantastic business opportunity. Change your eating patterns, change your life; get healthy, maybe wealthy, too.

From 8:00-9:00 p.m....

See a slide show and learn about a great new travel club, the TRAVEL 800 CLUB, that enables you to go anywhere in the world you want and save an average of 5% or more on your transportation alone. Also, you get rental car discounts, members only tours at wholesale prices, featured tours of the month, last-minute travel bargains, and a regular newsletter keeping you up-to-date on current travel news. We will also be planning some unique, fun trips for members in this area. Plus you can make money by letting others know about the club. So why not..TRAVEL ANYWHERE, HAVE FUN, & PAY LESS.

From 9:00-11 p.m....

Join us for drinks, conversation, and maybe some entertainment or getting-to-know-you-games by GAMEWORLD at a nearby restaurant or coffee house.

WHERE: At the BUSINESS OPPORTUNITY CENTER
      2412 14th Avenue, SF (near Taraval)

COST: $5 for dinner (reservations a must by noon Wednesday)
      $1 if you arrive after dinner

WHEN: PARTIES IN MAY:

     Wednesday, May 18   Wednesday, May 25

To make your reservation:

        GAMEWORLD (415) 658-2747

STRIKE IT RICH IN PERSONAL SELLING

Gourmet 'N Games Party

in a fabulous
San Francisco Mansion

Thursday, December 9   7:30 p.m.
2721 Pacific

Come to this exciting new program and find out how you can build a business with terrific-tasting natural foods you can prepare in minutes.

Also, get in on the ground floor of a new games company featuring unique "people" games, in which people interact and relate to each other in a fun party atmosphere...and players can get serious, too.

ENJOY A GREAT DINNER, PLAY GAMES, AND LEARN ABOUT HOW YOU CAN MAKE MONEY, TOO!!!

The cost is $7. For reservations call:

Gini Scott (415) 845-1649

or

Richard Foster (415) 482-4263

Make out your check to GAMEWORLD and send it in advance to:

GAMEWORLD
1314 La Loma
Berkeley 94708

WE HAVE A LIMIT OF 40 PEOPLE. SO GET YOUR RESERVATIONS AND CHECKS IN NOW TO MAKE SURE YOU CAN ATTEND.

247

Gini Graham Scott

Come to a
Gala GAME-FAIR

featuring

GAMES by Gameworld

Friday, May 27
at the GAMERY

7:30 P.M.

6537 Chabot Road, Oakland
(near College and Claremont)

Come to this exciting new program that combines food, fun, and a little business networking.

Play some great new "people" games which feature unique ways to interact in a fun party atmosphere...and players can get serious, too.

You can...explore your psychic powers with PSYCHIC; find out what you've always wanted to know about the opposite sex with MEN & WOMEN; enjoy a hilarious party game of playful pursuit with OH PEG IT!; give and take advice with ADVICE COLUMN; act out your wildest fantasies with PLAYING WITH POWER; and sell and promote your way to the top with MAKE A MILLION. The games are introduced by trained game leaders.

Also, sample some great gourmet foods at our GOURMET POTLUCK, and bring your own specialties to share. We provide the punch and juice; you bring the main dishes, salads, desserts, wine, and whatever else you want.

And bring your own business cards, flyers, samples, etc. too.

POTLUCK & NETWORKING: 7:30-8:15; INTRODUCTIONS: 8:15-8:30
GAMES & PARTY: 8:30 on.

Reservations required. We have a limit of 35 people. The cost is:
    For GAMEWORLD members - $2.50
    For non-members - $5.00

For reservations call: GAMEWORLD (415) 658-2747

Checks in advance to: 6537 Chabot Road, Oakland, Ca. 94618

STRIKE IT RICH IN PERSONAL SELLING

FOOD   FUN

 ## and GAMES

NIGHT

TWO UNIQUE PROGRAMS -- COME TO EITHER OR BOTH

LEARN ABOUT A QUICK TO PREPARE NUTRITIOUS FOOD PRODUCT
MADE POSSIBLE BY A UNIQUE HIGH-TECH FOOD PROCESS

HAVE FUN

AND FIND OUT HOW YOU CAN MAKE MONEY, TOO!

From 7:30-8:30 p.m. - Join us for a light dinner catered by Yurika, and
discover how you can get tasty, nutritious food
which is ready in minutes. These foods come in a
flexible pouch, are cooked in their own juice to
retain the flavor, and take five minutes to heat and
serve. Also, enjoy some easy to prepare bakery goods.

- Cost: $3. Includes entre, side dishes, and beverage.

From 8:30-10:30 - Play "People" Games -- Games of Social Interaction
and Communication. Essentially these are educational
and getting-to-know you games, dealing with themes
like: creativity, success, personal growth, relationships,
etc. which have been developed and marketed by
GAMEWORLD

- Cost: $2 for non-GAMEWORLD members. Includes
snacks and refreshments

at 6537 Chabot Road, Oakland
(near College and Claremont Avenue)

PROGRAMS IN MARCH:

Tuesday, March 22

To make your reservation for either event (we have a limit of 20):

GAMEWORLD (415) 658-2747

Gini Graham Scott

Get Healthy

with Games

Nights

TWO UNIQUE PROGRAMS -- COME TO EITHER OR BOTH
LEARN HOW TO GET HEALTHY - HAVE FUN
AND FIND OUT HOW YOU CAN MAKE MONEY, TOO!

From 7-8:30 p.m. - Discover how you can lose weight easily with Herbalife's weight control program based on sound nutrition and herbs

- Learn about healthy gourmet foods from Lifeline - packed with nutrition and ready in minutes

- Cost: $3. Includes entre and beverages.

From 8:30-10:30 - Play "People" Games -- Games of Social Interaction and Communication. Essentially these are getting to know you games, dealing with themes like: creativity, success, personal growth, relationships, etc. which have been developed and marketed by GAMEWORLD

- Cost: $2. Includes snacks and refreshments

at 6537 Chabot Road, Oakland
(near College and Claremont Avenue)

PROGRAMS IN MARCH:

Monday, March 14
Monday, March 28

To make your reservation for either event (we have a limit of 20):

GAMEWORLD (415) 658-2747

251

Gini Graham Scott

 NNOUNCING

the MLMMS

SUPER SALES

award

TO THE LEISURE MEMBER
WHO SPONSORS THE MOST
MEMBERS IN ONE MONTH

A FREE MEMBERSHIP IN LEISURE SINGLES
TO THE PERSON OF YOUR CHOICE

ALONG WITH A HANDSOME CERTIFICATE OF MERIT
YOU CAN HANG ON YOUR WALLS

AND WE'LL PRESENT IT TO YOU AND THE NEW MEMBER
AT ONE OF OUR REGULAR PROSPERITY PARTIES

So get out there...Sign up the world...You can do it...
We're behind you all the way.

Just keep those membership applications coming in.*

*And follow the appropriate filing procedures,
so we can keep track of who you sign up.

Chapter 15

WRITING EFFECTIVE LETTERS

When you contact people you don't know or don't see regularly, a good letter can be critical in sparking their interest. Letters can help you contact leaders of organizations, company heads, real estate and insurance agents, and others with a vast range of contacts. When they see a brief and compelling description of what you are doing, they become receptive to hearing more.

Note that this letter is not designed to be a direct mail sales letter that asks the recipient to act now. Rather, it is intended to introduce you and give you credibility, so you can follow up with a personal contact.

THE STEPS TO USING LETTERS EFFECTIVELY

A letter-writing approach involves certain key steps.

First, decide what key groups or types of individuals you want to contact (for example, church leaders, real estate brokers, leaders of social organizations).

Gini Graham Scott

Next, draft a letter that emphasizes how members of this group can use your product or service or how the group can earn money by marketing it to members.

Make a list of the groups or individuals you plan to contact.

Possibly make a preliminary phone call, either to find out the name of the person in the group to whom to send the letter, or to speak briefly to the contact person about the letter you plan to send. At times, you may find a preliminary phone call is all you need to interest the person in your program, and you don't need a follow-up letter. (See the section on phone techniques.) But commonly, you will need to send a letter.

Next, make copies of the letter and send it out with some literature about your program. Ideally, you should send it to a specific person. Leave space in writing your letter to insert a different name and address on each copy. Or preferably, use a word processor or word-processing service to type out multiple copies with the different names and addresses.

Follow up your letter with a phone call after a few days to set up a meeting or invite the recipient to a group meeting.

DRAFTING YOUR LETTER

In writing your letter, emphasize the features of your product, service, or business opportunity that are likely to be of special interest to the group you plan to contact. Use the following guidelines to write your letter:

Keep your letter brief and to the point—preferably no more than one page.

Make your letter look good. It should be on a business letterhead, and if you are just starting, you can create one inexpensively by following the guidelines for making flyers and brochures. Also, be sure to type it on a good typewriter. You want to go first class.

254

Keep your sentences and paragraphs short (no more than three or four lines per sentence, or eight to ten lines per paragraph). This way your letter is easy to read.

Leave plenty of space for the margins. Again, this promotes readability—and it looks more professional.

Start off with one or two sentences that attract attention, and quickly let the reader know what the letter is about and why he or she should read more. This way, you involve the reader and avoid the "junk-mail-toss-it-away" syndrome. If you have had a brief conversation with the recipient before writing, be sure to mention that the person already expressed interest, and now you are sending the information requested.

Select the one, two, or at most three benefits of your product which you think would be most attractive to your prospect and emphasize these. You are mainly trying to get your prospect to pay attention and to want to learn more about your program. Don't tell everything now. If you say too much, your letter can get boring or overwhelming. So home in on the key, most interesting points.

Include any details about your product, service, or business on a separate sheet, and note in your letter that you are attaching these materials.

Close with an invitation to action or an indication of what action you will take. Depending on your personal style, invite the person to call you to set up an appointment, or indicate that you will call in a few days to set up an appointment.

Either address your letter to a specific person, or if it is obviously a form letter, add a personal note to personalize it. You'll get a better response when you do.

Later, regardless of how you have written your letter or close, call to make sure your prospect has gotten the letter, has read it, or is interested. This follow-up is important, because even if you have invited the person to call, the person may never have received the letter, may have lost it, may not have read it, may have forgotten it, or may have meant to call but didn't get around to it.

So regard your letter as a door opener—and then you have to keep that door open and go through it.

SOME SAMPLE LETTERS

To illustrate how these letter-writing principles work in practice, the next section includes some sample letters directed to different groups of people. Each section begins with a list of key considerations to keep in mind in slanting a letter to that group. Note how each sample letter incorporates these key points.

A Letter to Friends and Neighbors

Key points to remember:

Make it friendly and chatty.
Subtly allude to your connection with this person to personalize the letter—but do so in a low-key way.
Indicate how you have personally benefited from the product features that are likely to be especially important to this person, and note that now you want to share these benefits, because he or she is a friend or neighbor.

A Sample Letter (Promoting a Consumer Discount Club)

Dear (Name of Friend or Neighbor):

Hi from your friendly neighbor across the street. I just got involved in a new program that has fantastic savings for consumers, and I thought this would be a great opportunity to be neighborly and let my neighbors know all about it, so they can benefit from it, too.

It's a consumer savings program that enables you to get all sorts of products you are already buying, at wholesale prices. It has just about everything, from groceries to more expensive items. And there are familiar brand name products, too. You can save about 20 to 50 percent on most purchases, sometimes even more.

I've already bought a new camera and saved almost $300, so I know the program works.

Also, you can make money by sharing the program with a few people you know. I know some people who are making a few hundred a week after two months, and one friend recently quit his regular job to do this full-time.

I think it's a tremendous opportunity to both save and make money, and that's why I'm so excited about it. I've enclosed some materials describing the program a little more fully and listing some dates when I will be having some meetings in my house. I hope you can attend, or if that's not convenient, I can let you know about other meetings and take you as my personal guest. Or let's sit down at your house or mine, and I'll tell you about the program personally.

Please let me know when you would like to attend a meeting or get together. Or if you'd like more information, please call. Hope to talk to you about this soon.

Sincerely,

John Smith
(your friendly neighbor)

A Letter to the Head of a Church Group or Social Organization

There are several key points to remember.

Be professional and businesslike, and use the appropriate business-letter form, including your initials and those of the typist (make one up if you wish) in the lower left-hand corner.

Make your business sound solid and impressive. If you're small, you can have someone other than yourself sign the letter with an appropriately impressive title. For example, when a friend did a mailing to ministers, her administrative assistant signed the letter as "Associate Community Service Director."

Emphasize how the product or service would benefit the group.

Show how the group or group leader could benefit economically by using the program as a fund-raiser, if this is an option.

Suggest that you can put on an interesting program for the group, and you would be glad to discuss this further with the group leader.

Mention any success other churches or group leaders have had using or marketing the product or service.

If you have had a brief conversation about the program or have been referred by anyone, be sure to note this.

A Sample Letter (Promoting a Consumer Discount Club)

Dear Reverend (Name of Minister):

I was delighted to hear about your interest in (Name of Program) when we spoke the other day. As you may recall, I was referred to you by (Name of Referral), and we talked about how much this program could benefit your group.

In brief, this program is of great benefit, because it offers your members an opportunity to save money on all kinds of goods they are already buying—groceries, general merchandise, and brand name items. At the same time, you can make a substantial monthly income for your organization or yourself, just by letting others know about the program.

I have already spoken at some church-connected social groups about this program as part of a presentation I call "Money-Saving Tips: How You Can Save without Spending a Cent." And some church leaders have used the program to organize a community project.

I would be glad to put on a special presentation for you and help you organize such a project. I can meet with you personally to discuss this—or if you like, come as my guest to one of our regular meetings.

I am enclosing some additional information on the program and some dates for regular meetings. Please call if you have any questions or to set up an appointment. I can meet with you at our offices or at your church offices—whatever is most convenient to you.

I look forward to hearing from you soon and sharing more about this wonderful program with you and your group.

Sincerely,

Joan Smith
Associate Community Service Director

JS:aj
encl:

A Letter to Outside Sales People about a Business Opportunity

This letter might go to real estate agents or insurance agents. Here are some key points to remember.

Be professional and businesslike in your approach (as just described).

Make your business sound solid and impressive, even if you're small, by using an appropriately impressive title, such as President, Director, or Marketing Director. For example, when a friend did a mailing to real estate agents, her administrative assistant signed the letters "Associate Marketing Director."

Emphasize the money-making benefits of the program.

Point out how the benefits of the product will enable the person to make money.

Suggest why this person might be in an especially good position to promote the product.

Invite the person to meet with you personally or attend a meeting.

Mention any successes other salespeople in this person's field have had in marketing the program.

If you have had a brief conversation about the program or have been referred by anyone, indicate this.

A Sample Letter (Promoting a Consumer Discount Club)

Dear Realtor (Name of Realtor):

I was pleased to hear of your interest in (Name of Program) when we spoke the other day. As you may recall, (Name of Program) is a terrific opportunity for realtors to make a substantial part-time income with only a few hours of work a week. And you can save money on purchases you would make anyway.

I have been contacting real estate agents in my area, because we have found that real estate agents are particularly successful in this business, since they have a wide circle of contacts who are likely to be interested in the program.

Since this program is relatively new in this area and has broad appeal, this is an excellent time to get involved now. Wherever the program has been introduced, it has grown rapidly, and you can be part of this tremendous growth here.

I am enclosing some material on the program and some dates of regular meetings. I would also be glad to meet with you personally at your convenience.

Please let me know when you would like to get together. I look forward to working with you, and will do everything I can to assist you in becoming successful in this fantastic new program.

Sincerely,

John Smith
Associate Marketing Director

JS:aj
encl:

A Letter to Merchants (If Your Program Permits You to Sell to Stores)

Key points to remember:

- Be professional and businesslike in your approach (as described earlier).

- Make your business sound solid and impressive (as described earlier).
- Emphasize that the product line would appeal to current customers, without detracting from products the merchant is currently selling.
- Show how the merchant can benefit from these added sales with relatively little personal effort.
- Point out how the merchant's customers who get involved in the program can help the merchant make money, too.
- Indicate that you will be glad to stop by during the day to present the program.
- Mention any success other merchants have had selling the products.
- Indicate that you are only contacting selected merchants in the area, and if he or she is interested, you will not contact any other merchants on the block—you will let him or her do this.

A Sample Letter (Promoting a Consumer Discount Club)

Dear Merchant (Name of Merchant):

I was pleased to hear you were interested in learning more about (Name of Program) when we spoke briefly on the phone today. As you may recall, you can use this program to expand your present product line, and you can do so relatively easily, since the product virtually sells itself.

It's a program that appeals to almost everyone, since it enables people to save money on all sorts of items. But the products are different from the ones you now carry, so the program won't detract from your own business. It will only help.

I am enclosing some materials on the program, including a full-color flyer. The flyer describes the full benefits of the program, and many merchants simply pass out flyers to customers in their store. Some hold brief meetings with interested customers at the end of the regular work day. So it's a very easy program to promote, and some merchants are now earning an average of $200 to $500 extra each week, just for a few hours' work.

Also, be assured, if you get involved, we will not contact any other merchants in your area, because we do not want to be in competition with you.

I would be glad to stop by your store at a convenient time to describe the program to you in more detail. Or you are welcome to come to one of our regular meetings. I will call you in a few days to set up an appointment. In the meantime, feel free to call if you have any questions.

Sincerely,

John Smith
President

JS:aj
encl.

Chapter 16

EFFECTIVE TELEPHONE TECHNIQUES

You have about four seconds to make a first impression. Researchers studying how people meet in bars found that people decide whether to continue their conversation in four seconds. And it's like that when you first call someone on the phone about your product, service, or business opportunity, except you have to make your impression with your voice alone.

Thus, you need to know the basics of making a good phone impression and how to adapt your technique to different situations and types of people.

In this section, we'll describe the basic principles of good phone techniques, then talk about how to apply these in different situations or with different people, and lastly provide some sample phone scripts to get you started.

SOME BASIC PRINCIPLES

The following principles are basic to all successful phoning, whether you are calling someone you know, are making a cold call to a stranger, are following up after sending a letter, or are responding when someone calls you because of an ad. Many of these principles apply in any kind of sales, too.

Getting Prepared before You Call

Have a general idea in advance of what you want to say. Start off with a basic script or outline of the key points you want to cover. Then you have an overall plan of action for what you want to say and to make sure you cover major points. You can modify what you say as the need arises, and you can train others to do some phoning for you. Some people like the flexibility of an outline; others feel more comfortable with a script. You can always revise your outline or script for the future, as needed.

List the key benefits of your product or service in order of importance. Then, you can go through those with the most appeal first, and if you encounter any objections, you can try to overcome these or go on to the next benefit.

Focus on one or two key products or services when you call. The company may have dozens of products, but emphasize those that you feel will have the most appeal first.

Before you call, review what you want to say and be ready to slant it according to the interests of the person you are calling.

Having the Right Attitude

Be enthusiastic and positive. Then, you convey a spirit of excitement about your products or business, whatever you say. You want to show that you think you are involved in a terrific program which is generating a lot of interest and excitement.

If you need to, take a few moments to put yourself in a positive, confident, calm frame of mind. Use affirmations, visualize the caller being excited—whatever you need to get your enthusiasm going.

Opening the Conversation with a Good Lead

Briefly explain who you are at the beginning of the conversation if the person you are calling doesn't know you. Give your professional credentials, and convey an image of authority with your tone of voice. Here's an example.

Hello. I'm Joanne Smith of Health Plus. We're a company that's promoting health and fitness through quality products and helping others earn money by promoting these products.

Start off with a good lead-in that attracts interest and suggests an immediate benefit in listening to you talk about your product or money-making opportunity. You want to say something that's catchy, even startling, to get attention. You can present this as a statement or a question, but in either case, keep your opener short and specific to spur your listener into wanting to learn more.

Some good openers include a leading question such as, "Could you use an extra two hundred dollars a month?" or a statement suggesting an urgent need to act now, such as, "I just heard about a great new gas saver that has a special offer on through this week."

Use the following examples to get some ideas of different approaches to use with people you know and those you don't. Note that a general lead-in is fine for those you know. The product and business opportunity approaches can be adapted for both.

Example of a General Lead-in with Someone You Know

"Hi. I just heard about an exciting new idea. Can I come over and let's talk about it?"

"I've been thinking about getting involved in a new project, and I'd like to get your opinion. Can we get together later today or tomorrow to talk about it?"

"I just discovered a great new program, and we both can benefit. When do you have some time so we can talk?"

Example of an Opener That Focuses on a Product or Service

With someone you don't know, emphasize a benefit that you know has broad appeal. With a personal contact, try to personalize your lead-in so it applies particularly to that person.

(To someone you don't know) "How would you like to save fifty dollars a month on your grocery bills?"

(To a friend who has been struggling to lose weight) "How would you like to be able to lose weight and keep it off permanently?"

(To a friend who you know wants something) "You know that new car you've been saving for? How would you like to hear about a way to get it in a few months?"

Example of an Opener That Focuses on a Business Opportunity

With strangers, you can appeal more directly to their need; with people you know, it's best to be more subtle, perhaps even using the third-person approach, so they don't feel on the spot.

(To someone you don't know) "Would you like to make more money than you are making now?"

(To a friend) "Do you know someone who would like to earn an extra five hundred to one thousand dollars a month?"

Keeping the Conversation Going Effectively

Get to the point of the conversation quickly. No one likes rambly calls, or calls that begin with someone asking a number of questions without explaining why. So establish your purpose quickly, and if someone calls you and isn't clear why he or she is calling, politely ask that person to describe his or her main purpose in calling.

Briefly describe the program (or expand slightly upon what the person you are calling already knows). As you describe it, emphasize the main benefits, and show by your confidence and air of authority that you know what you are talking about. And get the person excited to learn more. *Remember, your main purpose in calling is to get people to want to meet with you to learn more.*

So focus on a few key selling points and describe those briefly. For example, suppose you are promoting a health program, and a college student who is active in athletics calls about it. You can briefly say something like this:

It would be a great program for you. The program will help you in your training. The vitamin pills will give you extra energy. The athletes who have used them report playing better, and even breaking past records.

Vividly describe your product or service, so others can literally see it. This makes your product or service more emotionally appealing, and helps to hold your prospect's attention after a good lead-in. Through a vivid description, you make that product or service really come alive for people. For example:

It's a fantastic health program. You drink these terrific-tasting drinks that look and taste like malts, exercise about a half hour a day, and listen to tapes that teach you how to change your attitude. In a few days, you'll see the pounds melt away.

Mention any special features that make the program stand out, such as testimonials by name people, celebrity appearances on talk shows, and so forth. For example:

The famous football player (Name of Athlete) uses these products, and a panel of celebrities who have used them will be appearing on the Johnny Carson show.

But don't say too much. Don't give out details over the phone. If people ask, explain that you need to meet with them personally to go into detail. Or they can hear about all these details at a meeting. If you say too much, you may satisfy their interest, so they feel they don't need to know any more. And you take up too much of your valuable time in unproductive conversation.

If you talk about the business opportunity, it's better not to mention unfamiliar terms, such as network or multi-level marketing, unless the person knows what these are. Preferably, call the venture a home-based business. This makes the business sound simpler, and it avoids triggering any misconceptions many people have about direct sales or multi-level marketing. Also, MLM or network marketing can be difficult to explain if people have never heard of these concepts. When you meet personally, you can explain how the business works in your presentation. But for now, keep things simple and brief.

Stay in control of the conversation. Just as in any sales presentation, remember, you are in charge. Be aware of what you want to say and lead the conversation in that direction. If someone asks you a question that gets you off track, gently guide the conversation back or indicate that you will discuss this when you meet each other.

Ending the Conversation with a Good Close

Don't try to complete the sale on the phone. Unless you know someone really well—and even then—you normally can't close a sale on the phone. People, particularly strangers, need to see something concrete—literature, the product, or other people who are involved in marketing the program. So just focus on getting them to want to meet you or attend a meeting.

Keep the call under three minutes. That should be plenty of time to determine if the person is interested, explain who you are, and motivate him or her to want to learn more.

Wind up the call with a request for action, and, ideally, set up a specific appointment. For example, invite the person to a meeting, or better, make arrangements to pick up the individual so you can go together. Alternatively, arrange to meet at his or her house or yours. Or agree to send information, and then call to set up an appointment.

Ask for referrals. If people aren't interested themselves, ask if they know someone who might be. And be specific. Mention a particular type of product or business benefit, and ask if they know a particular type of person who might be interested in that benefit. That helps them think of specific people they know, whereas a general question is more likely to draw a blank. For instance, you might ask—

Do you know someone who would be interested in losing five to ten pounds in a month?

Or:

Do you know any other real estate people who might be interested in earning a few hundred dollars extra each week?

Responding to Calls about Your Ad or Letter

Plan your response in advance—just as you do when you call someone. Make an outline or mini-script, so you are prepared and can stay in charge of the conversation. Typically, plan to cover some of the points that follow:

Why the person is responding to your ad or letter, and what is most important to him. Then you can direct your message to that individual's "hot button." A good approach is to start with a question to draw the person out, such as, "What are you most interested in in my ad?" "How do you feel the program I described in my letter can help you?" "What kind of *home-based* business appeals to you?"

A brief description of the product or business.

A brief statement of the type of people you are looking for—to use the product or participate in the business.

A few questions to determine if the person is a likely consumer or business prospect.

A request to set up an appointment (as usual, suggest you only have a few openings, since you are busy, and determine if these are convenient for the person, or invite him or her to a general meeting).

A Sample Conversation Might Go Something Like This:

For a Call Responding to a Business Opportunity Ad:
Hello. Let me tell you a little about the business. We're the XYZ Company, and our company is involved in _____. The company has been growing extremely fast in the last few weeks, so we are looking for some people who would like to assist us and are interested in

running their own business to market this product.

You would be involved in all aspects of the process—sales, marketing, promotion, business management—and you would participate in training and motivating others, too. We are looking for people who have some skills in this area or an interest in learning this kind of business. We are scheduling meetings this week.

Now, if this sounds interesting so far, I need to have a little information about you. What kind of work have you done? Have you had any experience in management? Do you like working with people? Are you working now?

(Then, if the person sounds like a likely prospect—)

Okay, then, let's set up an appointment. First, let me get down your name and phone number. I have a few time slots available later this week. Which of these would be good for you?

For a Call about the Product You Are Advertising:

Hello. Let me tell you a little about the product we advertised. We're the XYZ Company, and we have a great line of products for people who are interested in losing weight. We put the ad in to invite people to our weekly health and nutrition parties. We start off with a brief discussion about some new findings about nutrition, and then show you how our program can work for you.

We're looking for people who really want to lose weight. Are you in any kind of diet program now?

Well, it sounds as if our program could really benefit you. Would you like to come to our next meeting? We limit the number of people at each meeting, so we can give you plenty of individual attention. I can make a reservation for you for our meeting on _____. [And, if the person can't make that one:] Well, our next meeting after that is on _____.

Setting Appointments

Try to pin the person down to making a firm commitment to meet with you. Make it clear when you set an appointment that it is definite, and confirm that the person understands this. Many people will say, "I'll try to make it" or "I'll let you know." But pin the person down, and emphasize why it is urgent to act now.

For example, if a person sounds uncertain about committing to a one-on-one appointment or you want to stress that the appointment is a definite one, you might say, "Okay, I've got this down in my calendar now. We'll be meeting together at [name the time and place], and I'll be counting on seeing you then."

Or to stress the importance of the meeting, you might say, "Okay, I've got our meeting set for _____, and I'll be over at your house then. If something should come up for you, please give me plenty of notice, so we can set up another appointment. I only have so many each week, and my time slots usually get filled very quickly."

When people do agree to come to a meeting, emphasize how important it is for them to come. Often people feel free not to show up for a meeting, since they feel they are just one of many people. So point out that their attendance is important.

For example, tell a prospect, "Okay, I'm putting you on my list for the meeting [date and place]. We can only accommodate a limited number of people, and I've made a reservation for you. If something should come up, please give me plenty of notice, so I can invite you to another meeting."

Arrange to take your guest to the meeting, rather than meet there. This way most persons feel more obligated to attend

273

and feel more important personally, because you are going out
of your way to bring them to the meeting. Again, make sure
your guest knows that it is a confirmed meeting. "Okay, I'll
pick you up at [time and date], and we'll go to the meeting
together. I'm putting this in my calendar as a confirmed date,
and I'll see you then."

*Instead of asking prospects for a time they can make it, it's
better to say you have a few time slots available.* Then, ask
which they would prefer. That gives your prospect the impression you are a busy person. If he or she can't make it, you
can always work out an alternate time.

*When you talk to people you know, set up a time to get
together before you go into details about the program.* Some
people use this "let's get together first" approach effectively,
although I personally feel more comfortable briefly telling
people the purpose of the get-together first. For example, Rick
Walsh and Ken Smith recommend this method in *Financial
Freedom*. They suggest that you "clear the night" first, before
you go into any sort of sales approach. As an example, you
might call a friend and say, "Hello, this is _____. I was
wondering if you and your wife had anything planned for next
Tuesday." If they do, find out if they are free another evening
the following week.

Walsh and Smith's rationale is that if you give your sales
message first and your prospects aren't free, you have to call
them again and give your message a second time. But, if you
get them to state they are free first, you have a clear field for
your pitch. On the other hand, I would rather determine if
people have any interest first, before setting up a meeting.

*When you set up a meeting, indicate that you will call back
on the scheduled date to reconfirm.* And ask your prospects
to call you at least a day in advance if they can't make the
meeting. Again, emphasize that this is important, since you
have a very tight schedule. This way, your prospect feels the

meeting is especially important, which decreases the likelihood of no-shows.

If someone cancels a meeting, put that person off for the next one. Don't sound as if you are available any time your prospect is. Make such persons feel they have to wait and that the appointment with you is very valuable, so they will be less apt to cancel next time.

Reconfirming Appointments

Reconfirm any appointments set for more than a day or two after you call. This way you reduce the risk of no-shows.

When you do call, do not ask if the person is coming. That gives persons a chance to rethink if they want to attend and reconsider how interested they are in the program. Instead, act as if the individual is coming and you are simply calling to reconfirm this.

Make a few comments to get your prospect reenthused, such as, "I'm calling to confirm that I will be seeing you tonight at seven. We're expecting a record turnout, since the company is introducing its new products tonight. I'm really looking forward to trying them out."

Briefly restate your agreed-upon arrangements. "I'll be by to pick you up at your house, thirty-four Davis Street, at seven." Or, "I'll meet you at the corner of Davis and Peach at seven, and I'll be sure to wait in case you're a little late."

Don't let the person start asking questions again about the program, since that will only make him or her reconsider. Instead, cut off any questions firmly but politely by indicating that they will be covered in the meeting itself and that the person will have plenty of opportunity to ask then.

If your prospect says he or she can't make it when you call, reschedule the meeting. But probe a little to find out why. If the reason is a serious matter that takes priority (such as someone sick in the family or a last-minute work assignment), be understanding and try to set the next meeting as soon as possible. Indicate that you are quite busy, but because of the situation, you will try to fit that person in right away.

On the other hand, if you sense that the person is putting you off because of uncertainty about the program, put the person off a little, too, to make him or her feel he or she is truly missing an opportunity. For example, say something like, "Oh, that's too bad. You'll really be missing a good meeting. The regional director is going to be in town, so the meeting should be super good." (Sometimes people reconsider at this point.)

Then, if you set another appointment, indicate that you have to set it a week or two away because of your other commitments. For example: "Okay, then let's set another meeting. However, it'll have to be next week, because I already have my calendar filled with other meetings, since the program is growing so fast. But I do have two time slots next week— Tuesday at five, and Wednesday at three. Which would be best for you?"

Some people send out a confirming note to remind their prospect of the time and place when they set up an appointment more than a week in advance. Rick Walsh and Ken Smith recommend this approach in *Financial Freedom*, because they find that people are better able to cancel an appointment when you call—but it is harder to say no to a piece of mail, for then the burden to break the appointment rests with them. I don't find it makes much difference and personally prefer the personal touch of calling. Use what feels most comfortable for you.

Following Up with No-Shows

Even with the best of phone techniques, some prospects will not show up. Distributors and sales reps have different ways of dealing with this. Some just figure that marketing is a numbers game and drop these people from their list. Others call back the people they know to find out what happened, but don't call back the people they don't know.

One effective approach that works for many is to call up the no-shows once in an upbeat way, suggesting that they missed a really great meeting, but have another chance. The value of this second-chance approach is that some people are a little skeptical about whether the program is really solid when you first call, particularly if they live in an area, such as San Francisco, where many new companies are constantly starting up, only to disappear in a few months. So the first time they hear about a new product or business opportunity people can easily say to themselves, "Oh, yes, another program." They have seen many companies come and go, and they may think this could be like the others.

However, when you call again after a week or two and report on how well the company is doing, they may be willing to listen a little more carefully. If you went to a meeting and are still excited maybe it's worth looking into the program a little further. That's why I suggest you don't give up on no-shows right away and call again.

If you do call again, don't put the person on the spot about why he or she didn't come. That will only make the person defensive and possibly hostile. For example, one friend hired a student to do some follow-up calling for her, gave her a script, and told the student to use it as a guideline, but put the ideas in her own words. Unfortunately, when the student made her first call, she immediately pounced on the poor man who answered, proclaiming in an accusatory tone, "I'm calling because you weren't at our last meeting for the XYZ Company. So why weren't you there?" Needless to say, he hung up, and my friend fired the student on the spot. But all was not lost. Afterward, when my friend called to apologize, the man's wife said he had been sick, and the man accepted the apology with good grace and subsequently did go to a meeting and bought some product.

In short, calling no-shows can be productive at times, as long as you keep these points in mind:

Be enthusiastic.

Express your regrets that the person couldn't come.

Let the person give you a reason for not attending if he or she wants to, but don't be too pushy.

Give new information that makes the program sound exciting and motivates the person to take a second look. For example:

Hello. This is _____ of the XYZ Company. I'm sorry you weren't able to make our meeting last night. It was really terrific. And that's why I'm calling you—to let you know about some brand new features just revealed last night that are truly revolutionary. [Describe them briefly.] I'm sure you'll find them really exciting, and we're having another meeting on Thursday, so you'll have another chance to look the program over and see that it's a really solid, fast-growing business opportunity.

And When Someone Calls You about Something Else . . .

Be ready to shift the conversation, so you can talk about your product or business opportunity. For instance, when a friend calls to invite you to a party, you might say, "I'd love to, but I'm not sure I can because I have been so busy." When your friend asks why, you explain. "I'm involved in this marvelous program in which I've been making some money on the side. It's a . . ." (and then you go on and tell your friend about it).

STRATEGIES FOR CALLING DIFFERENT TYPES OF PEOPLE

Targeting your phone approach to the type of person you are calling ups your chances for success. I have found that the strategies presented in this section are effective with the groups you are likely to contact:

friends and acquaintances
persons who have placed their own ads for
    jobs
    other direct sales programs
    party-plan selling
people with a wide network of contacts, such as:
    leaders of church and social organizations
    real estate and insurance agents

Calling Friends or Acquaintances

Decide if the person is most likely to be interested in your product, service, or business opportunity and emphasize that.

Sound enthusiastic and talk about the great product or business opportunity you discovered—how you want to let your friend, relative, acquaintance, or business associate know how to benefit, too. Stress the benefits you think this person might be most interested in.

Also, with personal contacts, it helps to personalize the benefits by showing how the program would help, given what you know about this person. This approach is particularly apropos when you are contacting a person who would probably be more interested in being a consumer first. For example:

Hi. This is _____. I'm calling because I've been involved in this fantastic weight loss program for the past month and have finally lost the weight I've been trying to lose for months. I wanted to let you know about it, because I know you've been trying a number of different diet programs, and I thought this might work for you.

Then, briefly describe some key features of the program. Alternatively, at times, it is best to use the third-person "do you know someone who would be interested" approach, because then your friend or associate feels under less pressure to show interest because he or she happens to know you. This third-person approach is especially useful when you're looking for people to join you in a business opportunity, since some people don't like to admit they need money. Here is an example.

"Hi. This is _____. I'm calling because I've been involved in this part-time business for the past few months, and now that it's growing so fast, I'm looking for a few other people who might be interested in starting their own part-time business. Do you know someone who might be interested? It's a fast-growing weight control program, and if someone is serious and works the program for a few hours a week, he or she can be earning a few hundred dollars a week on the side in a month or two, and then a few thousand or even more several months after that.

Then, if the person asks, briefly describe some key features of the program and how people make money with it.

Calling People Who Have Placed Their Own Ads

Another good source of leads for people interested in marketing your product or service is those persons who have ads in your local paper or advertiser, including those looking for jobs (especially in the sales or people-contact field), those involved in direct sales, network, or MLM programs (especially those with a related but not competing line), and those who are putting on home parties (if your product would fit in).

When you call, first try to learn more about what the person is looking for or is doing. Then you can slant your presentation accordingly.

Calling Someone Looking for a Job

My company has successfully used two different approaches for calling job seekers.

(1) We advised job seekers that we had three positions available: a salary position in our office doing routine work (primarily we have hired students for this); a commission position getting leads and inviting people to our product demonstrations and business opportunity meetings; and a chance to join a business where people can earn a substantial monthly income working on a part-time or full-time basis—from a few hundred a month to much more.

Because we presented these three options, people perceived us as a large organized company, which gave us almost instant credibility. So they were more open to hearing about the commission position and the business opportunity. Some people who originally only wanted a job told us over the phone they were now more interested in the business opportunity. Others came to our meetings with their options open, and after our presentation, most of them decided they were most interested in the opportunity, too.

Thus, we used this technique to gently redirect many job seekers into hearing about going into their own business. And if people still wanted a job, we did hire a few of them for routine clerical work, such as keeping our ever-growing mailing list.

(2) We told job seekers, particularly those having trouble finding a job, that they could make much more in becoming part of our business than they could on a regular job. Then we briefly described the program, product, and earnings potential, and invited them to a regular meeting or to a one-on-one or small group presentation at our office.

The best approach depends on your own style and your assessment of what the person needs and wants. But in either case, since you are calling the job seeker cold, you need to guide the conversation to quickly cover certain points.

- Does the person still want a job? Is he or she interested in part-time work?
- Your own credibility as a company with a bona fide income opportunity. The person may want a job, so you need to establish your authority in order to shift the person's thinking to recognize that starting a business as a distributor or sales rep offers a higher earnings potential.
- The person's background and major interests. By asking, you show you are personally concerned, and you can better direct your appeal to the individual's wants and needs and make the person feel he or she has to sell you on him/herself, too. In turn, you can better stay in control of the conversation.
- A brief description of the product, service, and business opportunity, emphasizing why the business would be good for this person.
- A brief indication of the earnings potential, without

exaggerating too much. To be credible, state figures people can relate to, particularly someone who has always had a job. Yet you can still dangle the carrot that big money is possible, so a person who wants more can imagine it.

- Close the conversation by inviting the person to take some action and meet with you, preferably in a small group or one-on-one meeting where you can talk on an individual basis.

Here's how a conversation with a potential job seeker that covers these points might go.

"Hello. Is this the person looking for a job? Are you still looking?" If not, ask, "Are you still interested in some additional part-time work?" If not, thank the person politely and call the next person. If you get a yes, go on.

"We have a position for someone who is looking for the kind of job you want. I represent [your company name], and we have a position that involves [list some of the activities that correspond to what this person wants]. But before I go into the details, I'd like to know a little more about your background, and what you are really looking for in a job." After the person explains, you continue. "Great, it sounds like there may be a perfect fit. We're looking for people who want to be independent, choose their own hours, work hard, be self-starters, and work with people. It's a great opportunity to create a real career for yourself and use your initiative and organizational skills in sales management. We help train you, too, and give you all the tools you need to be successful. Some people are earning anywhere from a few hundred to two to three thousand dollars a month in a few months. And some earn even more, based on a commission for what they do.

"Now, if this sounds good and you're really serious about this opportunity, I'd like to set up a meeting to go into more detail. I've still got a few time slots available Tuesday morning, if that's convenient."

Calling Someone in a Direct Sales or Party Plan Sales Program

You can locate local direct-sales and party-plan people from several sources, including your local newspaper in the sales-help-wanted section (look for the small ads that talk about unlimited opportunity, great potential, $1,000 plus monthly, home-based business, commission only, and so on); your local advertiser or flea market paper (under help wanted, business opportunities, and certain product categories such as health and nutrition products); and a directory from a local home-business or income-opportunity show.

People involved in direct sales or putting on party plans will respond in a variety of ways when you call. Some will be sold on the product they are advertising and will believe in doing only one product at a time. But others will be interested to hear about additional marketing opportunities, especially if they can sell the product to the same market they are already selling and therefore can supplement current sales.

So when you call, first find out what their product is (people don't always say in their ads), how actively they are marketing it, and for how long. Also, tactfully try to find out how well the product is doing. Then you can better assess how receptive they might be to a new product and can approach them accordingly.

For example, if these salespeople are well-established and have built up an extensive sales group, they might feel very protective about what they already have and not be very open. On the other hand, if you can point out how your product can supplement what they are doing and appeal to their sales organization, you might get a good response.

Similarly, newcomers may vary greatly in their response.

Some who have developed no strong loyalties and commitments might be readily attracted to an appealing new opportunity. Yet others might resist, feeling uncertain, for they are afraid to handle more than one product or fear dropping something they are in for something new and untried.

So get a sense of where the person is at when you call. One way is to pose as a potential customer or opportunity seeker. Then, ask questions. Afterward, you can continue to pose as a potential prospect, but also mention that you are using or promoting this great new product or service and you wonder how it might fit in with the advertiser's product line. When the person asks you about it (and he or she almost certainly will), describe it, dropping a few teasers to arouse interest. For example, mention how much you have earned, how quickly you have lost weight, how much you have saved, or whatever, to highlight some major benefits. Then, if the person still seems interested, you can suggest that perhaps you can work together on these two programs. So subtly, you have shifted the conversation from the advertiser's program to your own.

The direct approach can work well too if the advertiser has put enough in the ad to indicate what the product is, or at least the product category (such as health and nutrition). In using the approach, you call the advertiser, ask what company or particular products are represented, indicate you are familiar with the line and think highly of it, and then say you called because you represent a related but noncompeting product that would help increase his or her sales.

However, whichever approach you use, guide the conversation to cover some of the following key points, as appropriate (unless you already know the answer from the ad):

What product or company does he or she represent?
How long and how actively has he or she been marketing
   this product?

How committed is he or she to this company?

Does he or she currently market any other product lines? Or does he or she believe it is possible to market more than one product at a time?

How fast is his or her product or service selling? Or how fast is his or her organization moving? (Ask questions to get this information tactfully, such as, How much product does the *average* distributor move? or How many new people is *one* likely to recruit each month?)

Finally, point out how your own product or service can increase sales.

A conversation with an advertiser using the "I'm a customer" approach and covering these points might go something like this:

Hi. I saw your ad for the XYZ health and nutrition company, and it sounds interesting. Can you tell me more about your products?...

Very interesting. How long has the company been in existence?... How long have you been doing this?...

Hmmmmm. That sounds like something I might like to do. How much money might I be likely to make if I spent about ten to twenty hours a week marketing this? For example, what's your experience, or the usual experience, as best you can tell? How much product can the average distributor usually move each week?...

Yeah, that really sounds good. I might be able to work this in with the program I'm already involved in [then you go on to describe it].

A conversation employing a more direct approach might go like this:

Hi. I see you're marketing the XYZ Company's line of health products. I'm familiar with that product and think it's a great line. And that's why I called.

I'm involved in the ABC Company, which also has some health products. But they're different, and ABC has a nutritious food line, too. So I thought you might find this is a great way to increase your sales with almost no extra effort, since many people use the products of both companies.

Pause to see if this person has some interest. Plunge ahead if so.

I have several people in my sales group who are marketing both products. I don't think you should spread yourself too thin, of course. But if you've got two or three complementary products, that can work. For example, are you currently marketing any other products?...

Well, then, if this is your main product, I think you'll find our product can really add to your line. It's not at all competitive, and it virtually sells itself.

So, why don't we get together and talk some more? Then you set the appointment.

You can use a similar approach with people doing home parties. Simply indicate familiarity with their program. ("I see you're doing pleasure parties for women. I've been to one of them myself.") Then, point out how your own product could be introduced at the same time. ("You know, I bet those women would also love to see this new skin care line our company represents. They can feel sexier if their skin feels really fresh and clean.")

Calling Those with a Wide Network of Contacts

Persons who are heads of organizations, in outside sales, or in public contact positions where they see many people every day are especially good to contact because they know a large number of people. Some examples are heads of church groups or social organizations, real estate and insurance agents, and merchants.

These people will probably want to see a letter of materials they can review before they agree to meet with you (see the section on writing letters). But you can pave the way with a brief introductory call, where you explain to them or their secretary why the program might interest them and their group. The call should only last about a minute. If they are interested, send them literature, and after a few days, call again to follow up.

What to Say in Your Initial Call

In your initial call, get to the point quickly: how the program benefits these individuals and their group. Start off by saying you are calling about a program with these benefits and you would like to send them some literature if they are interested.

The advantage of this quick-to-the-point approach is that they know you intend to be brief, so they will be more receptive to listening—because they don't have to worry about a long sales pitch.

Finally, find out where to send the literature, and depending on your style, invite them to call back after they receive it or indicate you will call in a few days to follow up. In either case, plan to call back yourself, whether you invite them to call you or not.

A call might go something like this:

STRIKE IT RICH IN PERSONAL SELLING

To a Leader of a Church or Social Organization (about a Consumer Discount Club)

Hello. This is _____ of [your company name]. I'm calling about a new program that might benefit your group, since the program offers an opportunity to save money on all kinds of goods that people are buying anyhow. It would also be a great fund-raiser for your group, since you could organize it as a group project.

I can tell you a little more about it over the phone. Then, I've got some literature I'd like to send you. We have a number of presentations on the program in your area. Or if you prefer, I can meet with you personally, or one of our members can put on a presentation for your group.

To a Real Estate Agent (about a Consumer Discount Club)

Hello. This is _____ of [your company name]. I'm calling about a new program that real estate agents are finding very popular, because they can increase their goodwill by telling their clients about a new way to save money on all kinds of goods. Also, you can earn extra income when you tell your clients about the program.

I can tell you a little more about it over the phone. Then, I've got some literature I'd like to send you. We have a number of presentations on the program in your area. Or if you prefer, I can meet with you personally to discuss this further.

To a Merchant (If You Can Sell Your Product Line to Retail Stores)

Hello. This is _____ of [your company name]. I'm calling about a new program that many merchants are getting involved in, because they can substantially increase their income by putting out a few brochures about some exciting new products. And these products are not competitive with anything in your store.

I can tell you a little more about it over the phone. Then, I've got some literature I'd like to send you. We have a number of presentations on the program in your area. Or if you prefer, I can meet with you personally at your store to discuss this further.

What to Say in Your Follow-Up Call

Sometimes people will call you after reading the literature you have sent. But usually, you have to follow up yourself. The key points to cover in your follow-up calls are:

Have they read the material? (If not, recap some major points or offer to send them another brochure and call again.

Do they have any questions about anything they read? Are they still interested and do they want to learn more?

When can you set up a meeting? (Usually, they will want you to meet at their place of business. Or invite them to a meeting and offer to take them there yourself.)

Again, as in the initial call, don't go into too much detail on the phone. Your main objective is to set up a meeting to talk about the program in depth.

Chapter 17

TAKING YOUR PROSPECT TO AN OPPORTUNITY MEETING

Some types of direct sales or network marketing programs feature business opportunity meetings to recruit new distributors. These meetings range in size from small home gatherings to large splashy presentations with all the excitement of a massive company rally or political convention.

Some distributors take their prospects to opportunity meetings regularly. Others rely mainly on small one-on-one presentations and take prospects only occasionally.

The advantage of a good opportunity meeting is that it creates a high level of excitement—particularly in the case of the big ones because of the dynamics of the group.

When you get started in one of these programs, such meetings can be a good way to introduce your prospect to the product or business with a professional polish. Most good sales leaders or sponsors will put on these meetings for you or will be part of a network of people active in the program and can tell you when and where these meetings occur.

Gini Graham Scott

THE KEYS TO GETTING
SUCCESSFUL RESULTS

The keys to successful results when you take a prospect to a meeting are worth considering.

If you have set up the appointment several days in advance, call to confirm that you are going to the meeting that day. When you call, simply restate the arrangements you agreed to and advise the person that, as planned, you will pick him or her up (the better way) or that you will meet at a certain location (and indicate that you plan to wait, so the person feels committed to show up).

Also, when you call, *don't ask* if the person is still planning to attend. That provides the person with a chance to rethink the original decision and perhaps to change his or her mind, since the excitement of your original pitch may have faded. Just assume the person is coming, and you are calling as a courtesy reminder.

Pick up the person if you can. You want to make it as convenient as possible for your prospect to attend, and this way you know that he or she is coming. Otherwise, people frequently agree to meet you at the meeting, but don't show up, often because they feel less enthusiastic than when you first spoke to them. But if you pick them up, you help to reenthuse them.

Get to the meeting early, preferably about ten to fifteen minutes before the scheduled time. This gives you a chance to sign in (most meetings have some form of registration), and get a good seat so you can easily see and hear everything. Also, you can introduce your prospect to other people, tell him or her about what to expect, and get him or her enthusiastic about the benefits to be presented in the upcoming presentation.

As a result, your prospect will be more attentive and feel more positive when the meeting begins and thus will show greater interest in the program.

Have your distributor agreement and a packet of materials readily available to give your prospect at the end of the meeting. This way you can build on the enthusiasm created by the meeting, and you may be able to sign your prospect up immediately as a new distributor. In fact, the meeting leader will typically end by inviting prospects to get together with their sponsors.

So this is the time to invite your prospect to sign up, and if you notice any signs of hesitation, ask if he or she has any questions and answer them. If you can, finish your discussion and sign up at the meeting site. But if you have any trouble doing so (for example, the room is noisy or you have to leave the room because of a time deadline), invite your prospect to a nearby coffee shop to discuss the program there.

Try to get your prospect to sign up after the meeting; if you can't, follow up in a day or two. When you discuss the program after the meeting, be prepared to handle any objections, and if your prospect wants to think it over, try to get him or her to make a decision now by asking what he or she wants to think over. Do all you can to get the person to sign up now, when the enthusiasm of the meeting is at a peak.

But, if your prospect is determined to wait, accept this graciously and say you will call in a day or two. Then, do that. Don't let more than a few days go by, because your prospect is much more likely to cool off after a long delay.

Chapter 18

PUTTING ON AN EFFECTIVE ONE-ON-ONE PRESENTATION

A small one-on-one presentation of your product or business is a great way to get started. You just invite a friend or contact to meet with you at your house, at the friend's house, or perhaps over coffee, and then you share your story.

If your prospect is married, it's best to have both the husband and wife together so they see the program at the same time. Then, you won't hear the excuse, "But I have to talk it over with my spouse first." They may still want discuss and think about it, but they are better able to decide now.

Some distributors and sales reps use an expanded one-on-one format, and have perhaps from three to six people attend at one time. Their rationale is that it's too expensive in time to give a presentation to only one person or couple. Also, they may set up an appointment and the person doesn't show up. But if they have a small meeting for a few people, their time is spent more productively, since the meeting is more likely to occur, and someone is more likely to sign up. At the same time, the meeting remains small, so it preserves the intimacy of the one-on-one presentation.

HOW TO PUT ON YOUR PRESENTATION

When you make your presentation, be prepared. Plan in advance what you are going to say. This way, you can keep your presentation short, compact, and to the point, which makes for a more powerful presentation than a long rambly one.

Preferably keep your presentation to about a half hour. Otherwise prospects may start to lose interest. But if they have lots of questions, you know they are interested, and you can go longer.

Also, have any supporting materials organized and close at hand, so you can readily refer to specific items to make the point you want.

It's important to have more than a general idea of what you want to say, because if you prepare only casually, you are likely to forget major points. Or if you cover them, you may do so in a haphazard way.

Thus, *have an outline or script firmly in mind (or even written), and assemble your supporting materials in the order you want to refer to them.* You can use the Presentation Checklist (Chart 40) and the Order of Presentation Checklist (Chart 41) to get prepared.

Do some practicing initially until you are familiar with the major points you want to make and the sequence in which you plan to present them. If you prefer, have your outline or script with you when you make your first presentations, because then you are sure to cover everything and will feel more relaxed. Later, you will know the material and won't need a written copy with you.

CHART 40: PRESENTATION CHECKLIST

Items I Plan to Use in My Presentation	Items I Now Have (check)	Items I Need to Get for My Presentation
_____	_____	_____
_____	_____	_____
_____	_____	_____
_____	_____	_____
_____	_____	_____
_____	_____	_____
_____	_____	_____
_____	_____	_____
_____	_____	_____
_____	_____	_____
_____	_____	_____
_____	_____	_____
_____	_____	_____
_____	_____	_____

CHART 41: ORDER OF PRESENTATION CHECKLIST

The order in which I plan to use materials in my presentation:

1. _____   16. _____

2. _____   17. _____

3. _____   18. _____

4. _____   19. _____

5. _____   20. _____

6. _____   21. _____

7. _____   22. _____

8. _____   23. _____

9. _____   24. _____

10. _____   25. _____

11. _____   26. _____

12. _____   27. _____

13. _____   28. _____

14. _____   29. _____

15. _____   30. _____

Gini Graham Scott

SUPPORTING MATERIALS

Supporting materials are useful for creating interest and providing proof that you represent a good company with good products or services. Following are some suggestions.

Testimonials. Use either tapes or letters (videotapes if you have them). It's best to get these from several types of people to show that interest in your product is broad based. Also, it helps to have a testimonial from someone else in the same field as your prospect, so he or she can more closely identify with that person. And if you can, present those testimonials first.

If you use testimonial letters, they should be on a nice letterhead.

Include some identifying material about the person giving the testimonial if it's not already provided in the letter or tape— such as the person's name, town, occupation, sales record if good, and how long he or she has been a consumer or distributor with the company.

Slides. Some companies have slide-sound or slide-script presentations that are professionally produced. If available, these are ideal. Or if you feel creative, produce your own slide show or add some of your own slides to the company presentation to make it more personal. For example, show yourself and some friends using the product or service.

Graphs, Charts, Posters. Visual aids really help. They make your presentation seem more solid and interesting, and they graphically underline the points you make.

Ideally, develop suitable supporting materials into a pre-

sentation manual. Some companies and sponsors have already produced these, and if so, use them. Or, if you prefer, adapt this material or develop your own, to suit your personal style. (However, check company guidelines as to how free a hand you have, and get any necessary approvals.)

One advantage of a manual is that you can go over the major points of your presentation in a step-by-step fashion, because your manual keeps you right on target and helps you avoid forgetting major points—so you cover everything. If need be, you can always shift sections of the manual around for different presentations, or vary the sequence in which you present different sections in response to your prospect's interests.

Another advantage of a manual is that it looks impressive and backs up what you say graphically. Some techniques for making a good manual are described in the last section of this chapter.

Also, have a packet of materials to hand out after your presentation. While some people may be convinced from your presentation to buy or become a distributor on the spot, many will want to think it over, and if so, it is important that they can review something tangible, which reminds them of the major benefits you discussed in the presentation. In addition, *the materials can include additional supporting documents not mentioned in your presentation,* such as testimonials from satisfied product users or successful distributors, information on how or why the product works (particularly needed if you have a health or nutrition product or a high-tech product). These materials show that the program is really solid and that you are truly professional. Just giving out your business card is not enough.

WHAT TO COVER
IN YOUR PRESENTATION
(AND IN YOUR MANUAL)

Organize your presentation in the way that feels best for you—though in general, your presentation should cover the major areas described in this section. If you are using a manual and have supporting materials, arrange them to follow the same sequence, so your presentation flows easily.

Depending on your program, vary the sequence in which you make your presentation to emphasize the consumer benefits or the business opportunity. In some cases, it's appropriate to present only the consumer benefits; conversely, some people may be primarily interested in the business opportunity; but even so, it's usually best to discuss the product or service first, since a person must be sold on the product first before he or she can sell it.

Start with something to get your prospect's *attention*—the first step in selling anything. Then, *build interest* by showing how the benefits of the product or business opportunity will fill his or her needs. Then work on *arousing the person's desire* to buy or become involved in the business.

As questions or objections surface, your answers will help increase your prospect's *confidence* in the product, the company, and in you. Finally, help your prospect *make a decision and take action* on the grounds that this action will be beneficial and result in his or her satisfaction. If possible, encourage the person to act now, but if someone hesitates and is unwilling to decide now, give that person the space to review the product or opportunity, and ideally, provide an information packet to help him or her decide.

More specifically, include the following topics, as relevant, in your presentation or manual in any sequence that works best for you.

Introduction

Offer some attention-grabbing information that shows the value of your product and establishes credibility. This might include testimonials by users, claims by researchers, your experience using the product, a description of the company's fast growth, and a demonstration of the product or service.

A Description of the Product or Service

Include a discussion of how or why the product works, but don't get too detailed, unless the prospect asks questions. For example, some people find it sufficient to learn that a diet program worked for you and don't care what exactly is in the products. Others do. So sense the depth of your prospect's interest and knowledge, and respond accordingly. Also, you might include in this section a hands-on demonstration (if not part of the introduction) and photographs of the product or service in use.

A (Very Brief) Discussion of the Company for Consumers Only

Talk about how solid and stable the company is and its ability to produce the product or service. Some topics to cover include the company history in the business, names and backgrounds of key company officials, and reasons the company was formed and how it is organized.

A Discussion of the Backup Support You Will Provide

To Consumers

In some programs, your backup support doesn't matter much to consumers, since they order direct from the company. But in other cases, consumers may look to you for advice and assistance to help them in using the product or service. This is particularly true in the case of computer sales, diet programs, or health products, which require ongoing follow-up for proper use.

To Potential Distributors or Sales Reps

Prospective distributors and sales reps need the assurance you will be there to assist. Since some now shop around for the best sponsor or sales leader to help them in marketing a particular product line, you should be convincing in explaining what you will do to help. So play up your background and your plans to support them. For example, some topics to cover include:

your knowledge or expertise in the product area (for example, if you're promoting a health or diet product, it's great if you're a nutritionist)

your background in sales or marketing

the team of distributors you are working with

the kinds of activities organized by you or your sales organization (such as local meetings, rallies, newsletters, and so on)

A Brief Introduction to Network or Multi-Level Marketing

Many people still have not heard of network or multi-level marketing, so if you are looking to build such a sales group, include a section on how this form of marketing works.

In your explanation, illustrate how a marketing network grows, and show the difference when each person on the average contacts two, three, four, and five persons. However, point out that the program works differently for each individual, depending on how much effort he or she puts into it. (You can use Charts 1 and 2 in the beginning of the book.)

Since the issue of illegal pyramids may arise in discussing this type of direct sales, it helps to include a description or chart showing the difference. (Use Chart 3 in chapter 2.)

After a general discussion of this marketing approach, talk about why you think your company is an especially good opportunity—because of its...(fill in the strengths of the company: top-quality products, management, marketing plan, and so forth).

A Description of the Marketing Plan

If you are seeking distributors or sales reps, explain how the marketing plan works, too. Include some diagrams showing the basic structure of the plan as well as information on how the plan might work in practice. But be conservative. Use actual data from the company or other distributors if you have it. Alternatively, make conservative projections about how the organization is likely to grow or how much someone is likely to make.

Because of various regulations about what companies can say and cannot say in company literature, you may not be able to get information on potential earnings from the company or your sponsor. (Legally, companies cannot make projections about hypothetical earnings or they get in trouble with the post office and other authorities, though they can provide some examples of how much a distributor needs to qualify for different levels of bonuses or what a typical distributor makes.)

Despite these restrictions on showing hypothetical earnings, people are likely to ask anyway, so work out a few projections yourself if you can't get them from your sales group leader or sponsor. But when you use them, emphasize that they are completely hypothetical, and make sure people understand you have developed them yourself.

It is also useful to include testimonials from distributors who have been successful.

Some other materials and diagrams you might use include a chart showing the structure of the plan, a chart showing how the plan might operate in practice, and copies of checks showing the earnings of other distributors. (You can use a big check to illustrate, but don't imply that everyone is likely to do this well, since people don't earn that kind of money when they start a new sales program, and most don't make huge incomes each month. Simply say that this check shows what is possible. Also, to be more realistic, perhaps show your first few checks with the company or the checks of a few other distributors for their first few months. People have an easier time identifying with this.)

A Close That Encourages People to Get Involved

If it seems appropriate, *ask for the order*. Simply show your prospect an order blank or distributor agreement, and urge him or her to order or sign up now.

However, if your prospect seems sincerely hesitant, don't be too pushy. Instead, send the person home with some literature and possibly some samples. (For example, if you're promoting a health company, recommend that your prospect take some vitamin pills and call you in the morning to say how he or she feels.)

OTHER KEYS TO A SUCCESSFUL PRESENTATION

Besides being prepared with an organized presentation and supporting materials, take into consideration other elements that contribute to an effective presentation.

Adapt your presentation to your prospect. Use what you already know about your prospect and probe further during your presentation, if need be, to determine how to pitch your talk.

One decision is whether to emphasize the product advantages for the consumer, the business opportunity, or both. Some people may be interested only in the product, some mainly in how much they can make marketing that product; some are receptive to both alternatives. Adjust your talk accordingly.

If someone is interested only in being a consumer, let the person know you are also there to serve. And if there is a business opportunity as well, you can always bring up the topic later. In fact, people in network or multi-level marketing find that some of their best distributors start off as consumers only.

Your approach will differ, too, if you are speaking to someone who is only interested in part-time work compared to someone seeking a full-time business opportunity.

Also, adapt your style to what feels comfortable with that person and to the circumstances of the presentation. For instance, you can be more informal with a friend, while it's best to be more professional and formal with a person you don't know. Similarly, give a more organized, slick presentation to a businessman, but when you talk to a housewife or factory worker, present your case in a more down-to-earth, personal-experience way.

Then, too, some people are more relaxed, casual, and friendly, while others feel more comfortable when you keep your distance.

So play every presentation by ear, and in adapting your presentation to your prospect, take into account such factors as your relationship to this person (friend, business associate, stranger); your prospect's occupational background, educational level, and main interest in the program (consumer only, part-time distributor, full-time distributor); your prospect's experience in direct, network, or multi-level sales (for example, no knowledge, some experience, very experienced); and your prospect's personal style (relaxed, casual, informal, warm and friendly versus distant, reserved, aloof, and formal).

Frequently, we make adjustments intuitively as we interact with people. But being aware of these factors helps us further fine-tune the adjustments we make.

Know your facts. This way, you can come up with the answers if your prospect asks for details. Many prospects never ask. But some may, and you should know what to tell them. Otherwise, if you hem and haw, answer evasively, deflect the question, or admit several times that you don't know, you will lose credibility.

Don't make unrealistic claims. Some limited hype can give a prospect or a company pizzazz. But if there is too much of it, you lose credibility, too. For example, don't make extravagant claims for what a product can do. It can be tempting to do so for certain products, such as health products—but don't. People may not believe you, and if people start using the product themselves, they will soon find out what you claimed isn't true.

Likewise, avoid making untrue claims about a program's earning potential. Don't assure prospects they are guaranteed to make "big bucks" or any kind of income, because earnings depend on how much work a person does and consumer response, among other factors. Furthermore, only a small percentage of distributors and sales reps make the fantastic sums widely talked about in multi-level and network sales.

Also, if you make wild claims about possible earnings, using the incomes of the most successful distributors, most people will feel it impossible for them to achieve this much, even if they believe you, and they may not want to undertake a project that seems so overwhelming. By contrast, if you quote figures they can realistically aspire to, they are more likely to act.

Don't argue. If your prospect doesn't like the product or business opportunity, accept this. Not everyone is going to say yes, and if you can't convince your prospect after presenting your program and answering questions and objections, don't feel you have to keep struggling to gain acceptance. And don't feel you have done anything wrong if you can't convince someone. Just accept the fact that different people have different likes and interests, and go on and present your program to someone else.

HOW TO MAKE AN ATTRACTIVE PRESENTATION MANUAL

Once you decide on the general order of your presentation, organize your supporting materials and put them in an attractive binder to make your presentation even slicker.

Some companies have their own training manuals and marketing kits. But often these are extremely detailed and are more for your use than for making a presentation to others, since you want to feature your product in a brief and exciting, easy-to-understand way. It's important to have this detailed product information on hand or perhaps in the appendix of your manual, if someone asks about it. But it is best not to include it in the main section of your manual.

You can dress up your manual by placing individual sheets of paper in plastic sheet protectors. These protectors come in various styles, but the easiest to work with have a three-hole-punched side panel, so you can slip each sheet of paper into its own plastic pocket and don't have to punch holes into the paper itself.

Separate each section (such as "Introduction," "Product or Service," "The Company," "Sponsor Support," and "Marketing Plan") with a divider or introduce it with a title page. You can use rub-on letters to make headlines for this page. Either rub them directly on to the divider or title page, or make a master copy of your title page layout on white paper. Then run off a copy on colored paper or good bond paper.

Gini Graham Scott

Other excellent additions to your manual include charts, graphs, photographs, and other visual materials. If these are not provided by your company or sponsor, you can develop your own fairly easily. For example, cut some pictures out of magazines to illustrate a point. Or transform raw sales figures into a bar graph showing how sales have grown each year.

Some local touches help, too, to show how you have been using the program yourself, who is in your local organization, and what your group has been doing. For example, a section on the backup support your organization provides might include a directory of local people and where they live; a calendar of local activities; a copy of the local newsletter; a chart showing your immediate sponsor and the people in your immediate downline, so prospects can see how they will fit in your organization; and copies of checks received by local distributors or sales reps or by the leaders of your sales group.

You can also include an appendix for more technical product and marketing information. You won't plan to discuss this in your initial presentation, but you have it readily accessible for backup support if anyone asks.

Finally, after you decide what to include in what order, prepare a table of contents so you can easily refer to everything. Also, if your prospect wants to flip through your manual, a table of contents will facilitate this.

Chapter 19

DEVELOPING CUSTOMERS AND TURNING THEM INTO DISTRIBUTORS

One effective approach for building a sales group in network or multi-level marketing is developing customers first and then turning them into distributors. Many people don't use this approach; they zero in on people who want a business opportunity and almost exclusively try to recruit distributors.

But if you consider the vast number of people who are potential consumers versus those who are likely to be serious distributors in a network marketing or MLM business (a ratio of about ten or twenty to one), you'll see the possibilities. Once persons get hooked on the product, they almost automatically tell others about it. Then, if you show them how they can save money by becoming distributors and purchasing wholesale and point out that they can easily make money by doing what they are already doing—telling others about the product—you can readily gain a new distributor.

If you had tried to pitch the business opportunity first, the individuals might have been turned off. But now they like the product and have an ongoing relationship with you, so they are more receptive. Besides, if it's so easy to become a distributor and recruit others, as you did in sponsoring them, then why shouldn't they do it, too?

SOME SUCCESS STORIES

I have met dozens of MLM and network marketing distributors who tried the business-opportunity/recruiting approach without much success. People didn't show up at meetings. Or if they did, they didn't join. Then, if they did join, the distributor found it hard to keep them motivated.

But then these distributors shifted their approach to emphasize the product and being a consumer first. And that worked for them. For example, Bob, a distributor of health foods and vitamins, clipped a few vitamins to the back of his business card, and when he met someone who seemed tired, he would whip out his card and say, "Try them. They'll make you feel really good, and then call me in the morning." Janet, representing a travel program, would invite single people to a fun social evening at her house, and then she showed some slides describing how they could go on exciting low-cost trips. "I don't even try to market to people," she confessed. "But people sign up, and they bring others to sign up, too."

One key to this consumer-into-distributor approach is using the products yourself and telling the people you meet every day about them. For example, Joan, a former high school math teacher, built a business grossing over $10,000 a month in three months by talking to the people she met in supermarkets, at the post office, at the gas station—everywhere. She began by using the products—vitamins and a water dome that purified water. Then, she started talking about them enthusiastically to everyone she met. "I ask them if they're concerned about the water—and what vitamins they take." Then, she recommends what she is using and offers to get the products for them.

But Joan doesn't tell people about the business opportunity in the beginning, because she feels that might turn them off. As she explains, "Many people think multi-level or network marketing is like knocking on doors. But a satisfied customer is really your best distributor. When they see how good the product is, they think of other people they know who might use it. Then, they realize they could sell the product, too."

Another distributor, Barry, who also doesn't go out of his way to contact people, uses an effective three-phase approach to turn customers for his health products into distributors. First, he always has a few sample packs with him, gives out free samples, and asks people to call him the next day to let him know the results. When they call, he finds out about their level of interest. Do they only want to be a consumer and get the product wholesale? Would they like to tell a few friends about the product and make money, too? Would they like to start or expand a home business using this product?

Then, depending on their level of interest, Barry invites them to one of the following: (1) a small product seminar to learn more about the product and other health products; (2) a business opportunity meeting put on by some distributors in the company; or (3) a lunch together to discuss the business opportunity in depth.

Other distributors combine advertising, phoning, and other sales techniques with this consumer-first approach. For example, several distributors I know who are promoting diet and nutrition products advertise their products in a few local papers, and when people call, they talk only about the product. Then, they invite the callers to come to their office to try the product or they arrange to meet in the prospective customer's office or home.

When they have this first meeting, they focus on the product, too. They may mention in passing that there is a business opportunity for people who like the product. But they defer any discussion about this until the person has become an active consumer. That way the person develops a real commitment to the product and doesn't feel under any pressure to make it a business, which is what makes some people resist becoming consumers in the first place.

However, once persons become active consumers, they can be turned around. And some become extremely dynamic distributors. For example, Nancy was seeing a holistic physician who recommended a particular herbal remedy. She used it for several months. Then, after seeing dramatic changes in herself due to the product, she became a strong advocate and began telling others. Gradually, she built a business, and a few months later, her husband joined her in what had become a full-time effort.

MAJOR STRATEGIES

In summary, the network marketing and MLM distributors who have turned consumers into distributors have used most of these strategies:

- They use the product themselves and are highly enthusiastic about it.
- They use every opportunity to talk up their product, and they slip it into the conversation in a casual, informal way by describing it as something that turns them on or can help someone else.
- If the product lends itself to free samples, they give these out and ask the person to call them to report the results; or they call a few days later to follow up.
- If they advertise or use other promotional techniques,

they push the product only, although they may indicate there is a business opportunity, too. But they mention that only as an aside and focus on getting the person to try and use the product.

- They have some product on hand to supply the needs of their retail customers, and they order for their customers, as needed.
- They not only supply their customers with product, but they help them take it successfully. Such assistance is especially important with health or high-technology products, for consumers can easily use the products incorrectly and hence feel dissatisfied or frustrated.
- They invite people to product meetings or demonstrations to get more information on how to use the product and why it works the way it does.
- Once the consumer seems sold on the product, they explain that he or she can purchase the product at wholesale by signing a distributor agreement.
- They also tell the consumer that he or she can make money just by telling other people about the product. Then, if the consumer is interested they invite the person to a business opportunity meeting or they make an individual presentation.
- If the consumer decides to become a distributor, they continue to support and train that individual, just as they would any other distributor.

Chapter 20

PUTTING ON A SMALL MEETING IN YOUR HOME

After you feel comfortable giving individual presentations, a good second step is putting on product demonstrations or business opportunity presentations in your home for small groups. These might include prospects you have invited. Or, if you are working with a few active distributors, invite them to bring guests, too.

Basically, follow the same steps as in a one-on-one presentation. You might add a few gracious touches to make your presentation seem like a semisocial occasion. But keep things comfortable and informal. A few suggestions follow.

Keep your living room or other room where you are meeting arranged as it usually is. You don't want people to feel as if they are in a classroom or theater. If you need extra chairs, scatter them around the room or bring them out later. You want to make the place feel warm and homey.

Have coffee or light refreshments on hand and invite people to help themselves before the meeting starts. This way people can mix and mingle with each other. Some hosts enjoy making special hors d'oeuvres and creating a mini-buffet, which is fine, if you like to do that. But others recommend you don't do anything special and ask people to help themselves, because then your guests don't feel you are going to be trying extra hard to pitch them something they may not want.

Dress comfortably, but well. Dress a little more nicely than you might normally dress to present a good, serious, professional impression. But don't overdo it, because you will seem insincere, and if you dress much more formally than everyone else, others may feel uncomfortable. Essentially, you want to dress just a notch above everyone else, but not much more.

If guests are late or don't show, start the meeting anyway, no later than fifteen minutes after it was scheduled to begin. Frequently, people don't come, so don't worry about this or express concern to others. And don't hold the meeting up for latecomers, because that shows a lack of respect for the people who are there. They have shown enough interest to come—and on time—so pay attention to them. They are the people who are important to you—not the latecomers and no-shows.

Thus, put on the meeting for them, and if latecomers appear, invite them to quietly join the meeting. Indicate that you will be glad to meet with them later to answer their questions about what they may have missed. And *don't* try to start the meeting over for them—a sure way to antagonize the people who were on time.

To begin the meeting, get everyone together in the meeting room, invite them to sit down, and start by making everyone feel comfortable. If everyone knows everyone, a few introductory quips or comments are fine. But if some people are new, start off with introductions. Introduce yourself, and say a little about what you do and how you happened to get into this program. Then, ask the others to introduce themselves in turn and say what they do and why they are here, too.

Then, go into the presentation. As in the one-on-one meeting, you can organize your presentation in a variety of ways, as appropriate for your group, to cover such topics as:

- information on the product or service (including reports on the experience of users, such as yourself);
- a demonstration or hands-on experience with the product;
- a discussion of the company;
- a discussion of the backup support you and your organization provide;
- an introduction to network or multi-level marketing (if any guests are unfamiliar with it); and
- a close, in which you urge people to order or sign up.

Chapter 21

PUTTING ON A
SALES PARTY

The sales party or party plan approach is an excellent way to sell certain products. Pioneered by Stanley Home Products about fifty years ago, the party plan has been the mainstay of companies whose names are now household words, such as Mary Kay, Tupperware, and Avon.

Basically, to put on a sales party, you go to someone's home to sell to a group of individuals who may be interested in the product. Also, you look for consumers at these parties who would like to organize and host parties in their own home or perhaps put on a party like yours.

This approach lends itself particularly well to a product that needs to be demonstrated or needs a personal touch. For example, some products commonly sold via the party plan include cosmetics, jewelry, lingerie, household supplies, gifts, fine glassware, and recently, food. Typically, these products appeal to women, and usually women are the main participants at these parties. The salespeople for companies with these plans commonly have titles indicating they are specialists in the product, such as "beauty consultant" or "fashion representative."

ORGANIZING THE PARTY

Usually, to put on a sales party, you invite a woman to act as a hostess and invite several friends to her home to see your products. (Or if you have a product that appeals to men, too, ask a couple to host the event.) In return, you offer the hostess or host a free gift or percentage of the sales revenue. Or alternatively, some distributors offer the host or hostess $1 for each person present, apart from any gifts or percentages, on the grounds that the host's job is to get the guests there, while the distributor's job is to sell them.

As a variation on this approach, you can contact leaders of social and church groups and offer to put on a party for their group. In this case, the incentive for putting on the party might go to the organization as a whole.

To make sure the hostess or host understands what to do, go over some basics. The hostess should make the setting as comfortable and conducive to selling as possible. Most offer their guests something simple, like coffee and cookies; others include fancy hors d'oeuvres or even turn the event into a potluck before the presentation.

Whatever the arrangements, it is important that the hostess advise the guests they are coming to hear a sales presentation and should bring their checkbooks if they want to purchase anything. This way they come prepared to buy—and no one is miffed because they find the evening is more than a social occasion.

With this proper buildup, the sales party is a good setting for making sales. People who attend usually come for a mixture of reasons, including getting out of the house, doing something different, and finding a good bargain or unique product. A good presentation helps whet their appetite for the product, because it makes the product more exciting and desirable by showing how it is used. So the person can experience using the product, and your role as an authority on the product helps sell it, too. For example, you demonstrate how the cosmetics look and should be used by giving a facial, or you show how a decorative item would look on the wall.

Another reason the sales party can work well is that some guests may view making a purchase as part of the price they pay for an entertaining afternoon or evening. Then, too, some feel an obligation to buy because you and the hostess have entertained them. Further, the sales party creates a captive audience setting, where the excitement of one person is transmitted to everyone else, much as at an auction. When a few people start buying, suddenly others want to buy, too.

You can also use your creativity to turn a sales party into a theatrical event, which helps sales, too. For instance, Donna, a distributor for a high quality lingerie and lounge-wear line, reads poetry while the models walk about to show off different items, leads the audience in a creative visualization technique dealing with love, and has soft music playing in the background. Then, everyone has a chance to try the clothes on, and Donna concludes with a drawing for a door prize. She describes the event as akin to a theater piece, though it is designed to get the participants excitedly visualizing themselves in these clothes and therefore in the mood to buy.

Although your parties may start off small, with perhaps eight to fifteen persons at first, they potentially can become quite large as you do much more than put on a simple sales presentation. Donna, for instance, now gets invitations to put on parties for groups that sometimes draw hundreds of participants.

ATTRACTING PEOPLE
TO THESE PARTIES

While it is the hostess's job to attract people, you should give her some guidelines which you know work. Here are some examples.

Tell the hostess what to say to people to make them excited about coming to the party. Even give her a script and suggested outline—though make your suggestions low-key, so she doesn't feel you are being overly pushy and become resentful.

Advise the hostess that when she invites people, she should ask them to confirm if they are coming and call to cancel if they can't make it. Impress upon your hostess that it is important to do this, because otherwise people can get very lackadaisical about coming or not, and it becomes impossible to plan for the event.

Urge the hostess to check out the date in advance before she sets it to be sure there are no major conflicts that might affect those people she plans to invite. For example, one hostess scheduled a house party for the date of a big office party most of her friends were attending, so the sales party bombed.

Make up an attractive flyer, give the hostess a white master copy, and invite her to make up flyers to send to her friends. The flyer should announce the sales party and make it sound exciting. For example, use descriptions like "fun," "new," "a chance to see unique products." Also, the flyer should include a phone number to RSVP and directions to the event, unless the hostess is only inviting neighbors or people who have been to her house before. By sending a flyer, the event seems even more important. Then, after a few days, the hostess should call anyone who hasn't responded, to further enthuse people who might be still deciding about the value of attending the event.

Give the hostess an incentive for attracting people. Some distributors offer the hostess a 10–20 percent discount on her own purchases or a free gift; but it's more motivating to give her a percentage of the purchases made by the people she invites, or to give her a flat payment—say one dollar per person—for each person who attends.

When you put on a party, use your imagination to provide some dramatic flair. For example, one friend was the hit of the party when she presented a line of sensual items with a running commentary of deadpan humor. Another created a mini–stage show when she put on cosmetics demonstrations. A third put on fashion shows using the guests as volunteers to show off a clothing line. Use your own creativity to put "oomph" in your own program.

Also, be sure to let everyone know in advance that the products are for sale. Some distributors pass out a list of sales items and prices at the beginning of the program, so people can follow along as they show particular items. Others pass out their order forms after the presentation.

But in either case, people should know they have an opportunity to buy something. Then, at the end of the presentation, invite people to order. It helps to include some incentive to persuade them to buy now, rather than send in their order after they get home, because many people won't follow through. For example, if they order now, you might offer them a 10-percent discount or a free gift.

Just before the program breaks up so that people can buy, invite the guests to give parties of their own. Let them know they will receive a special gift if they do (although don't talk about getting a percentage of sales, because that makes them think about how the hostess will get a percentage of what they buy now). Also, if you are looking for additional distributors, say you'll be glad to talk to anyone who might like to put on his or her own party as a representative of the company like you. Indicate that you want to take care of any sales first; but you can meet after that with anyone who wants to set up an appointment to talk further.

After your presentation, ask people to bring up their orders. Meanwhile, as you fill these, the others can socialize and enjoy the snacks the hostess has prepared. Afterward, meet with anyone who wants to host a party or put on one as a company rep.

Finally, thank the hostess and give her any share of the sales or gifts that are due.

At many of these parties, you will find that most of the guests want to be customers, and a few may be interested in hosting a party. Finding a potential distributor takes longer.

However, even if no one wants to host a party at the time, you may be able to convert customers into hosts or part of your sales team later. The way to do this is through follow-up.

Some programs already have a system for this. For example, the Mary Kay representative normally follows up with each customer to find out how she (and sometimes he) is using the products and whether she (or he) needs anything else. The rep also uses this time to explore whether the customer might like to organize or put on a party, too.

You can do the same in any program. Just call your customers within a few days and offer to help if the person would like some consulting or needs more product. If the person seems to have become an avid consumer, ask if she (or he) would like to host a party, learn how to get the products wholesale, or put on a party like yours.

Then, tailor your follow-up according to what the person wants. As appropriate, set up another meeting to give him or her more product or help him or her use it; demonstrate how to organize and host a party; or explain how to become a company rep.

Chapter 22

OTHER CREATIVE WAYS TO PRESENT YOUR PROGRAM

The possibilities for marketing your program creatively are endless. And the more exciting, the more interesting you make your activities, the more enthusiasm you'll create for your product or service.

ATTRACTING PEOPLE TO HEAR YOUR MESSAGE BY CREATING AN EVENT

One way to attract people who may be potential customers or distributors is to present your program as part of an event that's interesting in and of itself. Such events are also a way to keep the present distributors in your organization excited and involved.

The important thing is to make your event enjoyable and fun. You want to appeal to people as consumers first—so they really like your product or how you present it. Then, if they are sold on the event, they may not only want to be customers but may be interested in promoting the product or service, too.

You are only limited by your imagination. Use the following ideas as a jumping-off point. Then plan events that fit your own product, your personal style, and the tastes of the people you expect to attend.

For example, we have used social interaction and communication games (published by Gameworld) as a means of attracting sizable groups of people to a fun event (usually about ten to twenty persons each time), and before that event we presented one or two product demonstrations. As "for instances," we have invited people to a Computer and Games Night; a Get Healthy with Games Night; a Food, Fun, and Games Night; a Travel and Games Night; and more.

At another successful series of events we call a Gala Game Fair, which averages about thirty-five to fifty persons, we started off with a mini-trade show. We invited people to bring their literature and demonstrate their products, and we provided an area with table space for this purpose. Usually six or seven persons came armed with products, and everyone had a chance to mix informally for about forty-five minutes to learn about them. Then, we played games.

A woman from Beverly Hills used a travel party approach to market a travel program to singles. She sent out invitations, using her list of hundreds of single partygoers, and prepared for a swinging Beverly Hills–style party with all the trimmings. She charged ten dollars at the door, served up exotic salads and party dips, let people mingle for about a half hour, and showed a brief travel slide show, which described both the program and some highlights of the marketing plan. Afterward, people had a chance to sign up with their sponsor or take literature home. Those who wanted—usually about half the guests—were able to party in earnest.

Other Possibilities

Here are some suggestions for other types of events that could help create enthusiasm for your program.

A Potluck Dinner and Product Presentation. Invite everyone to bring a dish, and coordinate what people bring, so you have a good mixture of courses. And if you are marketing a food product, so much the better.

A Get-Together for the Neighbors. Invite them by leaving flyers for them at their door or in their mailbox after the regular mail delivery comes (postal workers sometimes confiscate unofficial mail). On your flyer, explain that you are involved in an exciting new program, and you would like to invite your neighbors to a festive occasion to tell them about it. Also, note that this is a chance for the neighbors to get together to know each other better.

A Show-and-Tell Evening. Invite everyone to bring whatever they want, and encourage the performers to perform. You, of course, demonstrate your product or service.

A Movable Feast. This is a party that moves from one house or location to another within a relatively small area. You set up a few stops along the way—typically one for hors d'oeuvres, another for the main course, a third for dessert, and possibly a final blowout party. Then, at each place, you feature something different. For example, you might have an amateur performer at one, a dance lesson at another, a game at a third, and, of course, at one site your product or service presentation.

A Barbecue or Picnic. In this case, it's best to have a product that fits in with the ongoing activities, such as a low-calorie candy, a bakery product line, or toys and games. Then, in a fun way, people get to sample the product and perhaps buy it.

A Workshop or Class Dealing with a Topic Related to Your Product. This is a great way to get some free exposure, and perhaps even get paid for your advice. For example, suppose you're marketing a health product. You can work up a lecture or program on a subject such as "Techniques for Getting Healthy." Or if you're working with a food program, try offering a class on "Good Nutrition." You can advertise your classes or workshops locally, or offer to put on the program for some group.

A Health Fair, with Demonstrations of Health Techniques. It helps if you're promoting a health product, but since health is defined so broadly these days, almost any product can be worked in. The event might include people giving massages, demonstrating exercises, or leading a meditation. Also, you give a brief demonstration of how your product works to promote health. (Be creative if it's not specifically a health product.)

An Entrepreneur Exchange. A great promotional event. You can get a group you belong to to sponsor this or join a business group that puts these on. People come to these exchanges prepared to learn about other products and services and talk about their own. Usually, there is a table for product literature where people display their materials and business cards. Also, people have a chance to mix and mingle around. Sometimes there is a speaker on a business topic; sometimes not. In some cases, some or all of the attendees may have a chance to give a brief commercial about the product or service they offer, and this can vary from a few seconds to a few minutes, depending upon the size of the group. Commonly about twenty-five to fifty persons attend an average gathering, though some events may draw one hundred, two hundred, even more.

Frequently, the members of these groups are not marketing any product or service themselves, so this is an excellent opportunity to introduce your product to a new audience.

And you can probably think of many other ideas.

In putting on these programs, you should have two major goals:

1. To show off your product or service so that people will like it but won't feel under any presure to buy or sign up on the spot. You get their cards; you give out yours; later, you follow up.
2. To show that you are a fun, creative person to work with—so people will want to join your organization. As they can see by your participation in or organization of these events, they are not just buying or marketing a product. They also have a chance to become part of an enjoyable, supportive group of people. And that combination is hard to beat!

Part V

BUILDING A
SALES ORGANIZATION

Chapter 23

THE BASIC PRINCIPLES OF BUILDING AN ORGANIZATION

If you are involved in a network marketing, multi-level sales, or other direct sales program that encourages building a sales organization, you will want to start working on that as soon as you feel ready to start recruiting or sponsoring new distributors. If your company doesn't have such a program or you simply prefer to sell direct yourself, skip this section and go on to Part VI.

Once you have your first distributor, start training and helping that person learn the business, so he or she can start presenting the program and finding customers and recruits.

Initially, plan to spend most of your time looking for new distributors yourself, as well as continuing to make retail sales. But gradually, as you develop a distributor group, expect to spend less and less time yourself on sponsoring. In fact, after you get five or six active, first-line distributors, stop almost all sponsoring activity to concentrate on motivating and training your distributors and helping them build up their own organizations. Perhaps spend about 90 percent of your time working with them.

This principle is crucial. Until your distributors have developed their own groups, you don't have a solid organization yourself, because your distributors can easily get discouraged and drop out. You'll find they will start to become really enthusiastic only when they can see their own organizations develop and grow.

THE IMPORTANCE OF HELPING YOUR DISTRIBUTORS

You need to do everything you can to help your distributors who are serious. One of the most common reasons for failure in network or multi-level marketing is not doing this. Frequently, such neglect leading to failure is a problem for people with sales, and particularly direct sales, backgrounds. They get very excited about the program at first and feel like going out to sponsor the world. But if they do, they have no time to work with the individuals already signed up. So while they are sponsoring new persons, the first recruits are feeling ignored and confused about what to do, and so they drift away.

Thus, getting a lot of people on your front line is not the way to success in building an effective sales group. The secret is building a solid foundation in depth by helping your distributors gain their own success. You'll make less in the beginning, because you'll be giving up some of your immediate retail volume and first-level sales commissions when you take the time to work with your people. And in most network and MLM companies, the commissions are less as you go down each level.

But by building in depth, your organization will expand

exponentially, and you'll more than make up for the smaller commissions by the size of your organization on which you will collect commissions.

In fact, to promote this growth, many distributors enlist many new recruits under their active distributors—to help the latter build their organizations—rather than putting these new persons on their own front lines.

THE PRINCIPLE OF SPONSORING, TEACHING, AND DUPLICATION

You'll hear it again and again in network and multi-level marketing. The key to success is sponsoring, teaching, and duplication. That means when you sponsor someone, your responsibilities have just started because you must teach that person how to market the product and recruit others in order to duplicate yourself. Then, you have to teach that person how to teach those he or she sponsors to teach others how to market and recruit, too. Chart 42 illustrates this relationship.

In other words, the key principle is, *Teach those you sponsor how to teach those they sponsor to teach those they sponsor*, and so on down the line. For in this way, by sponsoring and teaching, sponsoring and teaching, *you duplicate yourself*.

This is how you build a strong chain of individuals—by sponsoring and teaching each of your first-level recruits how to sponsor and teach others to do the same. And like any chain, it is only as strong as its weakest link. So if anyone you sponsor drops out of the chain, reach down to the next link to connect it to your organization.

Thus, if you sponsor John and teach him how to market the product, and he sponsors Nancy but subsequently drops out, then you teach Nancy yourself. For then your organization can

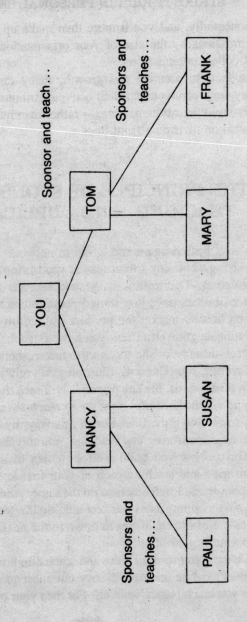

CHART 42: THE PRINCIPLE OF SPONSORING AND TEACHING

YOU

Sponsor and teach...

TOM

NANCY

Sponsors and teaches...

FRANK

MARY

SUSAN

PAUL

Sponsors and teaches...

continue to grow under Nancy. But if you don't reach down to Nancy, she is probably going to feel abandoned and drop out.

THE PRINCIPLE OF
ONLY SPONSORING PERSONS
YOU CAN WORK WITH

In order to carry out your teaching responsibilities effectively, you can't have too many people on your front lines. You should only sponsor as many people directly as you can work with effectively.

Many distributors believe you can only work with up to five, perhaps at most six or seven, active distributors at a time. Once one active distributor is successfully launched with his or her own organization and no longer needs your help, you can add another first-level distributor to take that person's place. But if you try to work with more than this recommended limit at one time, these distributors believe, you will be spreading yourself too thin.

Don Failla presents a case for this approach in *How to Build a Large Successful Multi-Level Marketing Organization*. He claims that in the military—in the army, navy, air force, marines, and coast guard—with rare exceptions, nobody directly supervises more than five or six persons because the military has found that this approach works best. So if these military agencies with over two hundred years of experience have come to this conclusion, Failla states, those in MLM should follow their example.

Some distributors, however, claim it is possible to work with more first-line people if you use a more efficient training approach. For example, I have heard many professional marketing people say that you can work with up to ten active first-level people if you supply them with good training materials, so you need to spend less time training them. Your distributors can simply read the materials to learn about some of the basics, and you don't have to spend that time explaining fundamentals. Instead, you can use your time more profitably to sponsor others, sell product, travel, or learn more about promoting the program yourself.

So, presumably, under this theory, you can give this book, *Strike It Rich in Personal Selling*, to your new distributors or recommend they get a copy, so they can read it for answers to their many questions about how to work the business.

Then, if you urge your own distributors to do the same with the persons they sponsor, so they can work with ten others, and their distributors can work with ten others, too, you can maximize your earnings exponentially, or so the theory goes. For then, supposedly, instead of your organization growing at a multiplication factor of 5 ($5 \times 5 \times 5 = 125$) or a multiplication factor of 6 ($6 \times 6 \times 6 = 216$), it zooms ahead with a factor of 10 ($10 \times 10 \times 10 = 1,000$). And at levels four and five, it expands at an even more dramatic pace.

Now this approach of giving out good training materials to reduce the time you spend on nonessentials with distributors is certainly valid to some extent. Also, this approach may substantially cut down on the total amount of time you spend with each person, so you can work with more first-level persons and perhaps work with some additional individuals by mail. Further, it may free you to spend more quality time with each of your distributors.

However, it is important to recognize that much of the time you spend with your distributors is not just for training; to stay motivated, most network marketing and MLM people also need personal and social contact. So your distributors not only want your knowledge; they look on you as a friend and supporter, too. They don't just want to read about basic principles, but they may want to hear about some of this material from you, too, or see how you put it into practice. So if you just hand your distributors a manual and expect them to get most or all of their training from it and stay active and motivated, that's not enough. *You have to truly give of yourself and show you care about them, too.*

BUILDING DOWN THREE LEVELS

To make the chain of individuals in your organization really solid, you must build down three deep, and you must explain to your distributors that they must build three deep and explain this to their recruits, too. This three-deep principle is illustrated in the three steps on Chart 43.

Until you have taught John to teach Nancy to teach Jack, you haven't fully duplicated yourself, because if Nancy isn't able to sponsor anyone, she is likely to drop out, and that will discourage John. Or she may fail to teach Jack, and he may have trouble continuing in the business. Thus, if you don't duplicate yourself, your whole organization can easily fizzle out.

This is why many marketing professionals in this field suggest reaching down to your second and third levels to work with the people there who have the most initiative. To locate them, you can ask each of your directly-sponsored persons who is the strongest, highest-initiative person on his or her first level, indicate you are willing to work with that person, and ask the best way to do it. Then, you can ask that person who is his or her strongest, highest-initiative person, and offer to work with that person, too. (However, if you do encounter any resistance along the way, don't be pushy. Just say you are making a standing offer and want to help whenever they would like your assistance.)

CHART 43: THE KEY TO BUILDING AN ORGANIZATION BY SPONSORING AND TEACHING DOWN THREE LEVELS

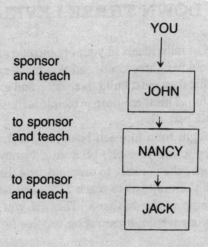

YOU

sponsor
and teach

JOHN

to sponsor
and teach

NANCY

to sponsor
and teach

JACK

STEP #1   YOU SPONSOR JOHN.

STEP #2   YOU TEACH JOHN HOW TO MARKET THE PRODUCT AND SPONSOR NANCY.

STEP #3   YOU TEACH JOHN HOW TO TEACH NANCY TO MARKET THE PRODUCT, SPONSOR JACK, AND TEACH JACK.

THEN JOHN KNOWS HOW TO DO IT AND HAS STARTED BUILDING HIS OWN ORGANIZATION SUCCESSFULLY.

Once you have located these serious second- and third-level persons, offer to help in various ways. For example, call them from time to time or send them mailings to keep them posted on what's happening; offer to speak at a meeting for them; or include them in your regular meetings and special programs if they live in your area. And be sure to let their immediate sponsor know how they are doing, too. Use Chart 44 for keeping track.

The value of this approach—working with the hot performers under you—is that it helps motivate those in between. They see those under them really moving, and that inspires them to do more, too. (Conversely, if one of your first- or second-level distributors doesn't catch fire, you can alway work with the hot performers he or she has referred to you and continue building your organization under them.)

Also, teach your first-level people to use this technique. For then you will truly build your organization in depth—and your distributors will build this way, too.

As you can see by Chart 45, reaching down three levels helps to spark everyone upline to the person you have helped. For example, you reach down to help Nancy, so she is able to sponsor and teach others, and that helps to keep John actively involved in the program, because he can see that it is working. Or if you reach down to help Jack, you will encourage Nancy, and her excitement will feed back up to John. It's a little like lighting a fire. The flame of excitement you light down two or three levels in your organization travels right up the line.

Then, when your first-level distributors have built their own solid organizations which are three levels deep, they can carry on without you. And then you have truly duplicated yourself.

Thus, *once you have sponsored someone, it's more important for you to help that person sponsor someone else than to*

CHART 44: NAMES OF SECOND- AND THIRD-LEVEL HOT PERFORMERS

First-Level Person Sponsored by Me:

Name: _____
Address: _____
City, State, Zip: _____
Phone: _____

Second-Level Referrals:

Name: _____
Address: _____
City, State, Zip: _____
Phone: _____

Third-Level Referrals:

Name: _____
Address: _____
City, State, Zip: _____
Phone: _____

Second-Level Referrals:

Name: _____
Address: _____
City, State, Zip: _____
Phone: _____

Third-Level Referrals:

Name: _____
Address: _____
City, State, Zip: _____
Phone: _____

find and sponsor another person yourself. That's the way you
build in depth.

THE PRINCIPLE OF BUILDING
AN ORGANIZATION
ON SOLID FOUNDATIONS

As you sponsor others and they do the same, your organization will gradually take shape.

Initially, this is likely to be a slow process, and you shouldn't
expect to see any major earnings for several months. Even if
your organization approximately doubles every few weeks, it
will be quite small in the beginning. For example:

Week 1	Week 2	Week 3	Week 4	Week 5	Week 6	Week 7
1	2	4	8	16	32	64

So it is only after the seventh week that you will really see
any major expansion. But once your organization takes off,
its growth can be tremendous.

The process is frequently compared by network marketing
and MLM people to building a house. You have to take the
time to lay down the solid foundations first. Then you can
build. Don Failla compares your initial sponsoring of five or
six persons to digging the foundations with a shovel or spade.
Then, as you teach them to sponsor, so that they bring in about
twenty-five second-level persons, that's like clearing the area
with a bulldozer. Next, when you teach these individuals to
teach others, so the total numbers about 125, he compares it
to bringing in the steam shovels and excavating down to bed-
rock, where you can build. Then, you can really start con-
struction in earnest, for when you are four deep, your

CHART 45: THE IMPORTANCE OF REACHING DOWN THREE LEVELS

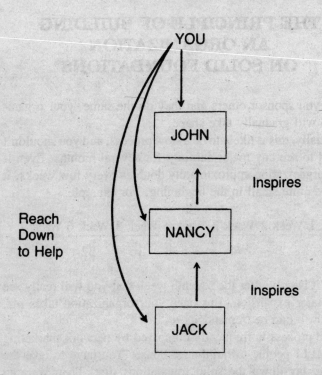

organization will spurt up quickly, and since you have created a strong foundation, it will stay up.

Before you get to this point, it can seem as if it is taking months and months—almost forever—for anything to happen. But if you have built deep, you will see the structure start to rise out of the ground and then grow rapidly.

The key to this rapid growth is building the solid foundation first. And that means working closely with your key first-level persons, and sometimes a few second- and third-level hot performers, training them so they know what to do and will sponsor and teach those under them to do the same.

Chapter 24

HELPING YOUR
NEW DISTRIBUTORS
GET STARTED

Once you have sponsored someone in a network marketing or MLM program, meet with him or her personally to help the individual get started. There are some basics you should go over with everyone, whether experienced in this type of marketing or not, and sóme special topics you should cover with newcomers.

THE BASICS TO COVER
IN YOUR FIRST MEETING

Get to Know Your New Distributor

If you don't know the person you are sponsoring well or at all, use this first meeting to get to know him or her better. You can do this informally, if this is your personal style and you are working with only a few distributors. Or if you prefer a more formal approach and have a number of front-line distributors, you can use an interview and questionnaire approach.

Debbie Ballard advocates this technique in *Secrets of Multi-Level Fortune Building*. She has an interview session with each new distributor in which she gets to know the person by asking about his or her work background, education, hobbies, interests, family life, and goals and objectives. She also asks the person to fill out a questionnaire, explaining that she is not trying to pry but wants the information so she can serve him or her better. Then, Ballard keeps the results in the distributor's personal file and refers to the card when she calls.

Go Over Company Products, Policies, and Procedures

At this first meeting, also go over the product, marketing plan, background of the company, and company literature, so the new distributor fully understands the program and knows where to go to find needed information. Usually, a new distributor will only recall the major highlights of your original presentation or opportunity meeting. So you need to go over key points in more depth, or at least indicate what the distributor should read to review these points.

It is also important to make sure your distributor clearly understands how to fill out the distributor application and product order forms. Go over them carefully, and ideally, provide a sample of how to fill these out (sometimes provided in company literature—or make copies of your own filled-out forms).

This review may sound elementary, but it is extremely vital, since you may lose commissions if orders are written incorrectly or if sponsorship information is unclear. So make sure your new distributor knows how to fill out company forms correctly and will advise his or her recruits about the correct procedures, too.

A good way to make sure everything is correct is to suggest that your new distributor process the first few applications and orders through you. Then, you can double-check to be certain the distributor has filled out the forms correctly and has printed clearly and hard enough. If not, you can readily correct any errors and advise the distributor accordingly.

Find Out about Your Distributor's Marketing Interests and Background

Another topic to cover is how active your new distributor wants to be, so you can assist accordingly and work within the person's limits.

It also helps to know what background this person has in marketing and direct sales, because this is an indicator of how much help she (or he) is likely to need. If someone already has a strong background in other direct sales, network marketing, or multi-level companies, she will already know the basic principles of this type of marketing and many sales techniques. But if she is new to the field, you will have much more training to do.

Suggest How Your New Distributor Can Start at Once

The specifics vary from program to program, but some of the things marketing people tell new distributors to do are: (1) make a list of all the people you know, (2) decide how many hours you want to devote to contacting people, (3) set up your goals for the week, indicating how many individuals you plan to contact and how many you intend to sell and sponsor, (4) allot a certain number of hours for reading about the program and for reading motivational and instructional literature, and (5) start at once!

Connect Your Distributor with Your Local Network

Let your new distributor know where any opportunity meetings are being held; also provide the names and numbers of key contacts in the area, including your group leader or upline sponsor.

Offer Your Assistance

Offer to put on some meetings for your distributors, too. Indicate that they can call you at any time to ask questions and get advice. Let them know you are only too glad to help.

HOW TO HELP A DISTRIBUTOR WHO IS NEW TO NETWORK MARKETING OR MLM

If persons are new, you need to explain the basics to them, and you may need a few extra preliminary meetings to do this. Some things to tell new distributors are discussed below.

• *Recommend or give some marketing materials to distributors to read.*
You can recommend or give them some books to read, like this one, that describe basic principles and techniques. Also, encourage them to read some motivational and success books.

Yet be sure that when you suggest these books, the persons understand you will continue to give them your support. If they need help or want to review with you anything they have read, you will be glad to assist.

• *Talk about the importance of setting goals.*

Explain how setting goals and writing them down is a crucial step toward achieving them. Also, note how breaking down larger goals into small, manageable day-by-day or week-by-week goals makes them easier to accomplish. Point out that building a sales organization will help them attain other goals, such as financial security or wealth.

• *Advise newcomers to look on their first month as a training period—but to start now!*

Keep newcomers motivated and reassured about their early progress. They should still get started immediately, but they shouldn't feel under pressure to produce results while they are getting familiar with the program and the techniques of network marketing or MLM.

Urge them to sell product and sponsor others as soon as possible, because this will give them a feeling of accomplishment. But make sure they understand that it's okay to take it slow, and they don't have to feel they are not doing enough or have failed if they don't start selling the product or building an organization from the beginning.

The virtue of this start-now-while-in-training strategy is that it has the advantage of getting your new people going right away. Yet it gives them permission to make mistakes and learn.

It's good to get your new distributors started immediately, too, while the excitement of signing into a new venture is still upon them. Encouraging them to get out and "do it now" builds momentum. Also, this approach speeds up the time when they get their bonus check. If people wait, they don't get their bonus check right away. And if the people they sign up wait, too, the whole earnings cycle is lengthened for everyone.

Moreover, if people wait to do anything, fears can build up that destroy confidence, such as the concern, "Do I know enough about my product, company, or sales techniques to present my program properly?"

But if a person gets started quickly, he or she can begin feeling the confidence that comes from an early success. Also, the person is less apt to lose out on sponsoring someone he or she plans to contact because someone else has already sponsored that prospect.

On the other hand, you want to balance this push to get started with the reassurance that the newcomer is still in training, so he or she is prepared for the possible mistakes and setbacks that may occur while he or she is learning.

You need to prepare newcomers for network or multi-level marketing in this way because they can easily get discouraged if things are slow at first. So, explain about the principle of building a strong foundation, and let them know they shouldn't expect to see large returns right away. As needed, go over the principles about how network marketing or MLM works and how their early hard work will eventually pay off handsomely because of the multiplication principle of this type of marketing. Stress that they should concentrate on learning about the product, how to get customers, and sponsoring distributors, and that you will help them do it.

In short, although you should tell your new distributors to regard this first month or so as a training period, you should urge them to get going right away, for, having just signed up, they still have that new-recruit enthusiasm. But if they wait to do something, this enthusiasm can easily be lost, and you will have to stimulate it again. *So give your new distributor some activities to do right away. Get him or her started now, even though in training.*

• *Urge newcomers not to compare themselves to experienced people in the program; they should focus on what they need to do to get started.*

This principle is important, because newcomers must understand and accept where they are starting and not think they are hopelessly behind, because someone with much more experience is doing so much better than they are. Frequently, people in network marketing or MLM look at the success of leaders who have massive downlines and are making tremendous incomes and think, "I'll never be able to catch up." So you need to point out that these leaders were at one time in their position, and they have to understand that it takes time and training to achieve this great success. But they can do it if they work hard. After all, if they were joining a corporation, they wouldn't expect to be one of the officers overnight. They would have to put in years and years of work.

Thus, they should focus on what they need to do right now and consider that they are spending the next few weeks in training learning the business. Also, they should think of their progress in light of their own goals, for they are building their own business. In other words, they must concentrate on running their own race. This way, everyone wins, for there is no "better" or "less than." Each person uses his or her own yardstick to measure progress.

• *Prepare your new distributor for rejection.*

Explain that not everyone will be interested in the program, so your new distributor doesn't start out with unrealistically high expectations and get let down. Explain about the typical averages: about three contacts for everyone who is interested; about three contacts with interested persons to get a sign-up; and about one in every three to five sign-ups become active.

Stress that your new distributor needs to discount rejection and continue ahead, because only a certain percentage of people contacted will be interested, so he or she should focus on finding them.

• *Tell new recruits a few proven things they must do to be successful in your program.*

Your new distributors could become successful using other strategies, of course. But by giving them a small list of things to do, they don't get stymied considering several alternatives. Instead, they have an immediate workable plan of action.

One distributor explains the success of the strategy this way: "I make my recommendations sound like a requirement, and I list these recommendations as specific steps my distributors must follow. That way people feel they have to do it, start doing something right away, and don't have time to think about all the alternatives and get confused about what to do next."

PUTTING ON MEETINGS
FOR YOUR NEW DISTRIBUTOR

In the beginning, your new distributor, even one with some network marketing or MLM experience, will be uncertain about the particulars of the program and the marketing plan, and therefore will lack confidence in presenting the program. Accordingly, to help your new distributor get started, offer to assist him or her in putting on his or her first meetings—even if these are with only one or two prospects.

Many successful network and MLM marketers recommend that their new distributor invite a few people over—then they will come and give the presentation. Others who are doing ongoing meetings invite the new distributor to bring guests. Or in some cases, when a new distributor is extremely busy but does have good contacts, these marketers offer to speak to their distributor's referrals without the distributor having to be present. Then, if the referral is interested the marketer signs him or her up under the new distributor.

Use whatever approach works best for you. Ideally, your

new distributors should be present to learn what to do, either by seeing your example or by presenting part of the meeting themselves. Then, after the meeting, it helps to go over what happened in it, to make your distributors more aware of what you included in your presentation and why. This is also a time to answer questions about the company or its products and to discuss the elements that contribute to an effective presentation (such as good visual aids, a varied tone, enthusiasm, and so on).

Initially, you may want to handle the whole presentation. But as soon as your distributors feel comfortable, encourage them to give parts of the presentation. Then, perhaps they might do the whole thing, while you offer moral support and backup in case they ask for your input on some topic or question raised in the meeting that they can't answer.

This process of training your distributors to put on meetings accomplishes three things:

1. It systematically prepares them to make effective presentations, and thereby gives them the confidence to do so.
2. When you present the meeting with skill, which comes from practice, this gives the program a solid, professional image, which makes the prospects invited by your new distributor more likely to sign up. If the new distributor had presented the program alone to them, they might have been more skeptical, particularly if they were friends and associates. But you are an outside authority figure, and so your presence makes the program and presentation seem more impressive, whether you actually lead the meeting or not.
3. When you assist your new distributors with presentations it helps to inspire and motivate them, be-

cause it shows you truly care about them and want to help them succeed.

STAYING IN TOUCH WITH YOUR NEW DISTRIBUTOR

Once you get your new distributors started, continue to stay in touch. Encourage your distributors to call you for help or just to let you know how things are going. But even if they don't call at first, contact them initially a few times to show you really do want to help.

When you do make contact, do so in a supportive way. Don't ask your distributors point-blank how many people they have sponsored or how many customers they have sold. That tends to put them on the spot and make them feel they are working for you. Or it makes them feel they should be doing more than they are doing, or that all you care about is how much money they are making for you. Furthermore, those who have some resistance to the idea of selling will be particularly disturbed.

Instead, when you call, be positive and encouraging, and offer information. You want to make your distributors *want* to do something, and not make them feel guilty if they haven't done something or haven't done enough. Some things you might call to tell them about are an upcoming meeting you are sponsoring; some company events you just heard about; a new technique someone is using that is working well; a training program you are planning for new distributors; an offer to meet with them personally to go over the program and answer any questions; a recommendation about an exciting new success or marketing techniques book you have just read; a request for information you can put in your local newsletter for distributors.

Then, as long as your new distributor seems enthusiastic and responsive and begins calling you occasionally, keep in contact.

In time, your distributor won't be as dependent on your assistance. But even so, stay in touch. Doing so helps to create a strong family feeling that will spread through your network, for your distributor is likely to emulate you and stay in touch with his or her own people, too. In turn, these bonds help to create and maintain a strong sales network. You are not just marketing the product, but are developing and continuing to express warm friendly feelings toward one another, which makes marketing the program satisfying and fun. And this helps to keep motivation and involvement high.

FOCUSING YOUR TIME ON YOUR BEST DISTRIBUTORS

At first, be encouraging and helpful to all of your distributors, because you don't know who is going to be the most serious and committed. But as you find out which distributors want to do the most, devote your time to them. They will be your most eager and productive distributors if you help them get started right. So invest your time most productively by giving most of your help to them.

You might think of working with your distributors in the following way. When they first come into the business, they are essentially unknown quantities—"silver ships," as Don Failla calls them. Or perhaps, think of them as newborn stars. Each one has the potential to make it to the top—as a ship whose cargo turns to gold or as a star that becomes a brightly burning sun. Conversely, any new distributor can fizzle out, just as a ship might lose its cargo or a star might explode or burn itself out. To some extent, you can help an individual become a shining star or gold-cargoed ship. But what the person brings to the business—in the form of personal traits, attitudes, values, and skills—will affect the outcome, too. It's just as it is when we're born, we all have a unique potential that can be developed so we can become successful in some way. But then our environment—our parents, friends, experiences, and so on—shapes us, too.

In a similar way, you play a key part in what your new distributor becomes. But if your new distributor doesn't respond, back off. You can only do so much. You can't keep an empty ship afloat or a burnt-out star burning.

So go on and *work with your distributors who show they really want to succeed and really want your help.*

There are certain signs to look for in selecting your most enthusiastic distributors.

They are actively interested in the products and the program, and they indicate this by buying and using the products or taking time to learn more about the business.

They are excited and enthusiastic about the business. They believe the program works, and they are eager to go out and promote it—or are already doing so.

They want to learn more, and they call you frequently to ask for additional information.

They ask you to help them in training and sponsoring others.

They are goal oriented, and have specific things they want to achieve.

They have a positive outlook, and as a result, it is enjoyable to work and socialize with them.

They have made up a list of people to contact, and are continually thinking about whom they might approach.

These are the people to work with and help, since they are actively and eagerly looking for your assistance. If you help them, they will build your organization.

But if you devote too much time to distributors who don't have this kind of spark—or don't develop it—this will pull you down. For example, when you call these distributors and offer to help, they will tend not to appreciate your offer. Rather, they may feel you are being pushy or trying to pressure them. Or they might regale you with complaints and gripes. And if you get too much negative input, you can lose your own enthusiasm and sense of direction.

So once you get this negative feedback from people, stay away and help your responsive distributors. Then, as they succeed, your other distributors may get inspired and come around, too.

Chapter 25

HAVING MEETINGS
FOR YOUR DISTRIBUTORS

Besides talking with your new distributors by phone from time to time, arrange regular meetings for distributors in the area. Individual meetings are particularly helpful in the beginning so you can develop a closer working relationship and deal with individual concerns. However, as soon as you have two or more distributors, have some group meetings, too. These are useful to plan joint strategies, discuss various problems and issues, and spark enthusiasm because of the dynamics of a group. For example, when you speak to one person, someone else who is just listening can sometimes gain more from the conversation and become more excited than the person to whom you are talking.

Different distributors use different types of meetings to build their organization. These include inspirational and motivational meetings; training meetings; sales, planning, and strategy meetings; brainstorming sessions; and social activities and events. And some meetings include a combination of activities or a little bit of everything. Examples of these are the "sizzle sessions" that many distributors have to inspire and train their people and to plan strategies.

In this chapter we'll describe each of these types of meetings in turn—though remember, you can always combine activities together. The main difference is in the primary focus of the meeting.

INSPIRATIONAL AND MOTIVATIONAL MEETINGS

These meetings emphasize overall goals and incentives rather than specific sales targets. Their purpose is to keep persons enthusiastic about the program and about working at it to become successful.

One approach that many distributors use is to help their group members feel more confident by going over success principles. To employ this approach, ask about topics such as having the right success attitude. Discuss those who have become successful and how they "made it." Invite motivational speakers and top distributors in your company to talk to your group. Or suggest that people read certain motivational and inspirational writings, and discuss these at the meetings. You can also invite some group members to give testimonials describing how they have accomplished some goal successfully. Or feature uplifting talks about becoming successful.

You might even combine these sessions with group-involving motivational activities, such as giving cheers ("Hip, hip, hooray, for..."), making expansive self-introductions ("I'm the *great*..."), singing upbeat songs ("Oh, I'm headed for the top"), and giving everyone in arms' reach a hug.

One distributor begins his inspirational meetings by having each person tell something positive that has happened in promoting the product or in building his or her sales organization. Then, at the meeting, participants talk about success principles, listen to inspirational tapes, discuss motivational books, and the like.

Another distributor for a health program uses his inspirational meetings to build confidence, so people continue to believe in themselves and have a "healthy attitude that's compatible with the program they're promoting." He has motivational speakers talk about the human potential and plays motivational tapes by well-known speakers such as Earl Nightingale. Also, he gives his people inspirational and positive books to read, such as *The Greatest Salesman in the World*, by Og Mandino. Then, at the meeting, people discuss these books.

A second approach at these motivational meetings is to go over the special incentives to success offered by your company that have extra appeal beyond cash alone because they are tangible symbols of success and status. For example, some of these company rewards may include diamond, gold, and silver jewelry, furs, boats, luxury cars, houses, and trips to exciting places like Hawaii, Japan, and Paris.

When you talk about these success symbols, you might put up attractive pictures and posters, or even a collage you have made from pictures in a magazine. Also, invite your distributors to create their own loose-leaf folders or booklets, called "wish books," in which they put pictures and write statements about the items they want. Then, they should look through these wish books frequently, so they can really feel they have these items.

TRAINING MEETINGS

When you have a few distributors, you can meet with them informally to train them individually. But as your organization grows, plan more-organized training meetings or workshops.

Some distributors put these on in conjunction with other meetings (for example, while new people are attending an opportunity meeting, the distributors can go to a training meeting). Others have weekly, biweekly, or monthly sessions. While some lead the training themselves, others bring in guest speakers to talk about various techniques.

As an example, Frances, a distributor for an education program, has regular seminar meetings to build business skills. The program covers such topics as effective advertising, telephone procedures, and techniques for networking with others. Also, participants practice doing meetings and observe others doing them. Then, they see an instant replay on videotape and discuss how to improve performance. Additionally, Frances encourages the participants to find what they do best and use these skills—some, for instance, are good at doing presentations, others at one-on-one sales. Then, at the end of the course, the participants get a certificate of completion suitable for framing.

But, however you do it, *continue training your people*. Besides helping individuals develop better sales techniques, these training sessions help them stay motivated, and they are another way of developing close feelings among those in your group.

At these meetings, you can review most of the topics covered in this book. In fact, use this book to help you put on a step-by-step training program. Here are some of the key topics to cover:

the principles of success
how to explain direct sales, network, and multi-level marketing
basic sales techniques
where to get leads
how to advertise

good telephone strategies
how to put on a good presentation
how to turn customers into distributors
how to build your own organization
how to train your distributors
how to set up your business
how to keep records

When you do trainings, involve participants as much as possible. For example, spend a few minutes explaining a basic point and follow this with a hands-on technique or demonstration that brings home your point. You can see some examples of how to do this in Chart 46. It lists a series of topics and a possible demonstration or technique for each one.

SALES, PLANNING, AND STRATEGY MEETINGS

A sales meeting should focus on setting and meeting specific sales goals. A planning and strategy meeting emphasizes developing ideas to plan and coordinate marketing strategies. The two types of meetings are thus somewhat different, although they are often combined.

The Sales Meeting

Help your distributors assess where they are now and where they want to be. Encourage them to examine how well they are doing in selling to customers and in sponsoring new distributors. Ask them to look at how much product volume is moving through their organization and to consider what that means to them in terms of their commission now.

Put a chart on the board to help them figure this out. Or

CHART 46: USING DEMONSTRATIONS
TO ILLUSTRATE A POINT

Topic Discussed:	Possible Demonstration:
The Principles of Success	A visualization experience. Participants see themselves being successful and having everything they want.
How to Explain Direct Sales, Network, or Multi-Level Marketing	A series of mini-presentations. You give the first description. Then, each person is invited to come up before the group and give an explanation in his or her own words.
Basic Sales Techniques	A series of improvisations. Invite each person in turn to do an improvisation of a person talking to a friend and trying to get him or her to become a consumer or distributor. The participant should use the basic principles of sales in the skit— getting attention, building interest, expressing conviction, encouraging desire, and asking for the order.
Where to Get Leads	Individual brainstorming. Invite everyone to take out a sheet of paper and think of leads in different categories.

STRIKE IT RICH IN PERSONAL SELLING

Topic Discussed:	Possible Demonstration:
How to Advertise	Designing ads. Ask everyone to write down his or her own ad appealing to different people. Then, ask participants to react to each ad. Or ask individuals to get into groups of six to eight each and decide which is the best ad and why.
Good Telephone Strategies	A series of improvisations. Invite each person to improvise making a cold call. One person plays a distributor, the other person someone being called for the first time. The distributor tries to get the person to attend a meeting. Then everyone comments on the technique.
How to Put on a Good Presentation	A series of practice sessions. Explain some basic principles. Then, invite some distributors to practice putting on a meeting for about five to fifteen minutes. Afterward, everyone can comment on what worked and what didn't.

Fill in Your Own Topic:

_____ _____

_____

_____

Gini Graham Scott

CHART 46: USING DEMONSTRATIONS TO
ILLUSTRATE A POINT (continued)

Topic Discussed: _____   Possible Demonstration: _____

_____

_____

_____

_____

_____   _____

_____

_____

_____

_____

pass out copies of Chart 47: Where I Am Now and Where I Want to Be. Then, ask them to set their goals for next month by writing down what they want to happen.

Suggest that they consider how much commission they are getting now for their personal and group product volume separately. Then, they can better assess both their personal and group performance.

CHART 47: WHERE I AM NOW
AND WHERE I WANT TO BE

Where I Am Now: _____

Where I Want to Be Next
Month: _____

How many customers do I
have now? _____

How many customers
do I want? _____

How many distributors do I
have now? _____

How many distributors
do I want? _____

How many new customers
did I get this month?
_____

How many new customers
do I want? _____

How many new distributors
did I get this month?
_____

How many new distributors
do I want? _____

How much product volume
am I selling myself to
customers? _____

How much product volume
do I want to sell? _____

How much product volume
are members of my group
selling? _____

How much product volume
do I want group members
to sell? _____

How much commission did I
get last month on my own
sales? _____

How much commission do I
want on my own sales?
_____

How much commission did I
get last month on my group's
sales? _____

How much commission do I
want on my group's sales?
_____

Emphasize that if they want to increase their own commission, they must increase their personal or group product volume by a proportionate amount. For example, if they and their group are selling $10,000 and they are netting a $1,000 commission, they must increase this volume to $20,000 to earn $2,000.

Then, ask them to break down their monthly goal into weekly and daily amounts. For example, if they want to obtain a combined personal-group volume of $20,000 a month, that means they and their group must sell approximately $5,000 worth of product each week and approximately $1,000 per day.

Also, they can break down those figures further to look at the amount of volume each distributor moves on the average, so they know better what to do with each distributor to increase overall group volume. For example, if a team leader determines that her average distributor is making about $100 a day in sales, based on a group volume of $1,000 for ten distributors, the leader knows very specifically what to do to increase her volume. Say she wants to double her commission, she knows that she should work on increasing her personal volume to $200 a day and encouraging her downline members to up their personal volume to that level, too. Then, once this goal is clearly set, the distributor can work on achieving it.

The Planning and Strategy Meeting

These meetings are designed to help you develop specific plans for achieving sales goals. Thus, they are often like problem-solving sessions. Or they can be used to lay out a weekly or monthly game plan for your organization and work out who does what.

One good approach to problem solving is to ask everyone

to state briefly what they have been doing for the past week to promote the program and what has worked or hasn't. Then, others in the group can make suggestions on what to do in the future.

Also, you can invite descriptions of particular problems that have been encountered. But the emphasis should be on finding solutions.

Group planning is extremely valuable at these meetings, too. Go over your plans for the next week or two and describe the various events that are scheduled. And if you are proposing or organizing a particular strategy, talk about that. For example, one distributor of a diet program worked out a group strategy that involved contacting health clubs. He divided his city and surrounding suburbs into regions, assigned each region to one active distributor in his downline, and then bright and early Monday morning, these distributors fanned out to make presentations at each health club in their area.

The key to good group planning is to have a general discussion about the proposed strategy, invite people to make comments and offer suggestions, weigh alternatives, and obtain an overall group consensus. This way everyone feels a part of the plan and will be supportive.

After you have general agreement, work out the specifics. Divide up the tasks to be done, either by getting volunteers to do them or by assigning them, so that everyone is clear about what the schedule is and who is supposed to do what.

For example, suppose your group is organizing a large opportunity meeting in a hotel. You need to assign specific tasks—one person to arrange for the room, another to handle refreshments, a third to coordinate sending out invitations and flyers, a fourth to organize a phone tree, and others to present different parts of the program.

Gini Graham Scott

BRAINSTORMING SESSIONS

Brainstorming sessions are a great way to develop new ideas for your program. You can use them for ideas on sales techniques, marketing strategies, events, whatever.

In brainstorming, you divide the meeting into two phases: (1) a creative, idea-generating phase, and (2) a critical, idea-evaluation phase.

Then, you follow the following common rules for a productive, creative session:

Phase One—The Creative Phase

Let everyone know they can say anything; the atmosphere of the meeting should be supportive.

Suggest a topic or ask for suggestions. Then, ask everyone to free-associate and come up with ideas. No matter what comes up, no matter how odd or outlandish these ideas may seem, people should say whatever comes to mind.

Have someone keep a list of all the ideas produced. Some brainstormers use a flip chart, on which one person records comments with a magic marker. Then, everyone can see the ideas as they are recorded, and it is easy to review these ideas later.

After the ideas stop flowing or the time set for free-associating is up, announce that the first phase of the meeting is over and it is time to evaluate the ideas.

Phase Two—The Critical Phase

Now shift into the critical, evaluation phase, where you review the ideas one by one.

Point to or read each idea in turn, and ask people to vote on the ideas they like. But limit the number of votes they have to three to five votes, depending on the number of ideas.

Record the number of people who indicate they like each idea.

Eliminate the ideas that people like the least, star those that people like the most—and double-star ideas that seem especially popular.

If there are still too many ideas to discuss, go through the process again to eliminate additional ideas. But this time, limit the number of votes even more—say to only one to two votes.

Next invite discussion of the most popular idea or ideas. Ask people to talk about why they like them or why they don't, and ask for suggestions on putting these ideas into practice. Come to a consensus if you can.

Now if you like, switch into Phase One again and brainstorm some more to generate additional ideas.

SOCIAL ACTIVITIES AND EVENTS

Don't forget that business should be fun. Also, you want to promote rapport among your distributors, so everyone works together as a better team. Occasionally then, have some activities that are just for fun. Some popular events include potluck dinners, theater parties, barbecues, picnics, dinner dances, and game nights.

And if your program has a lot of single members, use that to your advantage and organize activities for singles, too. For example, one travel club discovered that about 50 percent of its members were single, so it encouraged its distributors to put on parties and other events for singles. One distributor who was especially successful doing this was recruited to travel around the country on behalf of the company putting on workshops called "How to Put On a Good Party." And soon after this members in local areas began actively organizing events.

Social occasions are also a good time to honor local distributors in the company who have done especially well; and you should do so with some extra hoopla and pizzazz. The event may still be a party, but it becomes a motivational event, too.

For example, have a band, an emcee, and midway through the evening announce with appropriate flair that you will now give out some special awards. Then, let your emcee take it away and bestow the awards with the appropriate acknowledgments and flourish. Use ribbons, certificates, plaques, embossed cups, and the like for your awards. And perhaps design your own. People love it when you add your own creative touch—it shows you really care.

Examples of awards categories you might recognize include:

The distributors with the most sales for the month
The largest check for the month
The distributor making the most progress
A promotion to a new status in the company
The most positive person
The distributor with the most company spirit

SIZZLE SESSIONS

These are small get-togethers, usually with about five to fifteen, and sometimes as many as twenty persons, which can combine any of the above elements—inspiration, training, planning, brainstorming, and perhaps a little socializing. The main idea of these meetings is to create enthusiasm or "sizzle" and come up with plans and ideas. Participants should leave feeling charged up and ready to go.

You can organize these sessions in various ways. One distributor meets with a few people in a restaurant during off hours—generally midmorning or early afternoon—and as people arrive they relate something positive that has happened with their products or organization. Then, people share ideas about how to build the business and talk to others about it.

Another distributor holds weekly breakfast meetings as a way of kicking off the day and the week. Then, to make sure everyone is an active, positive participant, he has certain requirements to belong to the group. He asks people to take notes. He gives assignments. And people must contribute or they are asked to drop out. The focus is on coming up with solutions and strategies and building enthusiasm to "go out and do it."

But however you decide to put on your own meetings, the key to having a good sizzle session is to keep everyone involved, thinking positively, and focused on coming up with ideas for the topic at hand. You should only talk about your own products or company and avoid gossiping or reporting trivia about other individuals and companies, because that only brings down the energy of the meeting. Furthermore, the emphasis should be on finding solutions, not on sharing problems. This way everyone feels that creative "sizzle," and feels part of a warm, supportive, positive, dynamic group.

The Possibilities...

The possibilities for putting on creative, exciting meetings and activities are endless. A major goal of these events is to get people excited, eager to work toward their goal with the tools to do so, and feeling good! You can achieve this end in many ways.

As your meetings grow, you can become more creative in

what you do. Ideally have weekly meetings, so your distributors can get together on a regular basis. Then, keep the meetings exciting, lively, interesting, and fun, so people want to—even feel a need to—attend.

Encourage your distributors to bring their own recruits to the larger meetings, and if you have selected out especially active second- and third-level individuals to work with, invite them to attend, too.

In time, your distributors may develop their own meetings for the members of their own organizations, and encourage them to do so. In turn, your meetings can provide a model they can use themselves.

The major types of meetings are summarized in Chart 48.

CHART 48: TYPES OF MEETINGS

Inspirational and Motivational Meetings:
    Testimonials about positive experiences
    Guest speakers talking about success and motivation
    Discussions about success principles
    A review of company incentives for achievement

Training Meetings:
    Seminars on business skills
    Sessions to practice skills
    A review of topics listed in this training manual

Sales Meetings:
    An assessment of current product volume
    A review of sales goals
    A projection of future sales goals and product volume

Planning and Strategy Meetings:
    Reports of experiences in promoting the program
    Examples of strategies that worked and didn't

A review of alternate strategies and a decision about the best
  approaches
Discussions of plans for the next week or two
Dividing up tasks to be performed at group programs

Brainstorming Sessions:
  A creative, idea-generating phase
  A critical, idea-evaluation phase

Social Activities and Events:
  Fun activities, like dinners, parties, and barbecues
  Awards ceremonies to recognize and honor active local dis-
  tributors

Sizzle Sessions:
  A combination of inspiration, training, planning, brainstorming, and so on
  An emphasis on creating enthusiasm and developing plans
  and ideas

Chapter 26

OTHER WAYS OF WORKING
WITH YOUR DISTRIBUTORS

Besides having regular meetings, you can work with your distributors to build a solid organization in a number of different ways. These include—

- Organizing cooperative activities
- Passing on leads and sign-ups to members of your sales group or downline
- Developing techniques of communicating with members of your organization, such as telephone trees and newsletters
- Developing fast-start manuals and programs for your distributors

ORGANIZING
COOPERATIVE ACTIVITIES

You can help your distributors work together with you as a team by organizing and coordinating cooperative events. These can include some of the activities discussed in this section.

Jointly Organized Business Opportunity Meetings. Each person is responsible for a part of the program and contributes a proportionate share to the expenses. You can use various formulas for figuring out who contributes what—for example, five dollars each; two dollars per guest; or ten dollars for the group leader, five dollars for area leaders, two dollars for others.

An Opportunity-Meeting Network. A distributor in each area puts on a meeting, and these are announced on a single list or flyer which is circulated to all participating distributors and members of their groups. Any distributor in the network can invite guests to a meeting.

Cooperative Advertising. You combine forces with other distributors to do a joint meeting. Or you pool resources to place a large ad, and all of you share the leads. In some ads, individual distributors list their phone numbers and freely follow up when someone calls. In other cases, the head of the group places the ad, though all participating distributors pay. Then, as the responses come in, the group leader assigns them to the distributors—either by area or randomly.

Joint Participation as an Exhibitor at a Trade Show or Consumer Fair. Again, there are many sorts of arrangements. Several distributors can share the costs of the booth together, then share all the leads generated at the show. Alternatively, one person can pay for the booth, and the distributors who want to work it can contribute based on the number of hours they want to be there. In this case, everyone makes their own contacts at the show and follows up on their own leads. Or, you can create another system that works for you.

Sharing Office or Other Equipment. This is a good idea for expensive equipment such as computers and telemarketing devices. For example, one distributor bought a telemarketing system to share in making cold calls. (The device dials about sixty people an hour, and if they are interested, it records basic information about who they are.) He uses it to support his distributors by lending it to each of them for a short-term period. They use it for a few days to generate a lot of leads; then, they pass the equipment on to another distributor, and spend the next few weeks following up. Another distributor uses the same kind of device to develop leads out of a central office, which he shares with several members of his downline. Then, when leads come in, he refers them to these distributors according to geographical area.

An Open Invitation to a Large Opportunity Meeting You Put On. Your distributors can bring guests or just send people to your meetings if they can't attend themselves. Then, you sign people up for them.

PASSING ON LEADS TO MEMBERS OF YOUR SALES GROUP

Turning over leads and sign-ups to members of your sales group is an excellent strategy when there is a lot of local interest in your program and your organization is growing rapidly. You act as a central clearinghouse for your organization and pass on leads to first- or second-level members of your sales team or downline for follow-up.

This approach is especially good if you are advertising or actively promoting your program and are getting many inquiries. Rather than trying to handle all of them yourself and ending up with dozens of front-line persons you can't help properly, share your leads with your sales group and distribute them as best you can by geographic area.

Another advantage of this approach is that your active front-line people don't feel you are in competition with them for new recruits—so they can better look to you for support.

Think of it this way. It is as if you are an army commander or corporate head passing on assignments to your troops.

However, be sure you are referring your leads and sign-ups to active distributors who are willing to work with the people you assign them. Otherwise, you end up with these people further downline in your organization, and you have to work with them anyway, since the sponsor to whom you assigned them won't follow through.

You should also pass on people to your distributors when you meet them together or there is any confusion about who should sponsor this person. (For example, you tell Mary about the program, but Mary is a good friend of your distributor Brad.) The reason that you should give the priority to your distributors is that you don't want your distributors to feel you are in competition with them, for that only breeds resentment and alienation and makes them question your support.

So, remember this important rule: *Never ever compete with your distributors*.

Besides, when you pass on people to your distributors or let them do the sponsoring when there is any question about sponsorship, you benefit anyway, because the new recruit is still in your line. But if you sponsor a person, where your distributor feels he or she should do the sponsoring, only you benefit, and your active distributor may feel offended and less enthusiastic about working on the program in the future.

So practice the golden rule of network and multi-level marketing: *Pass on your leads when you can, and when in doubt, pass on your people, too.*

COMMUNICATING WITH
YOUR ORGANIZATION

As your organization grows, you need a quick way to get your message down to the troops, and you need to be able to inform, motivate, and inspire everyone on an ongoing basis. Good communication is essential.

Two effective approaches are the telephone tree and the organizational newsletter or progress report.

Telephone Trees

Telephone trees are great to spread the word quickly. For the best effect, have a short, snappy message that can be conveyed in a few sentences, such as: "A great meeting will be happening on Saturday, since the head of the company will be in town. It will be at the _____ Hotel, and we're expecting about one hundred people there. So come early to get a good seat." Longer messages can easily get garbled as they are passed on from one person to the next.

To make sure the message gets through accurately, write everything down and read the message to each person you contact. Then, ask that person to write down the message as you talk and pass it on exactly in this form.

You should structure a telephone tree so each person is assigned four or five persons to call when he or she passes on a message. Be sure each one agrees to participate in the tree before you give out any assignment. And don't settle for: "I'll try." You must have a commitment. Then, clearly indicate whom the person will be calling. This way you can be sure everyone is called who should be.

It's disastrous to your organization if you think someone is going to communicate a message down the line, but then he or she doesn't do so. Given the multiplier effect in MLM and network marketing, hundreds of persons could miss out on hearing the message this way.

Newsletters and Progress Reports

Newsletters or progress reports are important communication tools that can be used for certain key purposes:

To let people know where you are going and where you have been

To measure and recognize the progress made by you, your directly sponsored people, and notable achievers in your downline

In reporting the news, you should emphasize the positive and deemphasize the negative. You want to keep your newsletter inspirational and motivational. Besides informing people, your newsletter is another tool for promoting enthusiasm in your organization and encouraging your distributors to get ahead.

In some companies, local people, who may be from different sales organizations, get together to create a newsletter. This kind of group effort is most common in the beginning when the program is just getting going and groups are small. Working together helps generate more enthusiasm to build up the area. Typically, in this situation, distributors have open meetings, too, so anyone from any sales group or downline can come.

However, whether or not you have a company or local newsletter in your area, it's a good idea to create a newsletter for your own sales team, once it becomes sizable—say twenty or more persons. The newsletter will help everyone in your group stay in touch, and it promotes motivation.

Distributing Your Newsletter

One common way to distribute these newsletters is to send copies to your first-level distributors and request they make copies to pass on. If this works for you, fine. But sometimes distribution can bog down if you have someone who is inactive down the line.

So if you can, it's better to get the names and addresses of your downline members—either from their immediate sponsors or from the company. Many companies will send you a printout of your downline members at cost—about two cents a name.

Some distributors distribute their newsletters free to the first two or three levels of their downline, considering them a good motivator and training tool that is worth the cost. Others ask for a small subscription fee or contribution to cover costs, particularly if they are sending their newsletter to a large downline. Do whatever works for you. Perhaps ask some of the people on your first and second level what they think or what they are willing to pay for a newsletter, to help you decide.

What to Include in Your Newsletter

Feel free to be creative in your newsletter. Let it express your own style, whether that may be formal and businesslike or informal and chatty.

Some good things to include in your newsletter are reports about local activities, a calender of events, listings of active leaders who are putting on meetings and their phone numbers, announcements about recent awards, accomplishments, and large commission payments (which are a great motivator). Other possibilities include recent news about the company which you but not your distributors have received, because you have a higher status in the company, descriptions of strategies that have worked well, a discussion of common problems that come up and how to solve them, copies of ads and flyers other distributors can use (however, make sure you have company approval, if this is needed), and inspirational stories.

DEVELOPING FAST-START MANUALS AND TRAINING PROGRAMS

The more tools you can give your distributors to get them started quickly, the faster your organization grows. Two approaches are developing a fast-start manual designed specifically for your program, and creating a fast-start training program to help your people really know what to do.

The Fast-Start Manual

Such a manual is a great way to help people in your group get started. You can also use it to convince people to sign up with you or your group, because they can see that they will get excellent support from you, support that supplements any literature or training materials produced by the company. (Of course, be aware of company guidelines, if you mention the name of the company in your materials.)

Your manual might include a copy of the outline you use in your presentation; a copy of the presentation booklet you have put together for your one-on-one presentations; copies of flyers, ad copy, and brochures; lists of recommended books; promotional photographs of your product or service; testimonials; or anything else you have found useful in marketing the program.

The Fast-Start Training Program

A fast-start training program is an excellent approach if you are involved in the early phases of a new company, because it helps you quickly build up an active sales group. Then, once

Gini Graham Scott

you have recruited, trained, and motivated this team, the team members can introduce the program to other prospects in the more traditional way.

There are several facets to this approach to consider.

Have sufficient product and distributor kits on hand, so your distributors can get started right away. Some companies have their own variety packs and start-up materials. However, with others you have to purchase in case-lots and repack these materials to create your own fast-start kits.

Ideally, include one or two samples of all products, or if it's an extensive line, one or two samples of the fastest-selling items. Also, include company flyers, brochures, and any material you have prepared for your own group (in keeping with company guidelines, of course).

Use the distributor prices to figure your costs, and keep the cost of each kit to about fifty to a hundred dollars.

This approach does involve a substantial financial commitment, since you need sufficient product on hand to respond to the demand—perhaps two thousand to ten thousand dollars in product. However, consider having an investor or a team of investors who put in five hundred to a thousand dollars each.

Require recruits to pay for these kits with cashier's checks, money orders, or cash. No credit or personal checks—because you may be recruiting many people you don't know. Also, unless the company encourages local warehousing and gives distributors a bonus for doing this, add on a small service charge, say 10 percent, to pay for your time and to encourage distributors to order direct from the company.

Set up fast-start opportunity meetings and invite your first- and second-level persons to come to these meetings with at least one or two guests. Locate a facility, such as a hotel, that is large enough to hold a sizable group and can provide you with expanded space as your group grows. The facility also should have a solid, professional image, to show that you are going first-class.

Organize a good opportunity presentation and close by inviting all newcomers to sign up now with their sponsor. Indicate that they can take their starter kits with them right away.

Invite everyone to come to the next meeting with one or two more guests. And this includes the newcomers who have just signed up.

Provide additional training for those who have been to a meeting before. This way individuals don't have to sit through the same meeting again and again, and can learn some new techniques while the regular meeting is going on.

Some distributors in a new health program who used this technique divided their training program into three phases:

1. The Basics—how to fill out the company forms; how to prospect and invite people to opportunity meetings; highlights in the company manual
2. Advancing in the Program—techniques of building an organization; how to move up to the next level in the company
3. Excelling in Leadership—how to advance to the highest levels in the company by training others to create a strong, growing organization

The distributors who had been to the meeting before went to the appropriate training meeting, while their guests heard about the product line and the business opportunity.

Encourage your people who live in another area to attend your meetings a few times, even though they may have a long drive. Then, they can see how you organize the program and do the same thing in their own area.

Chapter 27

FINE-TUNING YOUR
SALES ORGANIZATION

Once you have your sales organization up and running, you need to keep it going so it will continue to produce. You might compare this process to running any machinery (you need to keep it well oiled) or to tending a garden (you need to keep it weeded to promote continued growth). In the same way, you must work with your organization on an ongoing basis to keep everyone happy, motivated, and working together as a team with you.

MAKING YOUR ORGANIZATION
RUN SMOOTHLY

When your organization runs smoothly, everyone is pulling together and supporting each other. People assist each other with meetings, attend events regularly, and share information and advice freely.

Managing your organization is like managing a team of baseball players. When everything runs smoothly, your team hits home run after home run. But when problems and dissension develop, everyone can strike out.

Thus, good rapport is essential, and when a team really works together, everyone knows it. You can feel the enthusiasm and excitement; sense the "positive vibes" in the air.

Two keys to running a successful organization are staying positive yourself and resolving potential problems quickly.

Staying Positive

As your team's leader, you play a crucial role in affecting how smoothly your organization runs. If you are positive, helpful, and supportive, you can help it run more smoothly. But if you become discouraged or otherwise express a negative attitude, your attitude can travel through your whole organization.

So, in general, no matter how you feel, you need to appear "up"—and of course, acting this way will help you feel this way, too. If you need one or two confidants to confide in when you're blue, fine, as long as they keep things confidential. But with others in the organization, keep the faith. They believe in you; they are following you. So don't let them down by appearing down. Stay positive, and they will, too!

Resolving Potential Problems Quickly

A second key to running a successful organization is sensing when there is a potential problem and acting quickly to nip it in the bud. This means using the skills of human relations. For instance, if you notice a conflict between two distributors, talk to them and try to resolve it. Or if you feel a distributor is not performing up to par because of a personal problem, offer to help if the person wants to discuss it.

Also, be aware of the special problems that may occur in

network or MLM organizations because of the way the sponsoring system works. If these arise, do what you can to smooth them out. For example, an issue that sometimes arises is who signs in under whom. Sometimes a distributor may feel that he or she unfairly lost a downline member to someone else. Or distributors may resist working together because they see themselves in competition for distributors, or feel they have nothing to gain in working together, since they are in separate lines.

The best thing to do in such a situation is to sit down with the people involved and help them work out a compromise. For instance, the person accused of unfairly signing up someone else's prospect might offer to give one of his or her next sign-ups to the other distributor. Or you might encourage your distributors in different lines to work together, because they will hold better meetings if they do and thus will both sponsor more people.

There are no clear answers for solving these problems, but you must do what you can to resolve them and encourage everyone to be mutually supportive. Otherwise, the petty bickering and resentments that may develop can hobble your organization and result in everyone performing less well than they could.

BUILD UP LOYALTY TO YOU, NOT TO THE COMPANY

Since some companies come and go in network and multi-level marketing, and since the popularity of a company's product line may peak and level off, you should work to build up loyalty *to you*, not to the company.

To do this, create your own identity as a company. Then, you are not merely a distributor for another company, but a marketing organization that happens to be distributing that company's product. It may be your only product line—and when you are getting started, it probably should be. *But you stand apart from the company.*

Then, if there are changes in the company or in the direction of your marketing efforts, most of your organization will stay with you.

However, to do this effectively, you must make your marketing decisions carefully. When people look to you as a leader, you must be worthy of that trust.

INTRODUCE NEW PROGRAMS CAREFULLY

To keep your leadership position, you must introduce any new programs carefully, keeping these three keys in mind:

Involve your sales group in the decision-making process
Avoid introducing too many programs
Use good planning in introducing a new program

Involve Your Sales Group in Making Decisions about New Programs

Before you initiate or recommend any changes in the programs you and your organization market, be sure you have researched your recommendations thoroughly, and include your reasons in a detailed letter or memo to everyone in your sales group.

Also, before you make a final decision on how to proceed, get some feedback from key people in your group. Find out how much support you really have for your idea. If you find that most people in your organization want to stick with the program they are already doing, it may be best to defer any change—or to build a separate organization if you decide to market the new product.

One way to get feedback is to send out a letter describing what you are thinking of doing. Enclose a brief questionnaire (along with a self-addressed stamped envelope to facilitate returns) to find out what people think. Then, tally up the replies and consider these in making your decision. If you get a clear go-ahead, great! But if not, it may be better to retreat or create a new marketing group. You may have spent months or years building up your present organization, and you certainly don't want to lose it by trying to take your people into something new if they don't want to go.

Should you decide not to pursue your proposed new direction, let your people know what you decided and why. One well-known distributor widely advertised a new program he was considering, but when he learned that 80 percent of his current organization wanted to stay with the current program, he decided to drop the new one and sent out a three-page letter explaining what he had done and why. Also, he returned the money anyone sent him to sign up in the new program, inviting that person to remain in the original program or to sign up in the new program under someone else.

Avoid Introducing Too Many Programs

Getting feedback from your sales group is fine, when you only do this occasionally. But be careful not to introduce too many new opportunities, or you will fragment the efforts of your people and lose their trust. Some distributors who jump on just about any "hot" new opportunity that comes along are sometimes called "multi-level junkies." And that's *not* what you want to do.

Sure, some of these new programs may be great. But you can't promote everything and shouldn't try. If you do, you will quickly lose your credibility and probably your organization. For it will appear as if once you have people started on a program you claimed was so great, you're off and running with something new.

Sometimes distributors think, "Oh, I've built up a sales group. Now I can make money with very little work by running each new program I join down the ranks." But that's the worst thing you can do. People who joined your group because they trusted you will start to feel used and exploited. And they will doubt your wisdom as a leader; if you hop around to the latest hyped-up program they will see that there is no selectivity, decision making, or real leadership in that.

Thus, if you want team loyalty and want your group to follow you, be cautious in how you proceed and present yourself as a serious, sincere, trustworthy leader who makes responsible decisions. Then, when you make a recommendation and back it up with supporting data, people will listen. They'll feel you have something worthwhile to say.

How to Introduce a New Program

When you do decide to introduce a new program to your sales group or downline, it should meet all the criteria discussed earlier for choosing a new program. In fact, it should meet even higher standards than usual for a company, product, and marketing plan, because you are not just selecting this program for yourself but are bringing in—or trying to bring in—your whole team.

So investigate thoroughly. If you can, meet with officers of the company. Look at the facilities and plant. Or if that's not practical, get information from some founding distributors.

Furthermore, it's best to introduce a program that's compatible with what your group is already doing. Then, your people don't have to discover new markets and can combine it with their current line. For example, if you're doing a weight control program, a new healthy gourmet-food line is fine.

Also, the program should preferably be something that is new, on which you have early information because you are active in network or multi-level marketing. This way, you reinforce your position as a leader who is in the know. In addition, you don't have the problem of introducing a program which some of your people may already be involved in. Instead, you can run the program down your organization and keep the same chain of command, assuming most or all of your people want to get involved.

Once you have made your decision, send out a letter explaining why. Also, let people know how you plan to work with this new program. For example, let people know if you are going to be developing special training materials or starting regular meetings in certain areas.

Finally, invite group members to join you if they wish. Advise them that it is best to keep the same lines of sponsorship; therefore they should check with their sponsors and first-line distributors to find out if they are interested. Then, individuals can sign up accordingly.

THE VALUE OF KEEPING LINES OF SPONSORSHIP

Do everything you can to encourage your team members to maintain their original lines of sponsorship, and maintain these yourself with your own sponsor.

Frequently, people switch lines, thinking, "I signed up under you in that; now you can sign up under me in this." Such an approach may be fine if your involvement in network marketing or MLM is only casual. But if you are seriously building an organization and want to keep it solid and working smoothly, keep the original lines wherever possible.

The problem with switching is that communication lines get confused; and switching creates confusion in handling records, in training, in almost everything.

Thus, if you are considering joining another network marketing or MLM company, always ask your sponsor if he or she is interested, and ask your people to do the same in your organization. In fact, if you have been a good sponsor and your sponsor has been equally supportive, both you and your people should *want* to maintain your original lines.

Just think of the sponsorship process as related to the functioning of any organization. Each organization develops its own structure and hierarchy, in which the people on top have more knowledge and experience. That's why they are there. Normally, they have been with the organization longer. Also, they have more contacts with others in the field by virtue of their higher position. Thus, you want to take advantage of that expertise by working with them or for them. For example, say you're an advertising account executive. You don't take on a new product and suddenly expect to have your boss work for you.

It's much the same in a network or multi-level marketing organization. You aren't working for your sponsor. But normally he or she has more knowledge and contacts, so it's best to continue to work together on new products with the same sponsorship arrangement. Everything runs more smoothly this way.

Part VI

ORGANIZING SPECIAL EVENTS TO BUILD YOUR OWN BUSINESS OR HELP YOUR SALES GROUP

Chapter 28

PUTTING ON A GOOD PRESENTATION

As you get more experience with your product and build up more contacts yourself or develop a growing sales group, it helps if you can put on good presentations to get customers for yourself or to assist your sales group. Initially, it's fine to do small informal meetings or refer your potential customers and recruits to meetings put on by your sales team leaders or by others in the program.

But eventually, think about putting on your own presentations. Depending on the kind of direct sales program you are promoting, these meetings can be an excellent way to gain customers for yourself more quickly or a great motivator for your sales group. Also, these presentations are a good selling point when prospective distributors are considering whose sales organization to join; they may be more receptive to joining your team.

To prepare, go to several presentations by others promoting your program. Notice what information they cover, how they present it, and what techniques seem to work especially well.

Also, notice what questions come up frequently so you can be prepared to answer them.

HOW TO PUT ON A GOOD PRESENTATION

To give a good meeting, keep it short and sweet. Present the essential facts in an interesting way and answer the questions that come up. The key to an effective presentation is to entertain and involve your audience as well as to inform. Since the average person remembers only about 10–20 percent of what he or she hears, you should emphasize and repeat key points, so the person remembers them. Use illustrations or demonstrations where you can, since a person remembers more—about 30 percent—if he or she sees something, too. To make your presentation more entertaining and involving, include a few anecdotes or personal experiences. Use these to teach key points and add color.

And don't worry about being nervous. As you get used to speaking, your nervousness will subside. Also, many of the most talented, well-paid speakers have a twinge of nervousness before they go in front of an audience. In fact, that tension makes them perform better, because they put that nervous energy into their performance.

The best way to reduce these anxious feelings is to be effectively prepared, and thus more confident. Then, as soon as you start your presentation, relate to your audience, concentrate on your material—not on yourself—and direct your excess energy into physical actions. Soon you'll be totally involved in your presentation and won't have a chance to feel nervous.

WHAT TO INCLUDE IN YOUR PRESENTATION

Plan on about forty-five minutes to an hour for your presentation. Structure it to be organized and compact. Preferably, ask your listeners not to interrupt with questions but to save them for the question period at the end. Allow about ten minutes for questions—but not much longer, because then people have a chance to bring up all sorts of trivia. It's better to invite those who still have questions to wait until the formal meeting breaks up. Then, go into your close and wind up the meeting. Afterward, you'll be amazed at how many of those seemingly burning questions disappear.

Expect to include most of the same basic information as you would in a good one-on-one presentation about thirty minutes in length. But then add a little bit more "sizzle," so your presentation has added impact.

Here are some ways to do this:

Start with or include a slide-sound presentation or film.
Use a flip chart with pictures, graphs, and other visuals.
Have different speakers present each part of the program.
Include a brief discussion on the techniques and attitudes
    that make for success.
Use a warm-up exercise to get everyone involved, such
    as asking each person to turn to a neighbor and relate
    a principal goal.

As in the one-on-one presentation, have informative handouts available that guests can take home with them. Meeting coordinators can work out the logistics for distributing these materials in various ways:

The distributor who brings guests provides an information
packet to each guest.

The meeting leader provides a flyer or two; the distributors provide their guests with the rest.

The meeting leader charges $1.00 to $2.00 at the door
to cover the cost of the handouts. The guests pay the
door fee, or the distributor pays for each guest.

Guests who want information packets pay for themselves; usually the cost is about $0.50 to $1.50.

In organizing your presentation, use the same basic categories described in chapter 18, "Putting On an Effective One-
on-One Presentation," and choose those appropriate to your
program. These categories are:

Introduction
Information on the product or service
Discussion of the company
Description of the backup support your organization provides
A brief introduction to network or multi-level marketing
A description of the marketing plan
A brief question-and-answer period
A close, in which you ask for the order

If you have several individuals who can do different parts
of the presentation, so much the better. That adds strength and
substance to what you are saying. And if you have someone
who is an especially good motivator, have that person lead off,
to get everyone's attention and increase the excitement and
interest level. Then have that person handle the close to have
everyone sign up.

THE IMPORTANCE OF PREPARATIONS

Other tips for a good meeting involve giving thought and effort to the preparations.

Prepare for the Meeting

It helps to have a good showing. To get one, you have to prepare and build excitement in advance.

If you have built up a sales group, encourage your group members to make calls and invite at least one or two guests each. Keep in touch with them to keep them motivated and find out how many persons they are bringing. If they are having any trouble inviting guests, give them some suggestions on what to do.

Some marketing people have a regular weekly meeting night, which is fine if you have a group that attends on a regular basis or—if your organization is growing rapidly—is excited by the momentum of weekly meetings.

However, if the numbers in your sales group aren't there yet, encourage your downline distributors to hold small meetings or to give one-on-one presentations themselves. Then put on a big, rousing meeting perhaps once a month. This way, you don't hype up everyone's energies only to have your attempt at a big meeting fall flat.

In any case, when you do put on a big meeting, *give your invited guests and sales team members plenty of advance notice and make the event seem special*. For example, put out a flyer announcing a special rally or presentation and highlight anything special about that meeting (such as a motivational speaker, the appearance of a company officer, or an awards presentation).

Also, decide in advance who is going to say what. If your group is fairly new at giving presentations, rehearse a few times first. Make sure everyone knows their part, and work out smooth transitions from one person to another. Also, work out a rough timetable for each part of the presentation, and remind everyone to stick to this. Likewise, determine in advance what product samples and audiovisual or other equipment you need for your presentation, and who is responsible for what. And give yourself plenty of time to prepare what you need.

You can use Chart 49 to help you prepare.

Find Out in Advance How Many Persons Are Coming

Advise the guests you invite yourself and the members of your sales group to let you know if they are coming and how many guests they are bringing, so you can be properly prepared. Even if they call the day of the event, ask them to let you know.

When meeting coordinators don't get this information, they have no idea about how many guests to expect. So they prepare too much or too little literature, food, product samples, and so on. Or they end up with a room that is much too large or much too small.

So, get some advance indication of attendance to help you better prepare. Not all of your guests and sales team members will let you know; and inevitably people will say they are coming and won't, and others will show up unannounced. But at least you will have some rough guidelines to use in deciding how much of everything to prepare.

Dress to Make a Good Impression

To make a good impression dress the part of success. The usual rule is to dress a little more formally than you might if you were giving a small informal presentation. (As may be recalled, at these gatherings, you dress a bit more upscale than you usually would, but not too much.)

Generally, males should wear a conservative suit or good sports jacket and slacks. Women should wear a dress, business suit, or fashionable pantsuit. At the smaller presentations you can dress more casually—but now you really want to look good. So dress for success!

Get Everything Properly Set Up in Advance

Arrive early with everything you need, and give yourself plenty of time before the meeting to set up.

Then, *check everything*! If you're going to boil water for a food demonstration, be sure the stove or hot plate works. Also, know how long it takes to bring the water to a boil, so you aren't waiting an extra half hour for everything to heat up. Likewise, if you're showing slides or a film, check the projector and the slides or film. You don't want to find that a bulb is out when you're ready to start, or discover you have slides missing or turned the wrong way as you talk.

Start on Time

Allow about fifteen minutes to a half hour for arrivals and socializing (in fact, you might state this in your invitations). Then, start on time or at most ten to fifteen minutes late.

People can get very impatient if they have to wait, and some people will have plans for later in the evening. So let the

CHART 49: GROUP PRESENTATION CHECKLIST

Date of Meeting _____

Location of Meeting _____

Speakers/Participants: _____

_____

Types of Materials Needed	Items Needed	Who Is Getting Needed Items

Equipment:

Literature:

Refreshments:

Other:

Topics Covered in Presentation	Speaker(s) Handling That Part of Meeting	Items Used in That Part of Meeting	Person Getting Item
1.			
2.			
3.			
4.			
5.			
6.			
7.			
8.			

latecomers miss whatever they miss. This way you show respect for the people who have come on time, and you show that it is important to come on time in the future.

GETTING A MEETING SITE

As your program grows, you will need to find a larger public or commercial site for your meetings. Besides being able to accommodate a larger group, such a location also contributes to your professional image. So unless you specifically want to emphasize home parties and informal get-togethers, start holding meetings outside of the home as soon as feasible.

Researching Possible Locations

It is helpful to research the possible sites for meetings in advance and to keep a table of these for making arrangements. Then you can quickly set up meetings, and if you have to, find alternate sites at the last minute. You can use Chart 50 for keeping track of these locations.

In selecting a place, take into account the following considerations and make a note of them in your records:

- *Convenience*. The meeting place should be centrally located and easy to get to by public transportation as well as by car.
- *Suitability*. The site should be in keeping with the kind of image you want to present. For example, it may be worth paying more to get a room in a nice hotel or restaurant, rather than paying less for a room in the YMCA.
- *Activities at the Site*. If there are many activities going on in the area, the place may be too congested or noisy to hold a productive meeting.

CHART 50: MEETING SITE LIST

Location	Address	Phone and Contact	Size	Equipment Available	Costs/ Arrangements	Other
•						

- *The Location of a Coffee Shop Nearby.* This is a real
plus. The advantage is you have someplace nearby where
you can take your prospect to relax and talk more about
the program if you wish, when the meeting ends.

Types of Places

You can rent conference or banquet rooms from hotels,
restaurants, bars, lodges, the "Y," and other public buildings.

If you know someone who puts on a lot of parties and events,
such as the program chairman of an organization or a creative
party caterer, ask that person for recommendations. And if you
happen to go to a place that looks suitable, ask to see the
manager about using it.

Working Out the Arrangements

Commonly, you have to put down a deposit and pay a certain
amount each time you use a room (about twenty-five to fifty
dollars a night is common for medium-sized rooms that hold
about twenty-five to forty persons). But try to get free arrangements if you can. For example, some restaurant and bar
owners will be open to a trial arrangement if they think you
will bring them more business. Then, if enough individuals
order drinks or buy dinner before or after the meeting, they
will let you continue to use the room without charge. Though
most owners will ask for money at first, it doesn't hurt to try
for a trade.

In the beginning, have a test meeting or two to see the kind
of response you get before you make long-term commitments.
This way, if attendance is low, you don't get stuck with a large
bill and can readily move the meeting to a more appropriate
location or cancel it entirely. Conversely, if you have overflow
crowds, you can move to a larger place.

Some owners and managers will permit you to pay in advance a few days before you want to reserve the space and will hold your reservation from week to week as long as you have regular meetings there. Others may ask for an initial two-to-four-week commitment, and thereafter may require you to pay in advance every two to four weeks to continue the arrangement. Some will let you pay on the night of your meeting. *Try for the most flexible arrangement possible, because it's hard to predict your needs in the beginning—and even on an ongoing basis.*

Estimating the Turnout

You can make a rough estimate of how large a space you will need based on the size of your own guest list or sales group (and of others sharing the room with you), and based on how actively you and your group will be recruiting.

If many guests are involved in recruiting, usually attendance will be good. However, if you are primarily depending on the draw of a newspaper ad or announcement, it is harder to predict the response.

If possible, ask people seeing your ad to RSVP and ask other distributors inviting guests to let you know in advance how many to plan for. Then, you are better able to plan accordingly and perhaps organize a second meeting if the response is great. Or if you don't get much response, you might possibly move to a smaller room in the same restaurant or hotel.

How to Arrange the Room

When you use a commercial meeting space, the standard theater or classroom arrangement with a podium, blackboard, flip charts, and/or audiovisual equipment usually works best.

It looks professional and focuses attention on the speaker.

Check in advance to see what equipment the management has, and arrange to supply the rest yourself. Find out, too, if the management will arrange the room the way you want it before the meeting, and if so, give the manager the necessary instructions. If not, allow extra time before the meeting to handle setting up. And if you need to return the room to its original arrangement after the meeting, allow time for that, too.

Chapter 29

PARTICIPATING IN A TRADE SHOW

Trade shows can be a great source of new contracts and leads. You can participate by yourself, although most distributors do combine forces with others to share costs or take turns working the booth.

In consumer-oriented shows, you can sometimes generate a high retail sales volume for a high-demand product. And some products, such as office supply products, move very well in business and trade shows. But if you're looking for new distributors for your sales group, don't expect the shows to be a major source of on-the-spot sign-ups. Some people may decide quickly. But generally, look on each show as a source of leads for prospects. Then, you or your sales group members can follow up after the show.

Some distributors do very well going to trade shows all over the country. However, unless you have a product that sells very well at the show or you are prepared for long-distance follow-up to recruit new distributors, stick to the shows in your area. You have a greater chance of sponsoring new recruits locally, where you can offer your strongest backup and training.

TYPES OF TRADE SHOWS

There are two main types of shows:

- Consumer shows, which:
    feature a particular product line (for example, health
        products or computers)
    are part of a fair or festival (such as a county fair)
- Professional and trade shows, which include
    conventions, workshops, and seminars for a particular
        profession;
    product shows for the trade (for example, gift shows
        and stationery shows);
    business opportunity shows (such as franchise, home-
        based business, and MLM shows).

Some of these shows, such as county fairs, are sponsored by your city or county. Others are organized by trade or professional groups; some are put on by private promoters.

Choose the shows that best feature your particular product. For example, if you are promoting a health product, you might consider a health fair, a county or city fair, a convention of health professionals, a home products show, or a business opportunity show featuring home-based or direct sales businesses (assuming you are seeking additional distributors).

SHOW POLICIES ABOUT COMPETING PRODUCT LINES

Shows have different policies about allowing competing products lines or sharing booths. Some shows—particularly consumer shows—have an open-booth policy, so that any number of product lines can be featured in the same booth and more than one company can sell the same products. However, in other shows—most notably in those featuring home-based businesses, network marketing, and MLM companies—the usual policy is only one booth per company and only one product line per booth. This way you are not competing against others with the same product. But you will have to act fast to get the space if you have a popular product.

So find out which policy the show is using. If it has open booths, find out about the likely competition before you sign up for a booth, and decide what's best for you. If there are already or are likely to be other booths with your product, it might be better to skip the show, since each additional booth dilutes your potential market. On the other hand, an open-booth policy gives you a chance to try out additional lines.

Conversely, if you are considering a one booth–one product show and want to be sure to be in it, make your commitment early so that you get a booth.

COSTS OF TRADE SHOW PARTICIPATION

Trade show fees range from a low of $50–$100 for a standard-sized booth at a small local show to about $400–$600 for such a booth at a professionally produced show. There have been shows where the cost was as much as $1,000–$1,200 for a booth, but the $400–$600 fee is more common.

A standard booth is usually eight by ten feet. Corner booths and booths at the entrance to the show commonly cost about $100 more. And larger booths or double booths cost proportionately more, too.

To figure your full costs of participation, include the cost of any product samples and literature you plan to give away, the cost of the products you hope to sell, and your expenses getting to the show and while at it (travel, hotel, food, and so forth).

If you are sharing a booth, figure out your share based on the amount of space you have in a shared booth with different product lines or based on the number of distributors sharing a common space.

Then, use these figures to decide if your participation is likely to be profitable and whether you want to participate on that basis.

For example, if you mainly expect sales to consumers, figure out how much you are likely to sell based on the size of the crowd expected and what your average profit is likely to be if you attain your sales goal. Then, compare your profit to the cost of being in the show. Also, add your time and effort into the equation. Your expected profits should be greater than expected costs to make participation worthwhile. If your expected profit isn't great enough to cover both your costs and some reasonable payment to yourself and anyone else running the booth (say at least ten dollars an hour), perhaps you shouldn't have a booth.

On the other hand, if the show is an arena for recruiting potential distributors as well as selling retail customers, take that into account in figuring your profit potential. To do this, make some projections about how many potential distributors you are likely to contact and how much income you might gain from those distributors.

To make a reasonable projection, make a rough estimate of the percentage of the population at the show that might be interested in your product line. (For instance, maybe 10 percent might be interested in a new time-management system, but 50 percent might be interested in a health product.) Then, if available, use the attendance estimates provided by the show organizer, or make your own estimate based on the type of show and previous attendance at similar shows, to figure out how many people might be attending and, of these, how many might be interested in your product.

Then, if you are looking for new distributors, estimate your potential earnings from those you are likely to recruit. In general, figure that about one-third of the persons you talk to will be interested in hearing more, about one-third of these will be interested in signing up as distributors, and about one-third to one-fifth of these will become active distributors. In other words, you can estimate that about 2–4 percent of those you talk to will be interested in a serious business opportunity working with you. Then, estimate how many distributors that might be and how much each is likely to earn for you.

Finally, if appropriate, combine your expected profits from retailing to consumers and signing up distributors, and ask yourself, Is that enough? How much profit am I likely to make from consumers? How many distributors am I likely to sign up? And will these earnings or potential earnings make my costs and my time for participating worthwhile? Then, make your decision on whether to be in the show or not on that basis.

Of course, you may have other goals besides immediate profits, such as getting your name known or conducting a market test, which more than offset not making a profit. Just be clear when you consider entering a show about your goals, expected profits, and costs, so you can make a good decision. Use Chart 51 to help you weigh the various factors.

SHARING A BOOTH

Although it's ideal to take a full booth so you can better feature your product, many distributors share a booth to cut down costs.

CHART 51: ESTIMATE OF COSTS AND PROFITS AT A TRADE SHOW

Cost of Participation

Basic Show Expenses	Total	My Share of a Shared Booth	
		% of Costs	Total Costs
Booth Fee	_____	_____	_____
Cost of Samples	_____	_____	_____
Cost of Literature	_____	_____	_____
Cost of Products for Sale	_____	_____	_____
Total	_____	_____	_____

Other Expenses

	Total	% of Costs	Total Costs
Travel	_____	_____	_____
Hotel	_____	_____	_____
Food	_____	_____	_____
Entertainment	_____	_____	_____
Other	_____	_____	_____
Total	_____	_____	_____
Total Cost of Participation	_____	_____	_____

Projected Gross Profits on Retail Sales and/or Signing Up New Distributors

Projected Profits on Retail Sales
1. Number of Consumers Expected at Show   _____
2. Percentage of Consumers Likely to Make Purchases   _____
3. Number of Consumers Likely to Make Purchases (multiply #1 × #2)   _____
4. Average Value of Each Expected Purchase   _____
5. Total Value of All Expected Purchases (multiply #3 × #4)   _____
6. My Share of the Profits (if shared) (multiply your percentage of profits by #5)   _____

Projected Earnings from New Distributors
1. Number of Persons Expected at Show   _____
2. Percentage of Persons Likely to Be Interested in My Product Line   _____
3. Number Likely to Be Interested in My Product Line (multiply #1 × #2)   _____
4. Number of Persons Interested in My Product Line Who Are Likely to Become Active Distributors (multiply #3 by 2–4 percent)   _____
5. Average Amount of Income Expected from Each New Distributor per Month   _____
6. Total Amount of Income Expected from New Distributors per Month (multiply #4 × #5)   _____
7. Total Amount of Income Expected from New Distributors in One Year (multiply #6 by 12)   _____

Projected Net Profits or Costs of Participating in Show
Projected Gross Profits on Retail Sales (use total from #5 or #6)   _____
Projected Earnings from New Distributors (use total from #7)   (+)   _____

CHART 51: ESTIMATE OF COSTS AND PROFITS AT A TRADE SHOW (continued)

Total Cost of Participation   (−)   _____

Projected Net Profit or Cost of Participating   _____

If you share a booth with another company, try to do so with a product line that is compatible but not competitive. For example, a booth with a vitamin product and diet program is fine. But if you both sell vitamin products and diet plans, better find two separate booths. It also helps to share with someone whose product line can enhance your product. For example, if you are selling health products, a line of soothing relaxation tapes would be a nice draw.

If you want to share a booth and don't know anyone, many shows with open-booth policies will help you find someone. They keep a list of those seeking to share booths, and as it draws near to show time, they give out their phone numbers. Then, it's up to you to make the arrangements. So let the show people know you are looking.

To be sure you have a booth and have control over it, you can contract for the whole booth and then seek people to share with you. Or alternatively, get the number of someone who has a booth and wants to share. The other possibility is getting a booth with someone after you agree to share.

Usually, distributors who share booths apportion costs based on the amount of space used. But who gets what space where is negotiable. Typically, the person who rents the booth and subcontracts it is the final arbiter.

Getting Your Distributors to Participate in Your Booth

Whether you take a whole booth or part of one, it's a good idea to split both the costs and the time running the booth with other distributors for your product. Ideally, if you are in a network or multi-level program, get members of your sales group to participate and contribute, with the understanding that all sign-ups will be distributed under them. Or alternatively, chip in with a few distributors from different geographical areas and work out some mutual understandings—such as that each person takes every *n*th prospect or can contact whomever he or she happens to talk to at the booth. Or perhaps you might assign prospects for follow-up by geographical area.

Work out a schedule of who will be in the booth when, so that you have all times covered and have the most people assigned at the times you expect the booth to be the busiest. (Usually, this is the late morning and early afternoon on Saturday or Sunday.) Two to three hours makes a good shift, if you are allotting times to be in the booth.

SETTING UP YOUR BOOTH FOR MAXIMUM IMPACT

The keys to setting up a good booth are:

    displaying your products effectively
    using eye-catching posters and good literature
    having a good booth arrangement
    using effective promotions, such as a free drawing, to
        attract people

Displaying Your Products

Organize your display to feature your most popular or eye-catching products. If you have room, set up a demonstration to get potential consumers and distributors involved. For instance, if you are marketing a food product, do a cooking demonstration or set out some free samples. If you sell vitamins, hand out a few on the back of business cards.

Using Posters and Literature

Put up a few posters which quickly relay the major benefits of your program. For example, in a travel club booth, you might feature a colorful poster of Hawaii and next to it a sign that boldly telegraphs your message: GO ANYWHERE IN THE WORLD YOU WANT AND PAY LESS.

And don't be too wordy on your posters. A few short, to-the-point messages are much more effective than a lot of words. In a consumer or trade show, people pass by quickly, and you have one to four seconds to catch someone's eye. If a poster is too wordy, no one will read it. You want catchy slogans, perhaps accompanied by pictures, to get someone's attention. Then use smaller flyers or handouts to go into detail on the key benefits of your program.

Similarly, select your literature carefully. Choose only a few pieces that will quickly highlight your product's major benefits. If people want to know more, they will ask, and you can always have additional materials on hand for backup, when they do. By the same token, if you start chatting with someone, selectively hand out the literature you think would appeal the most.

Arranging Your Booth

If you have the whole booth, try experimenting with different booth arrangements. The most usual arrangement is with the product or demonstration in front and you standing behind the booth. This format provides a sense of separation between you and the potential consumer or distributor, which helps to make you seem authoritative and professional.

On the other hand, if your product lends itself to an open booth with a display or demonstration, this arrangement creates an atmosphere of easy informality that draws people in and helps them relax. For example, if you are promoting health products, you might invite people to come and relax on a recliner while you massage their back with a vibrating wand. Passersby are likely to stop and watch, and that gives you the perfect opener to talk about your product.

Using a Free Drawing

A free drawing also pulls customers. Announce the competition on a sign with big bold letters and indicate what the prize will be. A good item is an introductory kit with samples of your product. Or offer a small amount of your most popular product. Some distributors also use drawings to give away slow-moving items in their product line.

In any case, whatever you offer, the idea of getting something free has broad appeal. People are attracted by the chance to get something free, whatever it is.

To run an effective drawing, have plenty of index-sized cards on hand. Preferably have preprinted cards that ask for the person's name, address, and both home and business phone numbers. Also, you might include some questions about the person's interests, to help you select those who are especially likely to become consumers and/or distributors. A sample card format is included in Chart 52.

A three-by-five card size is recommended, because you can file these in a standard file container. And since you will be using different follow-up approaches to different groups, you might want to separate your file into three sections or use a separate file container for each major interest category: consumer only, business opportunity only, or both consumer and business interests.

MAKING SURE YOU HAVE EVERYTHING YOU NEED

Be sure you have all the materials you need to set up your booth. Find out from the show organizers exactly what they are providing in your booth and what you have to bring. For example, most shows provide tables and chairs; in some you have to bring your own. Some shows permit you to tape signs to the wall, others require you to hang everything from a curtain.

Then, make a list of everything you need, noting what is already provided and what you still have to get. (You can use the checklist on Chart 53 for this purpose.) Include on your list the product samples and literature you need, as well as any display aids, like easels, posters, signs, hooks, string, wire, or tape. If you need any special equipment such as a projector to show slides, a tape recorder for tapes, or a cash box, list these, too.

Check off all the items you have and whenever you acquire anything else, note this. When you pack for the show, use your list to check off everything you pack. And use your list again after the show when you pack to go home. This way, by using a checklist, you bring everything you need ... and you take it back with you, too.

CHART 52: INTEREST CARD

NAME _____

ADDRESS _____

CITY _____ STATE _____ ZIP _____

PHONE (day) _____

PHONE (evening/weekends) _____

I am mainly interested in your product as (check one)

  A Consumer Only ( )   Business Interest Only ( )
  Both as a Consumer and as a Business Interest ( )

My usual occupation is: _____

Comments: _____

OPERATING YOUR BOOTH

You can run a booth yourself, but it's best to have at least one other person and perhaps several sharing your booth, even if they aren't in your own sales group. This way you can relieve each other, have some time to get around the show and enjoy it yourself, and can generally keep up each other's morale.

Another advantage of sharing a booth is that you look more organized and professional when you have a few people in your booth. Also, your booth looks more fun. Then, too, while one of you is in the booth talking up the program, the other

CHART 53: SHOW CHECKLIST

Items Needed for Show (cross out items not needed, add others)	Items Provided by Show	Have	Still Need	Repacking Checklist
Tables	_____	_____	_____	_____
Chairs	_____	_____	_____	_____
Company Name Sign	_____	_____	_____	_____
Posters	_____	_____	_____	_____
Easels	_____	_____	_____	_____
Cash Box	_____	_____	_____	_____
Box for Sign-Up Cards	_____	_____	_____	_____
Sign-Up Cards	_____	_____	_____	_____
Interest Sign-Up Sheet	_____	_____	_____	_____
Business Cards	_____	_____	_____	_____
Presentation Manuals	_____	_____	_____	_____
Product Samples	_____	_____	_____	_____
Literature	_____	_____	_____	_____
Miscellaneous Supplies				
Tape	_____	_____	_____	_____
String	_____	_____	_____	_____
Wire	_____	_____	_____	_____
Tools	_____	_____	_____	_____
Hooks	_____	_____	_____	_____
Pencils/Pens	_____	_____	_____	_____
Video/Sound Equipment				
TV Monitor	_____	_____	_____	_____
Slide Projector	_____	_____	_____	_____
Tape Recorder	_____	_____	_____	_____
Extension Cords	_____	_____	_____	_____
Lights	_____	_____	_____	_____
Other				
_____	_____	_____	_____	_____
_____	_____	_____	_____	_____
_____	_____	_____	_____	_____
_____	_____	_____	_____	_____
_____	_____	_____	_____	_____

can be just outside making comments to those who pass by to get them interested in stopping at your table to learn more. Also, the outside person can take some literature and talk to exhibitors in other booths about the program. Additionally, some distributors pass out materials if they talk to people in the aisles who are interested.

However, be careful to check on show policies regarding promotion outside of your own booth. Often the show managers frown on this, rightly arguing that any sales material should be distributed only in one's booth or in a designated literature area, since the booth holders have paid for the sales opportunity. So it is unfair for others to undercut these exhibitors by walking around handing out their materials. Sometimes show managers give this freedom to exhibitors, though not to anyone else who happens to be at the show. Thus, since different shows have different policies, check what is permitted at your show.

PRESENTING YOUR
PROGRAM EFFECTIVELY

As in any sales presentation, have a general idea in advance of the major points you want to make about your product. You only have a few seconds to capture attention and a few minutes to present the highlights. So focus on a few major benefits.

Opening Lines

Some distributors effectively call attention to their product by offering a few friendly and attention-getting comments about it as people walk by, such as:

"I'll bet you'd like to have some more energy right now." (to introduce a health product to someone who looks a little tired from the show)

"We have our free drawing for dinner going on right now. Here's a pen so you can sign up." (to get someone interested in a new food product)

Many distributors do well by waiting until a person starts looking at their posters or flyers or picks up a sample of their product. Then, they pick up on whatever the person seems to be interested in and describe it more fully. For example:

"That trip is just one of the many we offer. You can go anywhere in the world you want." (to promote interest in a new travel club)

"We have a dozen dinner products in the line now." (to someone who has just sampled one of your food items or is looking at food packages)

Avoid the relatively overused opening clichés "Can I help...?" or "Can I explain...?" Mostly, people tend to answer no.

Instead, *think of creative openers to get people interested and involved*. Inviting people to try something is always good: "Would you like to sample some of our great new carob drink?" "Would you like to relax and enjoy a massage?"

Other Attention Getters

Other good attention getters include video presentations on a TV monitor or slide-sound presentations on a self-contained slide projector.

Demonstrations in your booth also help draw a crowd. For example, at one show I attended, the most popular crowd pleaser was a cooking demonstration, in which a man energetically chopped up vegetables, popped them in a blender, and then handed out free drinks. Meanwhile, as he worked, he gave a running sales pitch, so when he had finished the demonstration, everyone watching had heard the major benefits of his product.

Alternative Approaches

Have a few alternative approaches in mind so you can easily vary your style depending on whether a person is more likely to be a consumer, a distributor, or both, and whether a person is interested in hearing a detailed presentation now or just wants a quick review and some literature.

Sketch out a general outline of what you want to say, and practice a few times until you get to be an old pro at giving your pitch at these shows.

Encourage Sign-Ups

Whatever opening approach you use, try to get everyone who expresses some interest to sign up on something—whether it's a list or a card for a free drawing. This way you build up a mailing list for further contact, and you can follow up later to sell product or talk up the business opportunity.

Part VII

RUNNING YOUR BUSINESS EFFECTIVELY

Chapter 30

SETTING UP YOUR OFFICE

Most people who start a direct sales, network marketing, or MLM business operate from their home on a part-time basis, so this chapter and those that follow will focus on how to run a home-based business. However, many of the tips will apply to running any small business.

For further details on laws, taxes, and business management, see a more specialized book or consult with an expert on the topic. These chapters deal with the basics.

THE ADVANTAGES OF WORKING OUT OF YOUR HOME

Starting a business in your home has numerous advantages, and many successful distributors and sales reps continue their operations at home because of the convenience. Let's discuss some of these advantages.

You have great flexibility and convenience. You can set your own hours and combine your work with your home life. But you do have to be careful to budget your time, so you don't end up working much more than you want. So be sure to schedule some hours to relax.

You are readily available to your customers and distributors, and you can meet with people who have full-time jobs in the evenings. However, protect yourself from intrusions when you don't want to be working by having a separate business and personal phone. Or use an answering machine to screen calls, and don't answer work-related calls until you want to work.

You have low start-up costs, because you don't have to finance a separate office until your business has expanded so you need one. Usually, your home is sufficient to stock the small amount of inventory needed to run most of these marketing businesses, since in most companies, distributors buy direct. However, you should set aside an area to stock a small supply of your most popular products, so you can supply individual retail customers and provide for your new distributors. But normally, you don't need to do any extensive warehousing (though some of the larger distributors in your company may do this).

You get a number of tax advantages because you can deduct that part of your home used for business purposes. To claim this area as a tax deduction, you must use it only for business purposes. For details on this subject, you can get the *Tax Guide for Small Businesses* free from the U.S. Government Printing Office.

SETTING UP A PRODUCT STORAGE AND DISPLAY AREA

Since you need to have at least some product and product literature on hand, set up an area in your house for your inventory, such as a large closet or part of your office. You might also have a display area with samples of your literature and product line. For example, some distributors use a dining room or den for this purpose, and some use their product display room as a small meeting hall, too.

To determine how much product and space you need, figure out how much product you need to supply your regular retail customers (based on how many customers you have and the average size of their order). Also, figure out how much product you need to assist your new distributors or sales reps who are just getting started. Then, keep about one month's supply on hand.

LOCATING YOUR OFFICE

When you get started, you will minimally need a small area where you can handle day-to-day calls, keep sales records, and keep track of other business matters. At first, a desk in one room may be enough, since most of your business activities—prospecting and talking to potential customers and distributors—will occur outside of your home.

But as your business expands, plan to set up an office with the necessary equipment and supplies. If your home is large enough a large room with a desk, filing cabinet, and other office equipment is an ideal place to set up shop, because of both the rent and tax savings.

However, if your home is not appropriate and you can afford a little extra rent, a shared office arrangement can be especially cost effective. There are some companies that provide such offices with support services designed especially for persons just starting off in business. They have names like Headquarters, Executive Suite, and Timesavers, and some companies are franchise operations, with offices in several cities. These companies rent you a small space in an office complex, and you can use their mailing address, telephone answering service, office equipment, conference room, and other facilities.

BASIC EQUIPMENT

You will need some basic equipment.

Filing Cabinets or Drawers

Most familiar are the usual two-to-four-drawer filing cabinets. However, you may find two other filing systems especially convenient: filing racks and filing drawers.

Filing Racks. These are about six inches deep, with several partitions, so you can place the whole rack on a desk or table and store files upright. One version is the step rack, which has four or five levels or steps, so it is easier to see groups of files. These open-file racks are excellent for files you use regularly, because your files are much easier to get at here than in a cabinet. Then, when you are ready to store something away, you can transfer the file to the cabinet.

Filing Drawers. These are about two inches high by nine inches wide and twelve inches deep, and they can be stacked one on top of each other. Most commonly they are grouped in stacks of three. They are especially useful for keeping copies of flyers, brochures, and other literature that you want to stock in quantity. If you can't find them in a regular office supply store, try an art store.

Long Tables or Desks

These are especially good to arrange your literature for a mailing. Also, you can use long tables or desks to keep your filing racks with open files.

Shelves

You'll need plenty of shelf space for your product supply and literature. Ideally, have some extra shelf space available so you can readily make use of it when your office expands. You can create shelves fairly inexpensively in two ways:

Get the metal put-it-together shelves at Sears or other big hardware stores.
Get some concrete blocks at a local building supply store and put these between individual shelves.

An Answering Machine

A real must. Besides the usual uses, you can use a machine to prescreen your calls before you answer. Or if you run an ad, use the machine to give a brief sales message, and ask interested callers to leave their name and number. You'll save a lot of energy by not having to repeat your message again and again yourself—and some people find a prerecorded sales message very professional and convincing. Another tip: use your company name, rather than your own name, to make your message sound more professional.

PRESENTATION MATERIALS

If you are going to be giving presentations, consider some excellent items (variously available at an office supply, art supply, or photo supply store).

An Easel. Use this to display products, signs, and so on. There are two types: a large easel that stands on the floor and a small easel you can place on a table or desk.

433

A Portfolio or Carrying Case for Signs, Posters, and Flip Charts. These are large, usually black, zip-up cases with a handle. They can comfortably hold about a dozen posterboard signs, a few flip charts, and perhaps fifty or sixty posters.

Flip Charts. These are good for temporary displays, before you transfer your final copy to signs or slides. You can write informally on these with magic markers before or during your presentation, and they give your talk an atmosphere of spontaneity. However, when you have signs or slides, people expect a more polished look.

An Attractive Leather or Vinyl Binder. Preferably, use a three-ring binder so it's easy to slip pages in and out. Get a good, high-quality binder if you can, since this quality look adds to the professionalism and eye appeal of your presentation.

Slide Projector, Slide Trays, and Carrying Cases. To give your presentation extra pizzazz, use slides.

SOME USEFUL SUPPLIES

Plastic Sheet Protectors. These are ideal for protecting the 8½ by 11–inch sheets you use in your sales presentation. The best kinds have a thin plastic spine down the side in which three holes are punched, so you can easily slip your document into the plastic protector and then put the whole sheet into a loose-leaf binder without punching holes in your documents.

Self-Adhesive Address Labels. These come on 8½ by 11–inch sheets, with twenty-one or thirty-three labels to a sheet. These are ideal if you will be doing large mailings, such as regular mailings to your sales group, and don't have a computer, because you don't have to retype the names each time. You simply place a sheet of white paper over a master typing guide and type each name and address once on this master sheet, following the lines on the guide.

Then, each time you want to print labels, you place the number of label sheets you need in a copying machine and copy the names from the master onto the labels. Then, you pull the labels off and affix them directly to each envelope.

You can also use these labels to make a master filing system. Simply type the name and address as you would for a standard label. Then, type the phone number and any comments in the next label section or on the lower part of that section so you can later cut it off when you use these labels for a mailing. Finally, print on the label sheets, and affix the two labels with the person's name, address, phone number, and comments, on a three-by-five card. Now you can use these cards to create your file.

Large Monthly Calendar. Get the kind with the big spaces, so you can write in events and appointments and have an overview of what you are doing each month. It helps to have a notebook-sized one you can carry with you. Also, you can get a large—about twenty by twenty-four inches—metal or plastic wall calendar, so you can see at a glance what's happening. I use two of these—one for the present month and one for next. Then, when the month is over, you simply wipe off what you have written with a rag or paper towel and start again.

Appointment Book. It should be small enough to carry with you. You can purchase the book style, or use the desk version with snap-out pages and take the next few weeks with you. I like the snap-out variety, since it enables you to leave most of the book at home. Thus, you need less space, and you aren't likely to lose all of your precious records if you happen to leave your book somewhere.

Personal Phone and Address Book. To keep the numbers you call frequently. In this case, you might consider having two books—a slightly larger one you leave by the phone at home and a smaller one you carry with you.

Notepads. Carry one with you wherever you go to jot down any ideas or names of contacts as needed. Preferably use a three-ring binder, so you can easily pull out sheets of paper and file them later.

Telephone Pads. Be sure to have one by each phone, so you can readily take down information whenever you have a call. I personally like the loose sheets that are about two inches square and come in a square plastic box, because they are easy to pull out and file. But just about any sort of pad—or index cards—will do.

Manila File Folders. These are ideal for keeping track of dealings with customers and members of your sales group, particularly your directly sponsored people—and any second- and third-level hot performers you work with yourself. It's helpful to keep one file for each person and include in it the following information: your copy of the person's completed application form; your copies of any purchase orders made by that person; any correspondence with that person; any notes

436

about that person's progress or your ideas for working with that person.

Colored File-Folder Labels. These come on a roll or sheet in a rainbow of colors. They're great for labeling your manila file folders and making your files look good. You can use the colors to separate the files into different categories. For example, if you are doing two programs, use one color label for each.

Colored Dots. These come in various colors and sizes from about ¼- to 1-inch diameter. The smaller ones are excellent for calling attention to specific information, names, and items. For instance, use the red dots on your distributor file folders to designate your most active performers. Or put the dots on the interest cards you use in prospecting to indicate the prospects with the most interest.

CREATING YOUR LETTERHEAD

You need a good letterhead to look professional. Since this is often your first introduction to a prospect or used in your initial follow-up after a preliminary call, it should look good.

To make a professional-looking letterhead inexpensively, you can have a typesetter set some headline type for you using cold type (less expensive because it's typed out on a machine, not set by hand). Or get a sheet of rub-on letters (such as Letraset, Instant Letter, Prestype), and do it yourself. Choose a large, bold-letter style for your company name, since that gives an image of class. Then, use a smaller but compatible letter style for your address and phone number. Ask the typesetter or art store clerk for advice if you aren't sure what lettering to choose.

You can lay out your letterhead on a standard 8½ by 11-inch sheet of paper, which is ideal for making quick copies (although professional artists use a board ruled with blue lines for an offset print job). Then, take your layout to an instant press.

For a full range of choice on your paper, go to a paper supply store. However, for convenience, you can use the paper available at your local press, although they have a limited selection and generally charge twice as much. Either way, choose your stock carefully. Remember, you are creating an image of your company. You should not only think about color, but about the texture and heaviness of the paper. Also, select a stock with matching envelopes.

The image of your company begins when your letter arrives, and the impression carries over and contributes to how people read what's inside.

SELECTING THE RIGHT PHONE SERVICE

Technically, the phone company expects a business to get a business service, which costs substantially more than a private line (about twice as much for the basic listing, and a premium on each call you make). If you want to list your phone number under your business name or advertise in the phone book, you will need a business service.

There are some pros and cons both ways. If your company is widely known like Amway, Shaklee, or Mary Kay, it can help to list yourself as a company distributor. Or if you are actively promoting your business or want to advertise in the phone book, it makes sense to have a business listing, too.

On the other hand, if you are still small, it is less expensive to use a personal listing, particularly if you plan to use the same number for your residence. I did this for a time and answered the phone with my business names during business hours—from 8:00 A.M. to 6:00 P.M. Monday through Friday. A phone company rep may tell you that you need a business line if you answer with the name of your company—for example, one rep who called during the day told me this. But, in general, the phone company is not in a position to do much investigating or follow-up on how you use your phone. So until it becomes an issue or you are ready to get a business listing, you can keep your phone expenses down by using your personal phone for business purposes.

Getting a Second Line or a Call-Waiting Service

Since you will probably be using your phone extensively, consider having a second line or a call-waiting service on your phone.

One easy solution to a business-versus-personal-line decision is to have a business line for incoming calls and a personal line for outgoing calls. This way you pay a few extra dollars a month for a business listing, but you don't pay the extra costs for making toll calls on a business line.

Call-waiting is an excellent feature to have if you are in an area that offers it, because a click sounds when someone else calls you while you are on the phone. Then, you can put the first caller on hold, find out who the second caller is, and decide which call to take.

But if call-waiting isn't available, a second phone is ideal, because you can use one to call out and the other for incoming calls. Then, if an incoming call goes on for a long time, you can call the caller back on your other line or ask him or her to call you on it. This way, you keep your incoming line free most of the time.

Other Phone Company Services

The phone company also offers a variety of other services in some areas which not everyone knows about, such as conference calling (so you can talk to more than one person at a time), call forwarding (so you can have your calls transferred to another number), convenience calling (so you can precode frequently called numbers into your phone and push a button or two to call these), and low rates for calls to designated areas.

The phone company reps don't always tell you about these services when you get a new phone—and when new services are introduced, you don't always find out either. So check sporadically with your local phone rep and find out about the various services offered.

Discount Phone Services

It's cost effective to use discount phone services if you spend more than twenty-five dollars or so on calls outside of your surrounding forty-mile area.

Besides the most well-known companies or services—Sprint and MCI—there are about a dozen of these services now. In these programs you usually have a basic set-up fee of about five to ten dollars, a monthly service charge of three to five dollars, and save about 15 to 50 percent on each call, depending upon when you call (the biggest savings are on calls when the evening, night, or weekend rates are in effect). Charges are in a state of constant change so check your options carefully.

TELEMARKETING SYSTEMS

Another possibility if you plan to do a great deal of calling is a telemarketing system. Today, there are dozens of these devices being marketed. You program the device to do the calling for you, and it runs quickly through a series of numbers. You can program in individual numbers, or set it to call a first number. Then, it will call every single number in sequence, or you can set it to call every nth number. (That way you don't call a company with a series of consecutive numbers again and again.)

When a person answers, the machine is programmed to start a sales message and ask the called party to answer several questions and leave a name, address, and/or phone number if the person wants more information. The machine might give a pitch that goes something like this:

Hi. I'm Bart. I'm a machine, and I have an important message for you if you'd like to lose weight. I'd like to ask you a few questions, and then if you're interested, a real person will get back to you. . . . Okay, ready? . . . Do you want to lose weight yourself? . . . Do you know anyone who would like to lose weight? . . . Would you like to earn some extra money telling others about how they can lose weight? . . . And now, if you'd like to talk to a real human about any of these things, please leave your name . . . and your phone number . . . and my master will get back to you real soon. And by the way, you sound really good for a human!

Only the person's answers are recorded, so you can get the information you need to follow up quickly from the tape.

And if someone hangs up at any time during the message, the device is programmed to go on and call the next number. According to current research, about 80 to 90 percent of those who receive a taped call hang up. But that's fine, because as noted previously, in any sales effort, only a small percentage of the people you contact are ultimately going to sign up anyway.

The advantage of the telemarketing approach is that you can run through the numbers faster to find that interested person. The machine can make about sixty calls an hour, versus about twenty to thirty when a live person calls. And the machine doesn't get discouraged or bored after making dozens of calls. It just gives your message in the same enthusiastic way again and again. Then, too, when you or another person calls, you have to figure your costs based on the amount of time spent, because your hours are worth money or you have to pay someone else's wages. But with the machine, you don't have to worry about time or pay.

In general, the price on these machines is fairly steep—about $6,500 to $7,500, if you buy them in cash. But most companies have long-term lease or purchase plans, so you can pay in affordable monthly amounts over time. Also, as an added benefit, some companies throw in excellent training manuals and tapes that teach you how to create an effective sales message to market your own program. And some companies will even make a tape for you.

TAKING CARE OF THE
BASIC LEGAL REQUIREMENTS

Regulations vary from city to city and state to state about what you need to do to run a business. And different companies have different policies as to what documents their distributors or sales reps need.

So check your company start-up manual for specific requirements and check if your city requires a business license. Initially, you can probably do business for a while and no one will notice you while you are small. But eventually, you need to have the appropriate documents on file, particularly to claim the tax deductions that go with running a small business. Here are some of the documents you will need.

A Fictitious Name or Doing-Business-As (DBA) Registration

You need this if you are using a name other than your own for your business. This registration not only lists your name as a matter of record, but it protects you from anyone else in your area using your name. You should use this procedure when you have a sole proprietorship or a partnership. Registering a name for a corporation is a different procedure, and you should see a lawyer if you are planning corporate status (or get a good book on creating a corporation yourself).

Before you file for a fictitious name, check around your area to make sure someone else isn't already using your name. Go through the phone book and city records. Then, the procedure is very simple. You file a fee—about ten or twenty dollars—at the city clerk's office and run an announcement about the filing in a publication of record (certain of your local papers will qualify; or use a legal newspaper that includes filings). The announcement costs about twenty dollars, too.

Then, if no one questions your use of the name, you get a legal document stating that this is your doing-business-as (DBA) name.

If you are thinking of using more than one fictitious name in your business, file them at the same time—it's cheaper that way—only a few dollars more for each additional name filed together.

A Resale License

The laws about whether you need a resale license to operate as an independent business owner or distributor are unclear, since state laws differ, and many states do not require certain types of business to register with the state department that collects the sales tax—the Board of Equalization. For example, small businesses under a certain minimum volume and services may be exempt. However, check, because you can be held liable for any taxes you should have collected, but did not.

At the moment, direct sales, network marketing, and MLM companies typically do not require you to have a resale license. If you do have a license, you should indicate your number. Then, when you make a product purchase at wholesale which you plan to resell, you don't pay the tax. On the other hand, if you don't have a resale license, you must pay the applicable state, county, and city sales tax for the products you purchase, unless the company pays the taxes for you. In both cases, when you resell the product at retail, you collect the tax from your retail customers or they pay it directly to the company when they order direct, if taxes are due (food, for example, is exempt).

Whether a resale license is required or not, there are advantages to having one. First, of course, you can purchase the products you resell without paying tax, and you can purchase a variety of items that you use to help sell these products without tax, too. For instance, if you make a training manual or slide show and resell it to members of your sales group, you can purchase the materials used in your manual or slide show (such as paper and film) without paying tax. The people who buy it will have to pay the tax, but you don't.

Secondly, when you have a license, you can qualify for a number of discounts available only to people with licenses. For instance, when you go to a trade show, you can purchase items at wholesale, which is usually 40–50 percent off. These can be for your business, such as for cabinets and desks, or for personal use, such as decorator pieces for the living room. If you don't use these items for resale purposes, you are legally required to pay the tax when you file your sales tax return. But you have gained a large discount, which you wouldn't have been able to get as a regular consumer.

To obtain a license, apply at your nearest State Board of Equalization. You will need to estimate your expected retail sales for the year and pay a deposit against projected earnings. For example, in California, the Board of Equalization requires that you deposit 6 percent of your projected taxable sales for your first three months of operation or a surety bond in that amount from your insurance agent (usually at a cost of 5 percent of the amount of the bond). Or if you project less than a certain amount, you will be required to pay the minimum deposit, which is about $100.

To minimize your deposit or bond, minimize your expected sales. Or advise the Board that you will sell much less than you actually expect. You will have to pay all your taxes eventually. But it is in your interest to pay as little deposit as possible.

A City Business License

Some cities require business licenses for home-based businesses, others don't. Check with your local city.

In return for this license, you pay a tax based on a percentage of your gross earnings. If your earnings are less than a certain amount, you pay the minimum tax, which may be as low as twenty-five to thirty dollars.

Generally, you get no special services or benefits in return for obtaining this license. Rather, this license simply indicates you have paid your current taxes and are in compliance with local business regulations.

OPENING UP A
BUSINESS BANK ACCOUNT

As soon as it is economically feasible, open up a separate bank account for your business. This way, you can separate your earnings and expenses in your business from your other income and expenses. Also, having a business account helps show the IRS, should an agent contact you, that you are truly in business. Then, too, it's more impressive to write checks on a business account when you pay your bills—it's all part of presenting yourself as a serious, successful business person.

If you are financially pressed in the beginning and don't have enough money to operate a viable second business account, you may want to consider some alternatives to the usual commercial account. (Normally, commercial banks require a minimum of $500 or more for free checking; and if you write many checks with a balance under the minimum, you will find your service charges on the account extremely high—figure on about fifteen to twenty cents a check.)

One way to keep down banking expenses is to combine your business and personal checking in the same account—and have your checks printed with your name and under that the name of your business. This way your checks help you appear to be a professional business person to others, but you still have the advantage of having a single personal account.

Secondly, you can cut banking costs by opening up your personal account in a savings and loan association, since you may be able to obtain many services with your account that you don't get at a commercial bank, such as no minimum balance for free checking and interest when your balance is $100 or more. As at a commercial bank, you can have your business name printed under your own name on the check.

If you do have one account, be sure to label any checks you write according to the purpose of the check, and use a coding system to indicate which business your check is for. (For instance, use the code letter H for your health business, C for your consumer club business.)

But then, get separate accounts as soon as you can. Using a savings and loan association enables you to separate your accounts sooner than you might at a commercial bank, because you don't need to maintain a minimum balance for free checking, although you may need $100 to open each account. Also, if you have two or more businesses, you can have an account for each one at no extra expense, since you can keep a small balance in each one. In fact, some savings and loans even give you free checks for each account.

Chapter 31

KEEPING RECORDS

You should keep records of your expenses and sales receipts for two reasons: (1) these records are required for tax purposes; and (2) they will help you better understand how your business is going.

If you are moving any extensive amount of inventory yourself, you should keep records of your inventory flow, too.

In some companies, you have to pay out bonuses to your distributors or sales reps who have not yet graduated to buying direct from the company, and in this case, your record keeping will be more complex. However, today, with the computer revolution, more and more companies use a system in which each distributor deals direct with the company, and the company pays all the bonuses directly. So your record keeping is simpler.

BOOKKEEPING METHODS

There are two types of bookkeeping methods, the double-entry system and the single-entry system.

As your company expands, you might consider using a

double-entry system, which employs ledgers and journals to keep your business records. In this system, which is generally the preferred method for keeping business records, you enter your transactions in a journal first and then post your monthly totals to the appropriate ledger accounts. These are divided into five categories: (1) income, (2) expenses, (3) assets, (4) liabilities, and (5) net worth. You keep track of your income and expenses on a yearly basis, but maintain your assets, liability, and net worth accounts on an ongoing basis.

When you're starting out, however, the single-entry book-keeping method is simpler to use, although not as complete. Basically, in this system, you record your income and expenses by making a daily summary of your cash receipts and expenses, and then you summarize both receipts and expenses on a monthly basis. You can use your checkbook and a record book of cash transactions for this purpose.

DOCUMENTING YOUR INCOME AND EXPENSES

If you have a separate business account, use this for all your business transactions, including credit card payments, and keep a petty-cash fund for small expenses. Otherwise, if you have a combined personal and business account, code your checks and income receipts, as noted, to indicate what business activities these are for.

Pay by check or charge account wherever possible to document your business expenses. Whenever you pay cash for a business expense, keep a receipt for the payment, or make a record showing the business purpose for which you spent this money. Also, if you use your car for business purposes, keep a record of your mileage, tolls, and parking expenses while involved in any business activity. You can use Charts 54 to 56 for recording your car, entertainment, and day-to-day business expenses.

Similarly, you should record your income from whatever sources, and note whether you were paid by check or cash. You can use Chart 57 for this purpose. Chart 58 is for recording sales.

Be sure to keep all canceled checks, receipts, paid invoices, deposit slips, and other business records, and file them in an organized way. For example, besides listing receipts and payments on the appropriate forms, you might put all your supporting papers in a series of envelopes or files that are dated in sequence to include transactions for every one or two weeks, and include income and expenses in separate envelopes or files. For instance, you might have separate income and expense files for January 1–15; for January 16–31; for February 1–15; and so forth.

If you are using the double-entry system, record your entries according to the five categories noted above, and classify asset accounts as current or fixed. Also, note the dates of acquisition, cost, depreciation, and any other relevant information.

Conversely, if you are using a single-entry system, you merely need to keep a daily record and monthly summary of income and expenses.

It's also helpful to categorize expenses according to the categories you will be using to report expenses on your income tax. Just attach a code number to each category and note that on the item. Then, on an ongoing basis or when you file your taxes, you can readily place items into the appropriate category.

Similarly, categorize your earnings according to the different programs you are working with and according to other sources of income.

For example, the coding system I use, which combines both personal and business expenses and income together, is the following:

1. Income (broken into categories of earnings from different programs and activities)
2. Advertising
3. Auto Expenses
4. Clothing
5. Contributions
6. Education
7. Entertainment
8. Equipment and Furniture
9. Insurance
10. Medical
11. Miscellaneous Business
12. Repairs and Cleaning
13. Shipping
14. Travel
15. Utilities and Rent

If you find large recurring expenses in a particular category, you might make these into a separate category. The point is to develop the category system that's best for you.

Then, use these records to keep track of how your business is doing and to prepare your tax returns. Or turn them over to your accountant, and let him or her take it from there.

KEEPING TRACK
OF YOUR INVENTORY

To keep track of your inventory of product and sales literature, keep some records of what you have on hand, what you have on order, what you paid, and how much people have paid you. You may not have much in stock if your company has a policy for all distributors to order direct from the company, but even so, keep some records. You can use Chart 59 to help you do this.

CHART 54: CAR TRAVEL EXPENSES

| Date | Speedometer Reading | | Parking | Tolls | Purpose of Trip |
	Beginning	End			

CHART 55: ENTERTAINMENT EXPENSE REPORT

Date	Amount Spent	Type/Purpose of Expense	Where Spent	Name of Company/ Guests Entertained

CHART 56: GENERAL BUSINESS
AND PETTY CASH EXPENSES

Date	Amount Spent	Type/Purpose of Expense	Category Code No.	How Paid	To Whom Paid

CHART 57: NONSALES INCOME

Date	Amount	Source of Income	Category Code No.	How Paid		
				Check	Cash	Other

CHART 58: SALES INCOME

Date	Items Sold	Sold To	Amount	Sales Type Retail/Wholesale	State	Taxes Due on Sale County	Taxes Due on Sale City	Exempt

CHART 59: INVENTORY RECORD FORM FOR PURCHASES AND SALES

Inventory Ordered

Date	Number Ordered	For Whom (if request)	Number Received	Date Received	Amount Due	Amount Paid

Inventory Sold

Date	Number Sold	To Whom	Amount Due	Amount Paid	Other

Chapter 32

HIRING SOME HELP

Most persons starting a new marketing or sales business at first do everything themselves. But as your activities and organization grow, you may need some additional help.

In fact, it's a good idea to separate the routine clerical and administrative work that anyone can do from the personal contact and sales activities better done by you and your distributors. This way, you can hire someone to do the routine work and thereby maximize the time you devote to the work that produces income.

THE ADVANTAGES OF HIRING
EMPLOYEES TO WORK FOR YOU

You can look at hiring extra help this way. On the average, you earn so much per hour when you contact people about your program. You can figure this amount by estimating how much time you spend in the field each month (see Chart 11 in chapter 5), and then dividing this into your earnings for the month.

If it costs you less than your average hourly earnings to hire someone to do the routine work, you can see that it's a real bargain to hire others to work for you, because this frees you to do the work that brings in the most money. And as business people know, you almost never make large amounts of money without having others help you.

Also, there are other advantages to hiring employees. The four major advantages can be summarized thus:

- *You multiply yourself cost-effectively.* Ask yourself: How much am I making or could I be making now? As noted, if you can hire someone to do some of the more routine business task you don't want to do at a rate lower than what you are or could be making, you are saving money by hiring someone else.
- *You create an impression of success* when you have employees doing your routine phoning and clerical tasks.
- *You build a cushion, so as your business expands, you have people in place to take on jobs you can no longer do.* Perhaps you can still do many routine tasks yourself, but by having other people handle them, you are training them for the future, so they can take over more activities as your business expands.
- *Your employees can do some things better than you, even if you are paying them less.* For example, you may be great on the phones, but a lousy administrator and record-keeper. Or you may be best as the brains behind the organization, but not that effective at making cold calls. So get the work you need done, done by the people who do it best.

DETERMINE WHAT YOU NEED

To determine your needs for help, make a list of the various duties you perform on a regular basis. (You can use Chart 60 for this purpose.) Star those activities which you *do not need* to do yourself, and double-star those activities which you *do not want* to do either. Then, using this information, decide which tasks you want to give to someone else.

Finally, decide how you would like to divide up the work. To help you decide, estimate how much time is required each week for each task. Then, consider: Do you want to have a single person do everything? Perhaps you might prefer to have a few people take one or more tasks each.

HIRING INDEPENDENT CONTRACTORS

I find it preferable to hire people for part-time or temporary work at first. This way you can see how they work out, and you have the flexibility of hiring people according to the flow of the work.

The simplest way to hire people as part-time or temporary employees is as independent contractors. This way you don't have to worry about withholding taxes and the other rules and regulations affecting regular employees.

However, to hire independent contractors, you must conform to certain rules. Most notably, you must give people the freedom to choose their own hours and where they want to work. However, if it makes the most sense to work at your place at certain times, you can give people that option and

CHART 60: LIST OF TASKS I MIGHT HIRE SOMEONE TO DO

(List all routine tasks you perform. Star [*] those you don't *need* to do yourself and double-star [**] those you don't *want* to do. Then, decide which tasks you want to give to someone else.)

Routine Tasks	Tasks I Don't Need*	Tasks I Don't Want**	Tasks I Want to Assign to Others Now	Name of Person(s) Given Task Assignment
Typing				
Filing				
Addressing Envelopes				
Stuffing/Mailing Envelopes				
Keeping Mailing List Up-to-Date				
Making Routine Phone Calls				

they can still work as independent contractors, as long as they still have some choice regarding when and where they work. (For example, I suggest several times when it would be convenient for people to work at my office, and then they can choose which is best for their own schedule.)

To avoid any confusion about employee status, make it very clear to the people you hire that they will be an independent contractor and perhaps ask them to sign a statement indicating they understand this and will not list you as an employer, should they file for unemployment insurance. (Chart 61 is a copy of an independent contractor form you can use for this purpose.)

CHART 61: INDEPENDENT CONTRACTOR'S AGREEMENT

This is to indicate that I understand I am performing work for _____ as an independent contractor.

I understand that I am not an employee, and as such, I am able to choose my own hours of work.

I further agree that I will not list _____ as an employer on any claims that I may subsequently make for unemployment insurance. Also, if I subsequently use this company as a reference, I agree to clearly indicate that I was an independent contractor and not an employee.

_____   _____
Date   Independent Contractor

KEEPING TRACK
OF YOUR EMPLOYEE'S
SKILLS AND INTERESTS

When you interview or hire a prospective employee, it's useful to get a general overview of what he or she can do and would like to do, so you can assign tasks accordingly. Also, it's helpful to keep a record of these skills and interests, so when you have a need for additional help in the future, you can review this material to see who would be good for a particular project. You can use the Employee Skills and Interest Checklist in Chart 62 for this purpose.

Then, for filing purposes, attach the Checklist to the Independent Contractor's Agreement for each employee, and keep a file for prospective employees and another for employees you have hired.

WHERE TO FIND EMPLOYEES
TO KEEP COSTS DOWN

Two of the best sources for employees who will do a good job at a low cost to you are colleges and universities—or high schools, if you live near one, since most students don't have cars.

To hire a student, call the student placement office and ask to advertise for an administrative assistant. Expect to pay about four to five dollars an hour. Normally, you should find it easy to get help, since there are usually many more students who want jobs than jobs for them. If you go to a commercial agency or hire a typist who advertises, you'll probably pay about twice as much.

CHART 62: EMPLOYEE SKILLS AND INTEREST CHECKLIST

Skills and Interests	Skills			Interest		
	Excellent	Good	Likes to Learn	High Interest	Slight Interest	No Interest
Telephone Sales/Follow-Up						
Door-to-Door Sales						
Contacting Organizations						
Handling Mailings/Mailing Lists						
Hosting Events						
Leafletting						
Typing (indicate words per minute)						
General Office/Clerical						
Art Skills (indicate types)						
Publicity/Promotion (describe)						
Speaking to Groups (describe)						
Writing (describe)						
Other Skills/Interests (list)						

NAME _____ PHONE _____

ADDRESS _____

CITY, STATE, ZIP _____

You might also be able to recruit some volunteer help from your university business administration department, if you can make your program sound exciting enough. To explore this possibility, talk to some professors and see if your program can be turned into a class or student project.

DECIDING WHOM TO HIRE

If possible, avoid hiring friends or relatives for routine work. Often friends and relatives will feel funny working for you, and if you aren't paying very much, they may feel resentful, even if they offer to work for very little to help out. Another problem is that if a friend or relative doesn't make a good employee, it's difficult to fire him or her. And when you do, you may not only lose an employee but a friend.

People use various systems to decide whom to hire: references, referrals from friends, tests, and so on. When I hire someone for routine work, I simply ask a few key questions: Have you done this kind of work before? Whom did you work for? What did you do? What are you studying? Why would you like to do this work now? What other kind of work would you like to do?

Then, if I feel good about working with this person, I ask him or her to fill out the Independent Contractor's Agreement and Employee Skills and Interest Checklist. Afterward, if I have some work I need done, I ask the person to stay and try it out for an hour or two. I indicate I will pay for this time, but that it should be considered a trial. Then, if the applicant likes the work and I feel he or she has done a good job, I offer more work—either now, if the person would like to stay, or in the future.

I use this approach because I am more interested in what the person can do now and how I feel about working with him or her than in past projects and references. I find that people can usually describe what they have done in the past so that it sounds good, and that they almost always can get someone to give them a glowing reference, so I feel that what they say doesn't mean that much. And remember, I am only hiring someone to do routine work—like typing, filing, and stuffing envelopes—on a temporary part-time basis. So I don't feel it's appropriate to ask all sorts of background questions. Rather, I prefer to put individuals to work on a trial basis and see what they do, because that's really what counts.

TRAINING YOUR NEW EMPLOYEES

At first I believe in supervising new employees closely, to be sure they know what they are doing. Then, gradually, I back off, so they can do more on their own. After I feel they know what to do and I feel I can trust them, I often let them work alone when I go out, and I give some employees a key.

I know some business owners worry about thievery and about employees slacking off when they aren't around. But I have found— at least with the employees I have hired—this has never been a problem, possibly because these are college students who are working toward building a solid future. So they are motivated to do well. Furthermore, I find giving them the key makes them want to do even better, because they experience the key as a sign I trust them, and they want to show they are worthy of that trust.

When employees do come to work when I am not around, I leave notes telling them what to do. And if I am not back when they go, I ask them to leave me a note indicating how many hours they have worked. And so far, I have never had an employee be dishonest in stating their hours. I might find out if they didn't tell the truth, since they may not know when I left or when I am coming back, although I give them a rough estimate. But I don't think this is why they have been honest. Rather, I feel they are working in a spirit of trust.

In any event, if you are able to let your employees come and go freely like this, there are some very practical applications—primarily it frees you to go out when you want. You don't have to stay around to watch and supervise your employees because you have trained them to supervise themselves.

PAYING EMPLOYEES

I usually pay the people who work for me regularly once a week, based on the number of hours worked. In the case of the employees who come in only occasionally, I prefer to pay them on a daily basis for the number of hours worked, since this simplifies bookkeeping. Also, I find student workers like getting their money right away, so they are highly motivated to work.

If I am not around when they finish work, I ask them to leave me a note about their hours. Then, I either give them a check for the correct amount if they come back to work within the next few days, or I mail them a check.

Chapter 33

DETERMINING
YOUR START-UP COSTS

Your start-up costs in a marketing or sales program can range from practically nothing to a few hundred dollars if you are pursuing it on a part-time basis, somewhat more if you are organizing a full-scale, fast-start effort.

CHART 63: START-UP EXPENSES WORKING OUT OF AN OFFICE IN YOUR HOME

Initial Start-Up Expenses	Average Range	
	Low	High
Distributor or Initial Training Fee	$10	$ 100
Start-Up Kit with Samples	25	200
Office Equipment (file cabinets, desks, tables, shelves)	0	500

STRIKE IT RICH IN PERSONAL SELLING

Initial Start-Up Expenses	Average Range	
	Low	High
Office Supplies (binders, presentation materials, letterhead, paper, stamps, file folders, pens, art materials, etc.)	25	250
Additional Phone Equipment and Services (answering machine, new phone lines, additional phone service)	0	300
Business Licenses (resale license, city license, fictitious name registration)	0	200
Accounting Service (do-it-yourself versus hiring an outside service)	0	100
Insurance	0	100
Personal Training	0	200
Advertising/Promotion (including flyers, brochures, newsletters, etc.)	10	200
Other	0	200
	$70	$2,350

The following list represents some typical ranges for direct sales, network marketing, and MLM programs. Use Chart 64, Estimated Start-Up and Monthly Expenses, to put yourself in the picture. Knowing what you do about your program, fill in your estimated costs for the distributor or initial training fee, start-up kit, and product samples. Then, estimate what you might spend for the other expense categories. Do this for your first month and for the next three to six months.

Average Monthly Expenses for the First Three to Six Months	Average Range	
	Low	High
Additional Product Samples (includes any product purchases required to receive commissions)	$50	$ 200
Additional Phone Equipment and Service	0	100
Additional Office Equipment	0	250
Additional Office Supplies	25	200
Accounting Service	0	100
Personal Training	0	100
Meeting-Room Rental	0	200
Advertising and Promotion	10	200
Entertainment	10	200
Part-Time Help	0	150
Other	0	200
	$95	$1,900

ADDITIONAL START-UP EXPENSES
WORKING IN A SMALL OFFICE

Additional Initial Start-Up Expenses	Average Range			
	Shared Office		Your Own Office	
	Low	High	Low	High
Rent (first month, last month, deposit, or start-up fee for shared office)	$250	$450	$ 500	$ 900
Equipment and Fixtures	0	200	250	2,500
Utilities and Phone Deposits	0	50	100	250
Insurance (for first six months)	0	0	200	500
Other	0	100	0	200
	$250	$800	$1,050	$4,350

Additional Average Monthly Expenses

Rent	$50	$150	$150	$500
Utilities and Phone Service	0	50	50	200
Other	0	100	100	200
	$50	$300	$300	$900

CHART 64: ESTIMATED START-UP AND MONTHLY EXPENSES

Types of Expenses	Estimated Start-Up Costs	Estimated Monthly Costs
Distributor or Initial Training Fee		
Start-Up Kit with Samples		
Additional Product Samples		
Office Equipment		
Office Supplies		
Additional Phone Equipment		
Additional Phone Service		
Business Licenses		
Accounting Services		
Insurance		
Personal Training		
Meeting-Room Rental		
Advertising and Promotion		
Entertaining		
Part-Time Help		
_____		
_____		
Total		

REFERENCES
AND RESOURCES

Because the direct sales, network marketing, and MLM field is changing so rapidly, this represents just a partial listing of books, magazines, and other resources.

MULTI-LEVEL MAGAZINES AND NEWSPAPERS

Multi-Level Marketing News
P.O. Box 1774
Fair Oaks, CA 95628
   (916) 965-9594
   An excellent source of information on all aspects of MLM. This magazine includes articles on success principles, recruiting, training, legal aspects of MLM, running a business, portraits of top distributors, and so on. The emphasis is on providing articles useful to people in any MLM company; there are no articles on particular companies. However, there are ads from companies, as well as from consultants and suppliers. $20 per year.

Opportunity 21
9968 Hibert Street
San Diego, CA 92131
(619) 566-3240

An excellent all-around newspaper that focuses on the multi-level marketing industry, but also has articles for those in other types of direct sales. There are articles on new companies, how-to information, and general industry news. $21 a year.

GENERAL MAGAZINES AND NEWSPAPERS DEALING WITH SMALL BUSINESS

Business Opportunities Journal
1021 Rosecrans Street
San Diego, CA 92106
(800) 854-6570 outside California
(619) 223-5661 in California

A monthly specializing in real estate, business, and investment opportunities. $30 a year; $4.50 per issue.

Entrepreneur (The Business Opportunity Magazine)
2311 Pontius Avenue
Los Angeles, CA 90064
(800) 421-7269 outside California
(800) 352-7449 in California

A monthly that focuses on small businesses, multi-level opportunities, and franchises. Contains a mixture of articles, product and business opportunity ads, and descriptions of American Entrepreneur Association manuals you can buy if you want to start a specific kind of business. $24.50 for a one-year subscription plus membership in the American

Entrepreneur Association; $44.50 for a two-year subscription and membership.

Financial Opportunities (A Nationwide Guide to Making Money)
3521 West Dempster Street
Skokie, IL 66076
   A tabloid format monthly which contains mostly advertising about money-making opportunities (though exercise due caution when you respond), as well as some articles on individuals who have started small businesses. $7.95 for one year; $15 for two years.

In Business (For the Independent, Innovative Individual)
Box 323
Emmaus, PA 18049
   Features advice on how to make money and save money and get more satisfaction from your business. Includes articles on how small-business people have gotten started. $13.95 for six issues; $19.95 for nine issues.

Inc. (The Magazine for Growing Companies)
P.O. Box 2538
Boulder, CO 80322
   (800) 525-0643
   Includes articles on fast-growing companies, marketing and sales techniques, new state-of-the-art office equipment, and so on. An excellent all-around publication about no-longer small but growing companies. $21 for twelve issues; $35 for twenty-four issues.

Income Opportunities
Davis Publications
P.O. Box 1931
Marion, OH 43305

Another publication featuring mostly ads for money-making opportunities, plus some articles on specific businesses and on those who have started their own businesses. Again, use your discretion when you answer the ads. $7.95 for one year.

Success (The Magazine for Achievers)
P.O. Box 3038
Harlan, IA 51537
  (800) 247-5470
Features articles on persons who have become successful in various fields and on techniques for achieving success. $18 for one year; $29 for three years.

Venture (The Magazine for Entrepreneurs)
P.O. Box 3108
Harlan, IA 51593
  (800) 247-5470
Features articles on new businesses, entrepreneurs who have made it, techniques for raising money for new ventures, strategies for making start-ups work. One of the best publications around on small business. $18 for one year; $32 for two years.

SUCCESS AND MOTIVATIONAL LITERATURE

There's lots of this around, starting with the first generation of success books written by Napoleon Hill. Some of the most popular books in this category include:

Napoleon Hill. *The Laws of Success.*
_____. *The Master Key to Riches.*

_____. *Think and Grow Rich*.

_____. and W. Clement Stone. *Success through a Positive Mental Attitude*.

Og Mandino. *The Greatest Salesman in the World*.

Norman Vincent Peale. *The Power of Positive Thinking*.

David J. Schwartz. *The Magic of Thinking Big*.

Other big names in the success field include:

Dale Carnegie
Robert Schuller
Zig Ziglar

TRADE ASSOCIATIONS

Direct Mail Marketing Association
6 East 43rd Street
New York, NY 10017
  (212) 689-4977
  An organization to contact if you use a direct mail strategy for your sales.

Direct Selling Association
1730 M Street, N.W., Suite 610
Washington, DC 20036
  (202) 293-5760
  The parent organization for direct sales companies. Companies must meet a minimum requirement to become DSA members, and dues are fairly steep (about $750 a year minimum). There are currently about two hundred members, and only a few of the bigger, more established network marketing and MLM companies are members.

National Mail Order Association
5818 Venice Boulevard
Los Angeles, CA 90019
   (213) 934-7986
   Another organization to contact if you are using a mail order approach to direct sales.

CONSULTANTS AND SEMINAR LEADERS

There are many excellent consultants and seminar leaders in direct sales, network marketing, and MLM. But now we have to toot our own horn. For consulting, training, seminars, classes, workshops, and so forth, we are:

Marketing Specialists
6537 Chabot Road
Oakland, CA 94618
   (415) 658-2747

"MANAGEMENT MUST MANAGE!"*

MANAGING   69986-9/$3.95US/$4.95Can
Harold Geneen with Alvin Moscow

"Sensible advice from the legendary practitioner of superior management, ITT Chairman of the Board Emeritus, Harold Geneen."*   *—Publishers Weekly*

THEORY Z   How American Business Can Meet the Japanese Challenge
William G. Ouchi   59451-X/$3.95US/$4.95Can

"Powerful answers for American firms struggling with high employee turnover, low morale, and falling productivity."   *—Dallas Times Herald*

HYPERGROWTH   The Rise and Fall of Osborne Computer Corporation
                     69960-5/$5.95US/$7.75Can
Adam Osborne and John Dvorak

The personal account of the Silicon Valley megabuck bust that stunned the business world.

An Avon Trade Paperback